# History of Education in India

**Pankaj Kumar Desai**

**AKHAND PUBLISHING HOUSE**
NEW DELHI (INDIA)

*Published by*
**AKHAND PUBLISHING HOUSE**
L-9 A, IST FLOOR, STREET NO. 42
SADATPUR EXTENSION
DELHI-110094 (INDIA)
CELL- 0-9013387535, 0-9968628081

History of Education in India


Edition 2010
ISBN 978-81-910525-2-7



Printed in India
at Asian Offset Printers, Delhi

# Preface

The history of education in India is very rich and interesting. One can trace the ancient India education to the 3rd century BC. Research shows that in the ancient days, sages and scholars imparted education orally, but after the development of letters, it took the form of writing. Palm leaves and barks of trees were used for education, and this in turn helped spread the written literature. Temples and community centres often took the role of schools.

When Buddhism spread in India, education became available to everyone and this led to the establishment of some world famous educational institutions Nalanda, Vikramshila and Takshashila. These educational institutes in fact arose from the monasteries. History has taken special care to give Nalanda University, which flourished from the fifth to 13th century AD, full credit for its excellence. This university had around 10,000 resident students and teachers on its roll at one time. These students included Chinese, Sri Lankan, Korean and other international scholars.

It was in the 11th century that the Muslims established elementary and secondary schools. This led to the forming of few universities too at cities like Delhi, Lucknow and Allahabad. Medieval period saw excellent interaction between Indian and Islamic traditions in all fields of knowledge like theology, religion, philosophy, fine arts, painting, architecture, mathematics, medicine and astronomy.

Later, when the British arrived in India, English education came into being with the help of the European missionaries. Since then, Western education has made steady advances in the country. With hundreds of universities and thousands of colleges affiliated to them, in fact scores of colleges in every discipline, India has positioned itself comfortably as a country that provides quality higher education to its people in specific and to the world in general.

The present publication provides a comprehensive account of the history of education in India since ancient Vedic and Buddhist period to the Islamic, the British and to the modern period. It describes in detail the activities and recommendations of various educational committees and commissions. It also discusses the progress and problems of education in basic, primary, secondary and higher education and also suggests remedies. It is hoped that the book will be of immense use to students, teachers, educational planners, administrators and the general public alike.

***Author***

# Contents

# 1

# Origin of Education

Education has taken place in most communities since earliest times as each generation has sought to pass on cultural and social values, traditions, morality, religion, knowledge and skills to the next generation. The passing on of culture is also known as enculturation, and the learning of social values and behaviours is socialisation. The history of the curricula of such education reflects human history itself, the history of knowledge, beliefs, skills and cultures of humanity.

In pre-literate societies, education was achieved orally and through observation and imitation. The young learned informally from their parents, extended family and kin. At later stages of their lives, they received instruction of a more structured and formal nature, imparted by people not necessarily related, in the context of initiation, religion or ritual.

As the customs and knowledge of ancient civilisations became more complex, many skills would have been learned from an experienced person on the job, in animal husbandry, agriculture, fishing, preparation and preservation of food, construction, stone work, metal work, boat building, the making of weapons and defences, the military skills, and many other occupations.

With the development of writing, it became possible for stories, poetry, knowledge, beliefs, and customs to be recorded and passed on more accurately to people out of earshot and to future generations. In many societies, the spread of literacy was slow; orality and illiteracy remained predominant for much of the population for centuries and even millennia. Literacy in pre-industrial societies was associated with civil administration, law, long distance trade or commerce, and religion. A formal schooling in literacy was often only available to a small part of the population, either at religious institutions or for the wealthy who could afford to pay for their tutors. The earliest known universities, or places of higher education, started teaching a millennium or more ago.

Universal education of all children in literacy has been a recent development, not occurring in many countries until after 1850 CE. Even today, in some parts of the world, literacy rates are below 60 percent. Schools, colleges and universities have not been the only methods of formal education and training. Many professions have additional training requirements, and in Europe, from the Middle Ages until recent times, the skills of a trade were not generally learnt in a classroom, but rather by serving an apprenticeship. Now-a-days, formal education consists of systematic instruction, teaching and training by professional teachers. This consists of the application of pedagogy and the development of curricula.

Education as a science cannot be separated from the educational traditions that existed before. Adults trained the young of their society in the knowledge and skills they would need to master and eventually pass on. The evolution of culture, and human beings as a species depended on this practice of transmitting knowledge. In pre-literate societies this was achieved orally and through imitation. Story-telling continued from one generation to the next. Oral language developed into written symbols and letters. The depth and breadth of knowledge that could be preserved and passed soon increased exponentially. When cultures began to extend their knowledge beyond the basic skills of communicating, trading, gathering food, religious practices, etc, formal education, and schooling, eventually followed. Schooling in this sense was already in place in Egypt between 3000 and 500 BC.

## Education in Prehistoric Age

Most of human history lies in prehistory, the period before the use of writing, and before written history. Throughout pre-history, most education was achieved orally and through observation and imitation. From the origin of our species, thought by many anthropologists to have been around 200,000 years ago in the African savanna, until about 10,000 BCE, most humans lived as hunter-gatherers. Some were settled in a given locale/region and others exhibited a nomadic lifestyle across a large territory. These bands or tribes had traditions, beliefs, values, practices and local knowledge which was passed orally for generations from person to person. The young learned informally from their parents, extended family and kin. At later stages of their lives, they received instruction of a more structured and formal nature, imparted by people not necessarily related, in the context of initiation, religion or ritual.

Some forms of traditional knowledge were expressed through stories, legends, folklore, rituals, and songs, without the need for a writing system. Tools to aid this process include poetic devices such as rhyme and alliteration. These methods are illustrative of orality. The stories thus preserved are also referred to as part of an oral tradition.

The advent of agriculture prompted the Neolithic Revolution, when access to food surplus led to the formation of permanent human settlements, the domestication of some animals and the use of metal tools.

Settlement, agriculture and metalwork brought new knowledge and skills to be learned and taught by each generation. As communities grew larger, there was more opportunity for some members to specialise in one skill or activity or another, becoming priests, artisans, traders, builders or labourers. Many skills would have been learned from an experienced person on the job.

The increased size of communities also brought changes to methods of leadership, politics and organisation, together with early institutions. Society became less egalitarian as chiefdoms, States, city-states and early civilisations replaced the earlier bands and tribes. For example, the Uruk period saw the emergence of urban life in Mesopotamia. These early city-states had strong signs of government organisation. The cities grew to cover up to 250 acres and up to 10,000-20,000 people by the end of the period.

In large settlements, social stratification began to develop, a hierarchical arrangement of social classes or castes within the society. There might be a king and nobles. There were often priests or other religious leaders, because religious beliefs in deities or spirits often formed an important part of a culture. In some societies, the status of women was lower than that of men; in some there were slaves. A person's social class, caste or gender might in turn determine or limit the occupations which he or she might follow and the education that he or she would receive. Before the development of writing, it is probable that there were already epic poems, hymns to gods and incantations, and other oral literature. In ancient India, the Vedas were learnt by repetition of various forms of recitation. By means of memorisation, they were passed down through many generations.

## Education in Ancient Civilisations

### Development of Writing Systems

Starting in about 3500 BCE, various writing systems were developed in ancient civilisations around the world. These writing systems would greatly increase the potential for passing knowledge onwards from one person to others. They would also bring the need for education in the skills of writing and reading.

The original Mesopotamian writing system was derived from a method of keeping accounts, and by the end of the 4th millennium BCE, this had evolved into using a triangular-shaped stylus pressed into soft clay for recording numbers. Around the 26th century BCE, cuneiform began to represent syllables of spoken Sumerian. Also in that period, cuneiform writing became a general purpose writing system yoyo wasp for logograms, syllables, and numbers. Symbols were imprinted on a wet clay tablet with a stylus, often made of reed. Large quantities of written tablets have been found in the Middle East.

In Egypt fully developed hieroglyphs that could be read in rebus fashion were in use at Abydos as early as 3400 BCE. Later, the world's oldest known alphabet was developed in central Egypt around 2000 BCE from a hieroglyphic prototype. One hieroglyphic script was used on stone monuments, other cursive scripts were used for writing in ink on papyrus, a flexible, paper-like material, made from the stems of reeds that grow in marshes and beside rivers such as the River Nile.

The Phoenician writing system was adapted from the Proto-Caananite script in around the 11th century BCE, which in turn borrowed ideas from Egyptian hieroglyphics. This script was adapted by the Greeks. A variant of the early Greek alphabet gave rise to the

Etruscan alphabet, and its own descendants, such as the Latin alphabet. Other descendants from the Greek alphabet include the Cyrillic alphabet, used to write Russian, among others.

The Phoenician system was also adapted into the Aramaic script, from which the Hebrew script and also that of Arabic are descended. In China, the early oracle bone script has survived on tens of thousands of oracle bones dating from around 1400-1200 BCE in the Shang Dynasty. Out of more than 2500 written characters in use in China in about 1200 BCE, as many as 1400 are identifiable as the source of later standard Chinese characters.

Of several pre-Columbian scripts in Mesoamerica, the one that appears to have been best developed, and the only one to be deciphered, is the Maya script. The earliest inscriptions which are identifiably Maya date to the 3rd century BCE, and writing was in continuous use until shortly after the arrival of the Spanish conquistadores in the 16th century CE.

Other surfaces used for early writing include wax-covered writing boards, sheets or strips of bark from trees, the thick palm-like leaves of a particular tree, the leaves then punctured with a hole and stacked together like the pages of a book (these writings in India and South East Asia include Buddhist scriptures and Sanskrit literature), parchment, made of goatskin that had been soaked and scraped to remove hair, which was used from at least the second century BCE, vellum, made from calfskin, and wax tablets which could be wiped clean to provide a fresh surface.

## Formal Education

In many early civilisations, education was associated with wealth and the maintenance of authority, or with prevailing philosophies, beliefs, or religion.

### *Middle East*

In what became Mesopotamia, the early logographic system of cuneiform script took many years to master. Thus only a limited number of individuals were hired as scribes to be trained in its reading and writing. Only royal offspring and sons of the rich and professionals such as scribes, physicians, and temple administrators, went to school.

Most boys were taught their father's trade or were apprenticed out to learn a trade. Girls had to stay at home with their mothers to learn housekeeping and cooking, and to look after the younger children. Later, when a syllabic script became more widespread, more of the Mesopotamian population became literate. Later still in Babylonian times there were libraries in most towns and temples; an old Sumerian proverb averred that "he who would excel in the school of the scribes must rise with the dawn." There arose a whole social class of scribes, mostly employed in agriculture, but some as personal secretaries or lawyers. Women as well as men learned to read and write, and for the Semitic Babylonians, this involved knowledge of the extinct Sumerian language, and a complicated and extensive syllabary. Vocabularies, grammars, and interlinear translations were compiled for the use of students, as well as commentaries on the older texts and explanations of obscure words and phrases. Massive archives of texts were recovered from the archaeological contexts of Old Babylonian scribal schools, through which literacy was disseminated. The Epic of Gilgamesh, an epic poem from Ancient Mesopotamia is among the earliest known works of literary fiction. The earliest Sumerian versions of the epic date from as early as the Third Dynasty of Ur (2150-2000 BCE).

Ashurbanipal (685-ca. 627 BCE), a king of the Neo-Assyrian Empire, was proud of his scribal education. His youthful scholarly pursuits included oil divination, mathematics, reading and writing as well as the usual horsemanship, hunting, chariotry, soldierliness, craftsmanship, and royal decorum. During his reign he collected cuneiform texts from all over Mesopotamia, and especially Babylonia, in the library in Nineveh, the first systematically organised library in the ancient Middle East, which survives in part today.

In ancient Egypt, literacy was concentrated among an educated elite of scribes. Only people from certain backgrounds were allowed to train to become scribes, in the service of temple, pharaonic, and military authorities. The hieroglyph system was always difficult to learn, but in later centuries was purposely made even more so, as this preserved the scribes' status. The rate of literacy in Pharaonic Egypt during most periods from the third to first millennium BCE has been estimated at not more than one percent, or between one half of one percent and one percent.

One thousand years later, in ancient Israel and Judah a basic education eventually became more widespread. The Torah includes commands to read, learn, teach and write the Torah, thus requiring literacy and study. In 64 CE the high priest caused public schools to be opened in every town and hamlet for all children above six or seven years of age. The expense was borne by the community, and strict discipline was observed. Raba fixed the number of pupils at twenty-five for one teacher; if the number was between twenty-five and forty an assistant teacher was necessary; and for over forty, two teachers were required. The standard education texts were all handwritten until the invention of printing. However significant emphasis was placed on developing good memory skills in addition to comprehension by practice of oral repetition. Although girls were not provided with formal education in the yeshivah, they were required to know a large part of the subject areas to prepare them to maintain the home after marriage, and to educate the children before the age of seven. Despite this schooling system, it would seem that many children did not learn to read and write, because it has been estimated that at least 90 percent of the Jewish population of Roman Palestine in the first centuries CE could merely write their own name or not write and read at all, or that the literacy rate was about 3 percent.

***India***

In ancient India, during the Vedic period from about 1500 BCE to 600 BCE, most education was based on the *Veda* and later Hindu texts and scriptures.

Vedic education included: proper pronunciation and recitation of the Veda, the rules of sacrifice, grammar and derivation, composition, versification and meter, understanding of secrets of nature, reasoning including logic, the sciences, and the skills necessary for an occupation. Some medical knowledge existed and was taught. There is mention in the Veda of herbal medicines for various conditions or diseases, including fever, cough, baldness, snake bite and others.

Education, at first freely available in Vedic society, became over time more discriminatory as the caste system, originally based on occupation, evolved, with the brahman being the most privileged of the castes.

The oldest of the Upanishads—another part of Hindu scriptures—date from around 500 BCE. These texts encouraged an exploratory learning process where teachers and students were co-travellers in a search for truth. The teaching methods used reasoning and questioning. Nothing was labelled as the final answer.

The Gurukul system of education supported traditional Hindu residential schools of learning; typically the teacher's house or a monastery. Education was free, but students from well-to-do families paid "Gurudakshina," a voluntary contribution after the completion of their studies. At the Gurukuls, the teacher imparted knowledge of Religion, Scriptures, Philosophy, Literature, Warfare, Statecraft, Medicine Astrology and History. The corpus of Sanskrit literature encompasses a rich tradition of poetry and drama as well as technical scientific, philosophical and generally Hindu religious texts, though many central texts of Buddhism and Jainism have also been composed in Sanskrit.

Two epic poems formed part of ancient Indian education. The *Mahabharata*, part of which may date back to the eighth century BCE, discusses human goals, attempting to explain the relationship of the individual to society and the world and the workings of karma. The other epic poem, *Ramayana,* is shorter, although it has 24,000 verses. It is thought to have been compiled between about 400 BCE and 200 CE. The epic explores themes of human existence and the concept of dharma.

An early centre of learning in India dating back to the 5th century BCE was Taxila, which taught the three Vedas and the eighteen accomplishments. It was an important Vedic/Hindu and Buddhist centre of learning from the 6th century BCE to the 5th century CE.

### *China*

During the Zhou Dynasty (1045 BCE to 256 BCE), there were five national schools in the capital city, Pi Yong and four other schools for the aristocrats and nobility, including Shang Xiang. The schools mainly taught the Six Arts: rites, music, archery, charioteering, caligraphy, and mathematics. According to the Book of Rituals, at age twelve, boys learned arts related to ritual (i.e., music and dance) and when older, archery and chariot driving. Girls learned ritual, correct deportment, silk production and weaving.

It was during the Zhou Dynasty that the origins of native Chinese philosophy also developed. Confucius (551 BCE-479 BCE) founder of Confucianism, was a Chinese philosopher who made a great impact on later generations of Chinese, and on the curriculum of the Chinese educational system for much of the following 2000 years.

During the Han Dynasty (206 BCE-221 CE), boys were thought ready at age seven to start learning basic skills in reading, writing and calculation.

In 124 BCE, the Emperor Wu Han established the Imperial Academy, the curriculum of which was the Five Classics of Confucius. By the end of the Han Dynasty (220 CE) the Academy enrolled more than 30,000 students, boys between the ages of fourteen and seventeen years. However, education through this period was a luxury.

Later, during the Ch'in dynasty (246-207 BCE), a hierarchy of officials was set up to provide central control over the outlying areas of the empire. To enter this hierarchy, both literacy and knowledge of the increasing body of philosophy was required: "....the content of the educational process was designed not to engender functionally specific skills but rather to produce morally enlightened and cultivated generalists". The Nine rank system was a civil service nomination system during the Three Kingdoms (220-280 CE) and the Southern and Northern Dynasties (420-589 CE) in China. Theoretically, local government authorities were given the task of selecting talented candidates, then categorising them into nine grades depending on their abilities. In practice, however, only the rich and powerful would be selected. The Nine Rank System was eventually superseded by the Imperial examination system for the civil service in the Sui Dynasty (581-618 CE)

## *Greek and Roman Empires*

In the city-states of ancient Greece, most education was private, except in Sparta. For example, in Athens, during the 5th and 4th century BCE, aside from two years military training, the state played little part in schooling. Anyone could open a school and decide the curriculum. Parents could choose a school offering the subjects they wanted their children to learn, at a monthly fee they could afford. Most parents, even the poor, sent their sons to schools for at least a few years, and if they could afford it from around the age of seven until fourteen, learning gymnastics, music and literacy. Girls rarely received formal education. At writing school, the youngest students learned the alphabet by song, then later by copying the shapes of letters with a stylus on a waxed wooden tablet. After some schooling, the sons of poor or middle class families often learnt a trade by apprenticeship, whether with their father or another tradesman. By around 350 BCE, it was common for children at schools in Athens to also study various arts such as drawing, painting, and sculpture. The richest students continued their education by studying with sophists, from whom, they could learn subjects such as rhetoric, mathematics, geography, natural history, politics, and logic. Some of Athens' greatest schools of higher education included the Lyceum and the Platonic Academy. The education system of the wealthy ancient Greeks is also called Paideia. In the subsequent Roman empire, Greek was the primary language of science. Advanced scientific research and teaching was mainly carried on in the Hellenistic side of the Roman empire, in Greek.

The education system in the Greek city-state of Sparta was entirely different, designed to create warriors with complete obedience, courage, and physical perfection. At the age of seven, boys were taken away from their homes to live in school dormitories or military barracks. There they were taught sports, endurance and fighting, and little else, with harsh discipline. Most of the population was illiterate.

The first schools in Ancient Rome arose by the middle of the fourth century BCE. These schools were concerned with the basic socialisation and rudimentary education of young Roman children. The literacy rate in the third century BCE has been estimated as around one percent to two percent. We have very few primary sources or accounts of Roman educational process until the second century BCE, during which there was a proliferation of private schools in Rome. At the height of the Roman Republic and later the Roman Empire, the Roman educational system gradually found its final form. Formal schools were established, which served paying students. Normally, both boys and girls were educated, though not necessarily together. In a system much like the one that predominates in the modern world, the Roman education system that developed arranged schools in tiers.

It has been argued that literacy rates in the Greco-Roman world were seldom more than 20 percent; averaging perhaps not much above 10 percent in the Roman empire, though with wide regional variations, probably never rising above 5 percent in the western provinces, and that the literate in classical Greece did not much exceed 5 percent of the population.

## EDUCATION IN MIDDLE AGES

### Middle East

During the 6th and 7th centuries CE, the Academy of Gundishapur, originally the intellectual center of the Sassanid empire and subsequently a Muslim centre of learning, offered training in medicine, philosophy, theology and science. The faculty were versed not only in the Zoroastrian and Persian traditions, but in Greek and Indian learning as well.

The House of Wisdom in Bagdad was a library, translation and educational centre from the 9th to 13th centuries CE. Works on astrology, mathematics, agriculture, medicine, and philosophy were translated. Drawing on Persian, Indian and Greek texts—including those of Pythagoras, Plato, Aristotle, Hippocrates, Euclid, Plotinus, Galen, Sushruta, Charaka, Aryabhata and Brahmagupta—the scholars accumulated a great collection of knowledge in the world, and built on it through their own discoveries. The House was an unrivalled centre for the study of humanities and for sciences, including mathematics, astronomy, medicine, chemistry, zoology and geography. Baghdad was known as the world's richest city and centre for intellectual development of the time, and had a population of over a million, the largest in its time.

The Islamic world developed a schooling system during the Islamic Golden Age. A systematic way of teaching and spreading knowledge was developed in purpose built structures. At first, mosques combined both religious performance and learning activities, but by the ninth century, the Madrasah, a proper school built independently from the mosque.

According to the modern definition of a university as an institution of higher education and research which issues academic degrees at all levels, the medieval Madrasahs founded in the 9th century are the first examples of a university. The University of Al Karaouine in Fez, Morocco is thus recognised by the Guinness Book of World Records as the oldest degree-granting university in the world with its founding in 859.

Also in the 9th century, Bimaristan medical schools were formed in the medieval Islamic world, where medical diplomas were issued to students of Islamic medicine who were qualified to be a practicing Doctor of Medicine. Al-Azhar University, founded in Cairo, Egypt in 975, was a Jami'ah which offered a variety of postgraduate degrees, had a Madrasah and theological seminary, and taught Islamic law, Islamic jurisprudence, Arabic grammar, Islamic astronomy, early Islamic philosophy and logic in Islamic philosophy.

The origins of the doctorate date back to the "license to teach and issue legal opinions" in the medieval Islamic legal education system. This licence was equivalent to the Doctor of Laws qualification and was developed during the 9th century after the formation of the Madh'hab legal schools. To obtain a doctorate, a student had to study in a guild school of law, usually for four years, and at least another ten years for a post-graduate course. The doctorate was obtained after an oral examination to determine the originality of the candidate's theses, and to test the student's "ability to defend them against all objections, in disputations set up for the purpose". After completing their post-graduate education, students were awarded doctorates giving them the status of faqih, mufti and mudarris, which were later translated into Latin as magister, professor and doctor respectively.

Philosophers such as al-Kindi (801-873) and al-Farabi (870-950) translated the works of Aristotle and applied his thinking to early Islamic philosophy. Al-Khwarizmi (790-840) wrote The Compendious Book on Calculation by Completion and Balancing, the first book on Algebra. He also wrote The Image of the Earth, an updated version of Ptolemy's Geographia, and participated in a project to determine the circumference of the Earth by measuring the length of a degree of meridian on a plain in Iraq.

Under the Ottoman Empire, the towns of Bursa and Edirne became major centres of learning. The Ottoman system of Kulliye, a building complex containing a mosque, a hospital, madrassa, and public kitchen and dining areas, revolutionised the education system, making learning accessible to a wider public through its free meals, health care and sometimes free accommodation.

In the 15th and 16th centuries, the town of Timbuktu in the West African nation of Mali became an Islamic centre of learning with students coming from as far away as the Middle East. The town was home to the prestigious Sankore University and other madrasas. The primary focus of these schools was the teaching of the Qur'an, although broader instruction in fields such as logic, astronomy, and history also took place. Over time, there was a great accumulation of manuscripts in the area and an estimated 100,000 or more manuscripts, some of them dated from pre-Islamic times and 12th century, are kept by the great families from the town. Their contents are didactic, especially in the subjects of astronomy, music, and botany. More than 18,000 manuscripts have been collected by the Ahmed Baba centre.

**India**

The first millennium and the few centuries preceding it saw the flourishing of higher education at Nalanda, Takshashila University, Ujjain, and Vikramshila Universities. Amongst the subjects taught were Art, Architecture, Painting, Logic, Mathematics, Grammar, Philosophy, Astronomy, Literature, Buddhism, Hinduism, Arthashastra, Law, and Medicine. Each university specialised in a particular field of study. Takshila specialised in the study of medicine, while Ujjain laid emphasis on astronomy. Nalanda, being the biggest centre, handled all branches of knowledge, and housed up to 10,000 students at its peak.

Nalanda was a Buddhist centre of learning founded in Bihar, India around the 5th century CE and conferred academic degree titles to its graduates, while also offering post-graduate courses. It has been called "one of the first great universities in recorded history."

Vikramasila University, another important centre of Buddhist learning in India, was established by King Dharmapala (783 to 820) in response to a supposed decline in the quality of scholarship at Nalanda.

British records show that indigenous education was widespread in India in the 18th century, with a school for every temple, mosque or village in most regions of the country. The subjects taught included

Reading, Writing, Arithmetic, Theology, Law, Astronomy, Metaphysics, Ethics, Medical Science and Religion. The schools were attended by students representative of all classes of society.

**China**

Although there are more than 40,000 Chinese characters in written Chinese, many are rarely used. Studies have shown that full literacy in the Chinese language requires a knowledge of only between three and four thousand characters. In China, three oral texts were used to teach children by rote memorisation the written characters of their language and the basics of Confusian thought.

The Thousand Character Classic, a Chinese poem originating in the 6th century CE, was used for more than a millennium as a primer for teaching Chinese characters to children. The poem is composed of 250 phrases of 4 characters each, thus containing exactly one thousand unique characters, and was sung in the same way that children learning the Latin alphabet may use the "alphabet song". Later, children also learn the Hundred Family Surnames, a rhyming poem in lines of eight characters composed in the early Song Dynasty which actually listed more than four hundred of the common surnames in ancient China.

From around the 13th century CE until the latter part of the 19th century, the Three Character Classic, which is an embodiment of Confucian thought suitable for teaching to young children, served as a child's first formal education at home. The text is written in triplets of characters for easy memorisation. With illiteracy common for most people at the time, the oral tradition of reciting the classic ensured its popularity and survival through the centuries. With the short and simple text arranged in three-character verses, children learned many common characters, grammar structures, elements of Chinese history and the basis of Confucian morality. After learning Chinese characters, students wishing to ascend in the social hierarchy needed to study the Chinese classic texts.

The early Chinese state depended upon literate, educated officials for operation of the empire. In 605 CE, during the Sui Dynasty, for the first time, an examination system was explicitly instituted for a category of local talents. The merit-based imperial examination system for evaluating and selecting officials gave rise to schools that taught the Chinese classic texts and continued in use for 1,300 years, until the end the Qing Dynasty, being abolished in 1911 in favour of Western education methods. The core of the curriculum for the imperial civil service examinations from the mid 12th century CE onewards was the Four Books, representing a foundational introduction to Confucianism.

In the period preceding 1040-1050 CE, prefectural schools had been neglected by the state and left to the devices of wealthy patrons who provided private finances. The Chancellor of China at that time, Fan Zhongyan, issued an edict that would have used a combination of government funding and private financing to restore and rebuild all prefectural schools that had fallen into disuse and abandoned. He also attempted to restore all county-level schools in the same manner, but did not designate where funds for the effort would be formally acquired and the decree was not taken seriously until a later period. Fan's trend of government funding for education set in motion the movement of public schools that eclipsed private academies, which would not be officially reversed until the mid-13th century.

## Japan

The history of education in Japan dates back at least to the sixth century, when Chinese learning was introduced at the Yamato court. Foreign civilisations have often provided new ideas for the development of Japan's own culture.

Chinese teachings and ideas flowed into Japan from the sixth to the ninth century. Along with the introduction of Buddhism came the Chinese system of writing and its literary tradition, and Confucianism.

By the ninth century, Heian-kyo, the imperial capital, had five institutions of higher learning, and during the remainder of the Heian period, other schools were established by the nobility and the imperial court. During the medieval period (1185-1600), Zen Buddhist monasteries were especially important centers of learning, and the Ashikaga School, Ashikaga Gakko, flourished in the fifteenth century as a centre of higher learning.

## Europe

During the Early Middle Ages, the monasteries of the Catholic Church were the centres of education and literacy, preserving the Church's selection from Latin learning and maintaining the art of writing. Ireland became known as the island of saints and scholars. Monasteries were built all over Ireland and these became centres of great learning.

Northumbria was famed as a centre of religious learning and arts. Initially the kingdom was evangelised by monks from the Celtic Church, which led to a flowering of monastic life, and Northumbria played an important role in the formation of Insular art, a unique style combining Anglo-Saxon, Celtic, Byzantine and other elements. After the Synod of Whitby in 664 CE, Roman church practices officially replaced the Celtic ones but the influence of the Anglo-Celtic style continued, the most famous examples of this being the Lindisfarne Gospels. The Venerable Bede (673-735) wrote his Historia ecclesiastica gentis Anglorum (Ecclesiastical History of the English People, completed in 731) in a Northumbrian monastery, and much of it focuses on the kingdom.

During the reign of Charlemagne, King of the Franks from 768-814 CE, whose empire united most of Western Europe for the first time since the Romans, there was a flowering of scholarship, literature, art, and architecture sometimes referred to as the Carolingian Renaissance. Brought into contact with the culture and learning of other countries through his vast conquests, Charlemagne greatly increased the provision of monastic schools and scriptoria in Francia. Most of the surviving works of classical Latin were copied and preserved by Carolingian scholars.

Charlemagne took a serious interest in scholarship, promoting the liberal arts at the court, ordering that his children and grandchildren be well-educated, and even studying himself under the tutelage of Paul the Deacon, from whom he learned grammar, Alcuin, with whom he studied rhetoric, dialect and astronomy, and Einhard, who assisted him in his studies of arithmetic. His great scholarly failure, as Einhard relates, was his inability to write.

The English monk Alcuin was invited to Charlemagne's court at Aachen, and brought with him the precise classical Latin education that was available in the monasteries of Northumbria. The return of this Latin proficiency to the kingdom of the Franks is regarded as an important step in the development of mediaeval Latin. Charlemagne's chancery made use of a type of script currently known as Carolingian minuscule, providing a common writing style that allowed for communication across most of Europe. After the decline of the Carolingian dynasty, the rise of the Saxon Dynasty in Germany was accompanied by the Ottonian Renaissance.

Cathedral schools and monasteries remained important throughout the Middle Ages; at the Third Lateran Council of 1179 the Church mandated that priests provide the oppurtunity of a free education to their flocks, and the 12th and 13th century renascence known as the Scholastic Movement was spread through the monasteries. These however, ceased to be the sole sources of education in the 11th century when universities, which grew out of the monasticism began to be established in major European cities. Literacy became available to a wider class of people, and there were major advances in art, sculpture, music and architecture.

During the 12th and 13th century in Europe, large numbers of Greek and Arabic works on medicine and the sciences were translated and distributed throughout Europe. Aristotle especially continued to be very important, his rational and logical approach to knowledge influencing the scholars at the newly forming universities which were absorbing, disseminating and elaborating the new knowledge and the developing thought during the 12th Century.

## History of Modern Education

Modern systems of education derive their origins from the schools of the high middle ages. Most schools during this era were founded upon religious principles with the primary purpose of training the clergy.

### Europe

Many of the earliest universities, such as the University of Paris founded in 1150, had a Christian basis. In addition to this, a number of secular universities existed, such as the University of Bologna, founded in 1088. Free education for the poor was officially mandated by the Church at the Third Lateran Council (1179), which decreed that every cathedral must assign a master to teach boys too poor to pay the regular fee; parishes and monasteries also established free schools teaching at least basic literary skills. With few exceptions, priests and brothers taught locally, and their salaries were frequently subsidised by towns. Private, independent schools reappeared in medieval Europe during this time, but they, too, were religious in nature and mission.

The curriculum of the educational institutions of this period was frequently based around the trivium and quadrivium and was conducted in Latin, the lingua franca of educated Western Europe throughout the Middle Ages and Renaissance.

In northern Europe this clerical education was largely superseded by forms of elementary schooling following the Reformation. In Scotland, for instance, the national Church of Scotland set out a programe for spiritual reform in January 1561 setting the principle of a school teacher for every parish church and free education for the poor. This was provided for by an Act of the Parliament of Scotland, passed in 1633, which introduced a tax to pay for this programe. Although few countries of the period had such extensive systems of education, the period between the sixteenth and eighteenth centuries saw education become significantly more widespread.

In Central Europe, the seventeenth century scientist and educator John Amos Comenius promulgated a reformed system of universal education that was widely used in Europe. This growth resulted in increased government interest in education. In the 1760s, for instance, Ivan Betskoy was appointed by the Russian Tsarina, Catherine II, as educational advisor. He proposed to educate young Russians of both sexes in state boarding schools, aimed at creating "a new race of men". Betskoy's work in Russia was soon followed by the Polish establishment in 1773 of a Commission of National Education. The Commission functioned as the first government Ministry of Education in a European country. Meanwhile, there was an increasing academic interest in education and the first attempts to create what might be considered academic rationales for teaching methods. This led, in the 1770s, to the establishment of the first chair of pedagogy at the University of Halle in Germany. Contributions to the study of education elsewhere in Europe included the work of Johann Heinrich Pestalozzi in Switzerland and Joseph Lancaster in Britain. Under the guidance of Wilhelm von Humboldt a new university was founded in

Berlin in 1810 which became the model for many research universities. Herbart developed a system of pedagogy widely used in German-speaking areas.

In the late nineteenth century, most of West, Central, and parts of East Europe began to provide elementary education in reading, writing, and arithmetic, partly because politicians believed that education was needed for orderly political behaviour. As more people became literate, they realised that most secondary education was only open to those who could afford it. Having created primary education, the major nations had to give further attention to secondary education by World War I.

In the twentieth century, new directions in education included, in Italy, Maria Montessori's Montessori schools; and in Germany, Rudolf Steiner's development of Waldorf education.

**India**

Education was widespread in the 18th century, with a schools in most regions of the country. The subjects taught included Reading, Writing, Arithmetic, Theology, Law, Astronomy, Metaphysics, Ethics, Medical Science and Religion.

The current system of education, with its western style and content, was introduced and founded by the British during the British Raj, following recommendations by Lord Macaulay. Traditional structures were not recognised by the British government and have been on the decline since. Gandhi, in a speech in London on October 20, 1931, described the traditional educational system as a beautiful tree that was destroyed during the British rule.

**Japan**

By 1603 Japan had been re-unified by the Tokugawa regime (1600-1867), and by 1640 foreigners had been ordered out of Japan, Christianity banned, and virtually all foreign contact prohibited. The nation then entered a period of isolation and relative domestic tranquillity, which was to last 200 years. When the Tokugawa period began, few common people in Japan could read or write. By the period's end, learning had become widespread. Tokugawa education left a valuable legacy: an increasingly literate populace, a meritocratic ideology, and an emphasis on discipline and competent performance. Under subsequent Meiji leadership, this foundation would facilitate Japan's rapid transition from feudal country to modern nation.

One of the things that amazed Europeans that arrived in Japan at the end of the Edo period was that the Japanese were very well educated. It is estimated that the literacy rate was already over 80% for men and somewhere in the 60s or 70s for women and much higher in cities like Edo and Osaka. Samurai curricula stressed morality and included both military and literary studies. Confucian classics were memorised, and reading and recitating them were common methods of study. Arithmetic and calligraphy were also studied. Most samurai attended schools sponsored by their han, and by the time of the Meiji Restoration of 1868, more than 200 of the 276 Han had established schools. Some Samurai and even commoners also attended private academies, which often specialised in particular Japanese subjects or in Western medicine, modern military science, gunnery, or Rangaku, as European studies were called.

Education of commoners was generally practically oriented, providing basic training in reading, writing, and arithmetic, emphasising calligraphy and use of the abacus. Much of this education was conducted in so-called temple schools, derived from earlier Buddhist schools. These schools were no longer religious institutions, nor were they, by 1867, predominantly located in temples. By the end of the Tokugawa period, there were more than 11,000 such schools, attended by 750,000 students. Teaching techniques included reading from various textbooks, memorising, abacus, and repeatedly copying Chinese characters and Japanese script.

The origins of education in Japan are closely related to religion. Schooling was conducted at temples for youngsters who wanted to study Buddhism to become priests. Later, children who were willing to study started to meet at places called, "Tera-koya" and learned how to read and write Japanese.

**Imperial Russia**

In Imperial Russia, according to the 1897 Population Census, literate people made up 28.4 percent of the population. During the 8th Party Congress of 1919, the creation of the new Socialist system of education was proclaimed the major aim of the Soviet government. The abolition of illiteracy became the primary task in the Russian SFSR.

In accordance with the Sovnarkom decree of December 26, 1919, signed by its head Vladimir Lenin, the new policy of likbez, was introduced. The new system of universal compulsory education was established for children. Millions of illiterate adult people all over the country, including residents of small towns and villages, were enrolled in special literacy schools. Komsomol members and Young Pioneer detachments played an important role in the education of illiterate people in villages. The most active phase of likbez lasted until 1939. In 1926, the literacy rate was 56.6 percent of the population. By 1937, according to census data, the literacy rate was 86% for men and 65% for women, making a total literacy rate of 75%.

An important aspect of the early campaign for literacy and education was the policy of "indigenisation" (korenizatsiya). This policy, which lasted essentially from the mid-1920s to the late 1930s, promoted the development and use of non-Russian languages in the government, the media, and education. Intended to counter the historical practices of Russification, it had as another practical goal assuring native-language education as the quickest way to increase educational levels of future generations. A huge network of so-called "national schools" was established by the 1930s, and this network continued to grow in enrollments throughout the Soviet era. Language policy changed over time, perhaps marked first of all in the government's mandating in 1938 the teaching of Russian as a required subject of study in every non-Russian school, and then especially beginning in the latter 1950s a growing conversion of non-Russian schools to Russian as the main medium of instruction.

**Africa**

Until at least 1900 CE, in most African countries south of the Sahara, children received traditional informal education on matters such as artistic performances, ceremonies, rituals, games, festivals, dancing, singing, and drawing. Boys and girls were taught separately to help prepare each sex for their adult roles. Every member of the community had a hand in contributing to the educational upbringing of the child. The high point of the African educational experience was the ritual passage ceremony from childhood to adulthood.

Nowadays, many sub-Saharan African countries have low rates of participation in formal education. Schools often lack basic facilities, and African universities may suffer from overcrowding and the difficulties of retaining staff attracted overseas by higher pay and better conditions.

Africa has more than 40 million children. According to UNESCO's Regional overview on sub-Saharan Africa, in 2000 only 58% of children were enrolled in primary schools, the lowest enrollment rate of any region. The USAID Center reports as of 2005, forty percent of school-aged children in Africa do not attend primary school.

## Recent Trends

Today, right to education has been described as a basic human right: since 1952, Article 2 of the first Protocol to the European Convention on Human Rights obliges all signatory parties to guarantee the right to education. At world level, the United Nations' International Covenant on Economic, Social and Cultural Rights of 1966 guarantees this right under its Article 13.

Overall, illiteracy has greatly decreased in recent years. In some countries this has been the result of deliberate government action. Illiteracy and the percentage of populations without any schooling have decreased in the past several decades. Among developing countries, illiteracy and percentages without schooling in 2000 stood at about half the 1970 figures. Among developed countries, figures about illiteracy rates differ widely. Often it is said that they decreased from 6% to 1%. However, the National Adult Literacy Survey of 1993 showed that more than 20% of the adults in the USA were functionally illiterate. These findings were confirmed in a 2003 follow-up study. Illiteracy rates in less economically developed countries (LEDCs) surpassed those of more economically developed countries (MEDCs) by a factor of 10 in 1970, and by a factor of about 20 in 2000. Illiteracy decreased greatly in LEDCs, and virtually disappeared in MEDCs. Percentages without any schooling showed similar patterns.

Education is becoming increasingly international. Not only are the materials becoming more influenced by the rich international environment, but exchanges among students at all levels are also playing an increasingly important role. In Europe, for example, the Socrates-Erasmus Programe stimulates exchanges across European universities. Also, the Soros Foundation provides many opportunities for students from central Asia and eastern Europe. Some scholars argue that, regardless of whether one system is considered better or worse than another, experiencing a different way of education can often be considered to be the most important, enriching element of an international learning experience.

Although the field fo education is well-developed, it faces numerous challenges. In some developing countries, the number and seriousness of the problems faced are naturally greater. People in more remote or agrarian areas are sometimes unaware of the importance of education. However, many countries have an active Ministry of Education, and in many subjects, such as foreign language learning, the degree of education is actually much higher than in industrialised countries; for example, it is not at all uncommon for students in many developing countries to be reasonably fluent in multiple foreign languages, whereas this is much more of a rarity in the supposedly "more educated" countries where much of the population is in fact monolingual. There is also economic pressure from those parents who prefer their children making money in the short-term over any long-term benefits of education. Recent studies on child labour and poverty have suggested that when poor families reach a certain economic threshold where families are able to provide for their basic needs, parents return their children to school. This has been found to be true, once the threshold has been breached, even if the potential economic value of the children's work has increased since their return to school. Teachers are often paid less than other similar professions.

A lack of good universities, and a low acceptance rate for good universities, is evident in countries with a relatively high population density. In some countries, there are uniform, over structured, inflexible centralised programes from a central agency that regulates all aspects of education.

India is now developing technologies that will skip land based phone and internet lines. Instead, India launched EDUSAT, an education satellite that can reach more of the country at a greatly reduced cost. There is also an initiative started by a group out of MIT and supported by several major corporations to develop a $100 laptop. This laptops should be available by late 2009 or 2010. The laptops, sold at cost, will enable developing countries to give their children a digital education, and to close the digital divide across the world.

## References

Coulson, Joseph. (1999). *Market Education: The Unknown History.* Transaction Publishers.

Cordasco, Francesco. (1976). A Brief History of Education: A Handbook of Information on Greek, Roman, Medieval, Renaissance, and Modern Educational Practice". Rowman & Little field.

Hartmut Scharfe (2002). *Education in Ancient India.* Brill Academic Publishers.

Michael Chiappetta (1953) "Historiography and Roman Education," *History of Education Journal* 4, no. 4 . 149-156.

Yun Lee Too, (2001) *Education in Greek and Roman antiquity.* Boston: Brill.

# 2

# History of Education in India

The history of education in India began with teaching of traditional elements such as Indian religions, Indian mathematics, Indian logic at early Hindu and Buddhist centres of learning such as Taxila and Nalanda before the common era. Islamic education became ingrained with the establishment of the Islamic empires in India in the middle ages while the coming of the Europeans later bought western education to colonial India. A series of measures continuing throughout the early half of the 20th century ultimately laid the foundation of education in the Republic of India.

One can trace the ancient Indian education to the 3rd century BC. Research shows that in the ancient days, sages and scholars imparted education orally, but after the development of letters, it took the form of writing. Palm leaves and barks of trees were used for education, and this in turn helped spread the written literature. Temples and community centers often took the role of schools.

When Buddhism spread in India, education became available to everyone and this led to the establishment of some world famous educational institutions Nalanda, Vikramshila and Takshashila. These educational institutes in fact, arose from the monasteries. History has taken special care to give Nalanda University, which flourished from the fifth to 13th century AD, full credit for its excellence. This university had around 10,000 resident students and teachers on its roll at one time. These students included Chinese, Sri Lankan, Korean and other international scholars.

It was in the 11th century that the Muslims established elementary and secondary schools. This led to the forming of few universities too at cities like Delhi, Lucknow and Allahabad. Medieval period saw excellent interaction between Indian and Islamic traditions in all fields of knowledge like theology, religion, philosophy, fine arts, painting, architecture, mathematics, medicine and astronomy.

Later, when the British arrived in India, English education came into being with the help of the European missionaries. Since then, Western education has made steady advances in the country. With hundreds of universities and thousands of colleges affiliated to them, in fact, scores of colleges in every discipline, India has positioned itself comfortably as a country that provides quality higher education to its people in specific and to the world in general.

## Early History

Early education in India commenced under the supervision of a Guru. The education was imparted on the basis of caste and the related duties that one had to perform as a member of a specific caste. The Brahmans learned about scriptures and religion while the Kshatriya were educated in the various aspects of warfare. The Vaishya caste learned commerce and other specific vocational courses while education was largely denied to the Shudras, the lowest caste. The earliest venues of education in India were often secluded from the main population. Students were expected to follow strict monastic guidelines prescribed by the guru and stay away from cities in ashrams. However, as population increased under the Gupta empire centres of urban learning became increasingly common and cities such as Varanasi and the Buddhist centre at Nalanda became increasingly visible.

Nalanda was the highest learning centre not just of India but also of the entire South Asia. Students from foreign countries like China, Japan, Korea, Sri Lanka used to come here for higher studies. It had around 10,000 students and teachers on its roll cards. The University had eight colleges. And one of the colleges had four-storied building. It was one of the earliest examples of residential cum learning complex.

Varanasi was famous for religious teachings. In the South, Kanchi was famous for its studies while the Vallabhi University was no less. Huan Tsang in his records mention the university to be at par with Nalanda and Vikramshila universities.

Education in India in its traditional form was closely related to religion. Among the Heterodox schools of belief were the Jain and Buddhist schools. Heterodox Buddhist education was more inclusive and aside of the monastic orders the Buddhist education centres comprised of urban institutes of learning such as Taxila and Nalanda where grammar, medicine, philosophy, logic, metaphysics, arts and crafts etc. were also taught. Early secular Buddhist institutions of higher learning like Taxila and Nalanda continued to function well into the common era and were attended by students from China and Central Asia.

On the subject of education for the nobility Joseph Prabhu writes: "Outside the religious framework, kings and princes were educated in the arts and sciences related to government: politics (*danda-niti*), economics (*vartta*), philosophy (*anviksiki*), and historical traditions (*itihasa*). Here the authoritative source was Kautilya's Arthashastra, often compared to Niccolò Machiavelli's "The Prince for its worldly outlook and political scheming." The Rgveda dating from 1500 BCE mentions female poets called brahmavadinis, specifically Lopamudra and Ghosha. By 800 BCE women such as Gargi and Maitreyi were mentioned as scholars in the religious Upanishads. Maya, mother of the historic Buddha, was an educated queen while other women in India contributed to writing of the Pali canon. Out of the composers of the Sangam literature 154 were women. However, the education and society of the era continued to be dominated by educated male population.

The formal admission ceremony was known as 'Upanayana'. With the accomplishment of this ceremony the child had to leave his home for the 'ashrama' where he would receive education. It was supposed to be the re-birth of the child and was known as 'Dvijya', which means, "twice born". Sanskrit was the language of teaching. It was supposed to be the language of learned men. The academies of higher learning were known as 'Parisads'. The education system involved of three basic processes, which included 'Sravana', 'Manana' and 'Nidhyasana'.

In the 'Sravana' stage of education, students received 'shrutis' knowledge, which was passed orally from one generation to another. The second stage was 'Manana' which means that pupils had to think themselves about what they have heard. They have to make their own inferences and assimilate the lesson taught by their teacher into the life. The third stage 'Nidhyasana' means complete comprehension of truth and its use in the life.

In ancient India women were given the equal right to education and teaching. Women seers like 'Gayatri' were prominent participants in educational debates and the proceedings of the 'Parishads'. (Assemblies) It was mainly the Brahmins followed by Kshatriyas that received education at the Gurukuls while the boys from the lower caste learnt their family trade from their fathers.

## Early Common Era

Chinese scholars such as Xuanzang and Yi Jing arrived in Indian institutions of learning to survey Buddhist texts. Yi Jing additionally noted the arrival of 56 scholars from China, Japan, and Korea. However, the Buddhist institutions of learning were slowly giving way to a resurgent tradition of Brahmanism during that era. Scholars from India also journeyed to China to translate Buddhist texts. During the 10th century a monk named Dharmadeva from Nalanda journeyed to China and translated a number of texts. Another centre at Vikramshila maintained close relations with Tibet. The Buddhist teacher Atisa was the head monk in Vikramshila before his journey to Tibet.

Examples of royal patronage include construction of buildings under the Rastrakuta dynasty in 945 CE. The institutions arranged for multiple residences for educators as well as state sponsored education and arrangements for students and scholars. Similar arrangements were made by the Chola dynasty in 1024 CE, which provided state support to selected students in educational establishments. Temple schools from 12-13th centuries included the school at the Nataraja temple situated at Chidambaram which employed 20 librarians, out of whom 8 were copiers of manuscripts and 2 were employed for verification of the copied manuscripts. The remaining staff conducted other duties, including preservation and maintained of reference material.

Another establishment during this period is the Uddandapura institute established during the 8th century under the patronage of the Pala dynasty. The institution developed ties with Tibet and became a centre of Tantric Buddhism. During the 10-11th centuries the number of monks reached a thousand, equalling the strength of monks at the sacred Mahabodhi complex. By the time of the arrival of the Islamic scholar Al Biruni, India already had an established system of science and technology in place. Also by the 12th century, invasions from India's northern borders disrupted traditional education systems as foreign armies raided educational institutes, among other establishments.

## Late Middle Ages

With the advent of Islam in India the traditional methods of education increasingly came under Islamic influence. Pre-Mughal rulers such as Qutb-ud-din Aybak and other Muslim rulers initiated institutions which imparted religious knowledge. Scholars such as Nizamuddin Auliya and Moinuddin Chishti became prominent educators and established Islamic monasteries. Students from Bukhara and Afghanistan visited India to study humanities and science.

Islamic institution of education in India included traditional madrassas and maktabs which taught grammar, philosophy, mathematics, and law influenced by the Greek traditions inherited by Persia and the Middle East before Islam spread from these regions into India. A feature of this traditional Islamic education was its emphasis on the connection between science and humanities. Among the centres of education in India was 18th century Delhi was the *Madrasa Rahimiya* under the supervision of Shah Waliullah, an educator who favoured an approach balancing the Islamic scriptures and science. The course at the *Madrasa Rahimiya* prescribed 2 books on grammar, 1 book on philosophy, 2 books on logic, 2 books on astronomy and mathematics, and 5 books on mysticism. Another centre of prominence arose in Lucknow under Mulla Nizamuddin Sahlawi, who educated at the *Firangi Mahal* and prescribed a course called the *Dars-i-Nizami* which combined traditional studies with modern and laid emphasis on logic.

The education system under the rule of Akbar adopted an inclusive approach with the monarch favouring additional courses comprising of medicine, agriculture, geography, and even from texts from other languages and religions, such as Patanjali's work in Sanskrit. The traditional science in this period was influenced by the ideas of Aristotle, Bhaskara, Charaka and Ibn Sina. This inclusive approach was not uncommon in Mughal India. The more conservative monarch Aurangzeb also favoured teaching of subjects which could be applied to administration. The Mughals, in fact, adopted a liberal approach to sciences and as contact with Persia increased the more intolerant Ottoman school of manqul education came to be gradually substituted by the more relaxed manqul school.

The middle ages also saw the rise of private tuition in India. A tutor, or Riyazi, was a an educated professional who could earn a suitable living by performing tasks such as creating calenders or generating revenue estimates for nobility. Another trend in this era is the mobility among professions, exemplified by Qaim Khan, a prince famous for his mastery in crafting leather shoes and forging cannons.

## Colonial Era

During the 19th and 20th centuries most of the Indian princely states fell under the British Raj. The British rule during the 19th century did not take adequate measures to help develop science and technology in India and instead focused more on arts and humanities. Till 1899 only the University of Bombay offered a separate degree in sciences. In 1899 B.Sc and M.Sc. courses were also supported by the University of Calcutta (Now Kalkata). By the late 1800s India had lagged behind in science and technology and related education. However, the nobility and aristocracy in India largely continued to encourage the development of sciences and technical education, both traditional and western.

While some science related subjects were not allowed in the government curriculum in the 1850s the private institutions could also not follow science courses due to lack of funds required to establish laboratories etc. The fees for scientific education under the British rule were also high. The salary that one would get in the colonial administration was meagre and made the prospect of attaining higher education bleak since the native population was not employed for high positions in the colonial setup. Even the natives who did manage to attain higher education faced issues of discrimination in terms of wages and privileges.

One argument for the British detachment towards the study of science in India is that England itself was gradually outpaced in science and technology by European rival Germany and a resurgent United States of America so the prospects of the British Raj adopting a world class science policy towards its colonies increasingly decreased. However, Deepak Kumar notes the British turn to professional education during the 1860s and the French initiatives at raising awareness on science and technology in French colonies. The British themselves undertook science initiatives in Canada and South Africa. Growing awareness for the need of technical education in India gave rise to establishment of institutions such as the Indian Institute of Science, established by philanthropist Jamshetji Tata in 1909. By the 1930s India had a total of only 10 institutions offering engineering courses. However, with the advent of the second world war in 1939 the "War Technicians Training Scheme" under Ernest Bevin was initiated, thereby laying the foundation of modern technical education in India. Later, planned development of scientific education under Ardeshir Dalal was initiated in 1944.

The Madras Medical College opened in 1875, and imparted medical education to women so that they could treat the female population who traditionally shied away from medical treatments under qualified male professionals. The concept of educated women among medical professionals gained popularity during the late 1800s and by 1894, the Women's Christian Medical College, an exclusive medical school for women, was established in Ludhiana of Punjab.

British education became solidified into India as missionary schools were established during the 1920s. New policies in 1835 gave rise to the use of English as a medium of education of western science. Fritz Blackwell writes: 'With the establishment of five universities in major cities in the middle of the century and the increase in primary and secondary schools, political consciousness also increased. The curriculum was Western, and the response was impressive; for example, the University of Calcutta in 1900 was reportedly the largest university in the world, with more than eight thousand students. Further, a number of Indians, including Gandhi and Nehru attended university in England.'

## Present Educational System

The present educational system of India is an implantation of British rulers. Wood's Dispatch of 1854 laid the foundation of present system of education in India. Before the advent of British in India, education system was private one. With the introduction of Wood's Dispatch known as Magna Carta of Indian education, the whole scenario changed. The main purpose of it was to prepare Indian Clerks for running local administration. Under it the means of school educations were the vernacular languages while the higher education was granted in English only. British government started giving funds to indigenous schools in need of help and thus slowly some of the schools became government-aided.

Contemplating on the new system which was introduced Mahatma Gandhi expressed his anguish in following words,

> "I say without fear of my figures being challenged successfully, that today India is more illiterate than it was fifty or a hundred years ago, and so is Burma, because the British administrators, when they came to India, instead of taking hold of things as they were, began to root them out. They scratched the soil and began to look at the root, and left the root like that, and the beautiful tree perished. The village schools were not good enough for the British administrator, so he came out with his programe. Every school must have so much paraphernalia, building, and so forth. Well, there were no such schools at all. There are statistics left by a British administrator which show that, in places where they have carried out a survey, ancient schools have gone by the board, because there was no recognition for these schools, and the schools established after the European pattern were too expensive for the people, and therefore they could not possibly overtake the thing. I defy anybody to fulfil a programe of compulsory primary education of these masses inside of a century. This very poor country of mine is ill able to sustain such an expensive method of education. Our state would revive the old village schoolmaster and dot every village with a school both for boys and girls."

## References

Blackwell, Fritz (2004), *India: A Global Studies Handbook*, United States of America: ABC-CLIO, Inc.

Elder, Joseph W. (2006), "Caste System", *Encyclopedia of India (vol. 1)* edited by Stanley Wolpert, 223-229, Thomson Gale.

Prabhu, Joseph (2006), "Educational Institutions and Philosophies, Traditional and Modern", *Encyclopedia of India (vol. 2)* edited by Stanley Wolpert, 23–28, Thomson Gale.

Raman, S.A. (2006). "Women's Education", *Encyclopedia of India (vol. 4)*, edited by Stanley Wolpert, 235-239, Thomson Gale.

# 3

# Education in Ancient India

India has a rich tradition of learning and education right from the antiquity. These were handed over generations to generations either through oral or written medium. The highly esteemed Vedas have come to down to us. They existed for nearly 2000 years before they were known in India. It was the knowledge of acoustics that enabled ancient Indians to orally transmit the Vedas from generation to generation.

Institutional form of imparting learning came into existence in the early centuries of the Christian era. The approach to learning was to study logic and epistemology. The study of logic was followed by Hindus, Buddhists and Jains, one of the most important topics of Indian thoughts was pramana or means of reliable knowledge. The Nyaya schools upheld four pramanas—perceptions are liable by analogy or comparison, word (Sabda), and pronunciation of a reliable authority such as the Vedas. The Vedanta school added one more to it i.e. intuition. It is probably while studying the process of inference that the schools of true logic arose.

Ancient Indian postulated syllogism though not as accurate as that of Aristotle. Yet, they recognise some of the major fallacies of logic like reduction and absurdum, circular argument,infinite regression, dilemma, and ignorance. In the field epistemology, Jains contributed the most. There were not only two possibilities of existence and non-existence but seven more. Although the modern logicians might laugh at this pedantic system of ontological and epistemological reality they concede that the world is more complex and subtle than we think it to be. Regarding institutional form of education the first was the guru-sishya system.

According to sacred texts, the training of the Brahmin pupil took place at the home of a Brahmin teacher. In some texts the guru is depicted as the poor ascetic and it is the duty of the student to beg for his teacher. The first lesson that was taught to the student was the performance of sandhya and also reciting of gayatri. The family functioned as a domestic school, an asrama or a hermitage where the mental faculties of the pupils were developed by the teacher's constant attention and personal instruction. Education treated as a matter of individual concern, did not admit of the method of mass production applicable in industry. The making of man was regarded as an artistic and not a mechanical process. Indeed, the aim of education was the developing of the pupil's personality, his innate and latent capacities. This view of education as a process of one's inner growth and self-fulfillment evolved its own technique, its rules, methods and practices.

The thinking principle, Manana Shakti was reckoned higher than the subject of thinking. So the primary subject of education was the mind itself. According to the ancient Indian theory of education, the training of the mind and the process of thinking, are essential for the acquisition of knowledge. The chase counts more than the game. So the pupil had mainly to educate himself and achieves his own mental growth. Education was reduced to the three simple processes of Sravana, Manana and Niddhyaasana.

*Sravana* was listening to the truths as they fell from the lips of the teacher. Knowledge was technically called Sruti or what was heard by the ear and not what was seen in writing.

The second process of knowledge called *Manana* implies that the pupil has to think out for himself the meaning of the lessons imparted to him orally by his teacher so that they may be assimilate fully.

The third step known as *Nidhyasana* means complete comprehension by the pupil of the truth that is taught so that he may live the truth and not merely explain it by word. Knowledge must result in realisation.

The admission was made by the formal ceremony Upanayana or initiation by which the pupil left the home of his natural parents for that of the preceptor. In this new home he had a second birth and was called Dvijya or twice-born. Besides these regular schools of instructions, there were special institutions for the promotion of advánce study and research. These are called in the Rig Veda as Brahmana-Sangha, Academies of learned most its discussions hammered into shape the very language of the country, the refined language of Sanksrit (Samkrata) as the Vehicle of highest thought. These Academics were called Parisads, there is a reference to the Pancala Parisad in the Upanishads, in whose proceedings even kings participated, learning was also prompted by discussions at public meetings which were a regular of rural life, and were addressed by wandering scholars known as Carakas. These scholars toured the country to deliver public discourses and invite discussion.

What might count as earliest literary congress of the world was the congress of philosophers which was codification of Brahmanical philosophy by discussing the subject under the direction of the master philosopher, Yajnavalkya. In these deliberations at the highest level, a lady-philosopher named Gargi was a prominent participant beside men like Uddalaka Arni. Obviously, in those days women were admitted to the highest knowledge and did not suffer from any education disabilities. There was equality between the sexes in the filed of knowledge.

The Rig Veda mentions women Rais called Brahmanávadinis. To begin with, in ancient India; the main subject was the Veda. The teacher would instruct handful of students seated on ground. For many hours daily they would repeat verses after verses of the Vedas till they attain mastery of at least one of them. To ensure correctness of memory, the hymns were taught in more than one way. Soon the curriculum was expanded. The limbs of the Veda or the six Vedangas were taught—the performance of sacrifice, correct pronunciation, knowledge of prosody, etymology, grammar, and jyotisha or the science of calendar. Also in the post-Vedic era, teachers often instructed their students in the six schools of Philosophy.

The writers of Smritis maintain that young women of upper class underwent this kind of training. This is a doubtful contention. Princes and other leading Kshatriyas were trained in all the manifold sciences to make them fit for government. Most boys of the lower orders learnt their trades from their fathers. Some cities became renowned because of their teachers. Chief among them were—Varanasi, Taxila from the day of Buddha and Kanchi in the beginning of the Christian era. Varanasi was famous for its religious teachers. Taxila was known for its secular studies. Among the famous men connected with Taxila was Panini, the grammarian of the fifth or fourth century B.C.: Kautilya, the Brahmin minister of Chandragupta Maurya and Charaka one of the two leading authorities of Indian medical sciences. The institutions imparting Vedic knowledge that exists even today.

## Education in Later Vedic Period

History unveils the fact that there was a well-planned system of education in later Vedic period. Education at that time began with the ceremony of Upanayana. The student wore the skin of antelope, the girdle of Kusa grass and collected fuel for worshipping god Agni. Begging for his preceptor was also one of his daily duties. The pupil lived with his teacher. Begging for alms was prescribed for the pupil to produce in him a spirit of humility. The student as a rule studied with his preceptor for twelve years.

There were many scholars, who after completing their education wandered in quest of knowledge. They were called Charakas. There were also associations for advanced study and research. One such association was Panchala-parisad. Kings also organised conferences where philosophers participated in discussions. King Janaka of Videha organised one such Conference that was presided over by sage Yajnavalkya.

The ultimate aim of education in later Vedic period was the attainment of highest knowledge, the knowledge of Brahman or Atman as the supreme reality. The purpose of education in later Vedic period was thus to achieve the utmost knowledge—the knowledge of soul and God. As stated by the scholar, Dr. Radha Kumud Mookerjee, "The ultimate aim of education was the attainment of highest knowledge, the knowledge of Bramha or Atma as the sole and supreme reality. But it can be attained only by complete conquest of desire and renunciation of the world". There were many ladies like Gargi and Maitreyi who took part in philosophical discussions.

Education in the later Vedic period was strategically limited to the main three upper castes. The guru shishya tradition as one of the most sacred traditions of India was accepted in the sphere of education in later Vedic period. The subjects of study during that time included the four Vedas, Grammar, Mathematics, Mineralogy, Logic, Ethics, Brahma-Vidya, Biology, Military Science, Astronomy, and Medicine. Dhanur Vidya or war tactics was also a part of education in later Vedic period.

There had been a vast progression in the sphere of education in the later Vedic period. Debates among scholars used to be held to decide religious and philosophical disputes. The debate between Yojnavalkaya and Gargi in the Sabha of Janak is an unforgettable historical truth. Kings used to give away prizes to winners in debates.

Literature also flourished as an immediate effect of the advancement of education in later Vedic period. As remarked by one of the scholars, "The age of the later Vedic literature of Brahmans and Upanishads is universally admitted as the golden age of literature and intellectual progress of which the highest level is registered in the works known as Aranyakas and Upanishads".

## Gurukul System

India has a long history of organised education. The Gurukul system of education is one of the oldest on earth, and was dedicated to the highest ideals of all-round human development: physical, mental and spiritual. Gurukuls were traditional Hindu residential schools of learning; typically the teacher's house or a monastery. Education was free, but students from well-to-do families payed Gurudakshina, a voluntary contribution after the completion of their studies.

At the Gurukuls, the teacher imparted knowledge of Religion, Scriptures, Philosophy, Literature, Warfare, Statecraft, Medicine and Astrology. The first millennium and the few centuries preceding it saw the flourishing of higher education at Nalanda, Takshila, Ujjain, and Vikramshila Universities. Art, Architecture, Painting, Logic, Grammar, Philosophy, Astronomy, Literature, Buddhism, Hinduism, Arthashastra, Law, and Medicine were among the subjects taught and each university specialised in a particular field of study.

Takshila specialised in the study of medicine, while Ujjain laid emphasis on astronomy. Nalanda, being the biggest centre, handled all branches of knowledge, and housed upto 10,000 students at its peak. British records show that education was widespread in the 18th century, with a school for every temple, mosque or village in most regions of the country. The subjects taught included Reading, Writing, Arithmetic, Theology, Law, Astronomy, Metaphysics, Ethics, Medical Science and Religion.

The schools were attended by students representative of all classes of society. The current system of education, with its western style and content, was introduced & funded by the British in the 20th century, following recommendations by Macaulay. Traditional structures were not recognised by the British government and have been on the decline since. Gandhi is said to have described the traditional educational system as a beautiful tree that was destroyed during the British rule.

A Gurukul is a type of ancient Hindu school in India that is residential in nature with the shishyas or students and the guru or teacher living in proximity, many a time within the same house. The Gurukul is the place where the students resided together as equals, irrespective of their social standing. The students learn from the guru and help the guru in his day-to-day life, including the carrying out of mundane chores such as washing clothes, cooking, etc.

The guru-shishya parampara is a hallowed tradition in Hinduism. Other religious groups in India have adapted it into different forms that fall within their religious ideology and framework such as Jainism, Buddhism, and Sikhism. At the end of a shishya's (student) study, the student offers a "guru dakshina," since a guru does not take fees. A guru dakshina is the final offering from a student to the guru before leaving the ashram. By the colonial era the Gurukul system was almost dead in India excepting in a few remote regions. An exception was Kerala where the warrior Nair clan and their own military Gurukuls called Kalaris. In the past, some efforts have been started both genuine and others driven by monetary gains, whereby this gurukul tradition is in the phase of resurrection.

Gurukula is not a religious school in Hindu tradition but rather a secular academic institution based on universal spiritual principles. Vivekananda College near Madurai is an NAAC -accredited 'A' grade autonomous college that is run under a Gurukula system. There are many Vedic Gurukulas in modern India which follow ancient tradition. Government of India provides financial and other help to Vedic teachers who establish such Vedic gurukulas for imparting Vedic education without asking for any fees from the students; the leading government institution offering such assistance is Sandipani in Ujjain, named after the guru of Krishna, which also helps Vedic gurukulas in preparing students for examinations held by recognised Sanskrit universities.

## Guru-shishya Traditions

The guru-shishya tradition, lineage, or parampara, is a spiritual relationship in traditional Hinduism where teachings are transmitted from a guru to a 'Shirhya' or *chela*. Such knowledge, whether it be vedic, agamic artistic, architectural, musical or spiritual, is imparted through the developing relationship between the guru and the disciple. It is considered that this relationship, based on the genuineness of the guru, and the respect, commitment, devotion and obedience of the student, is the best way for subtle or advanced knowledge to be conveyed. The student eventually masters the knowledge that the guru embodies.

Beginning in the early oral traditions of the Upanishads (c. 2000 BC), the guru-shishya relationship has evolved into a fundamental component of Hinduism. The term Upanishad derives from the Sanskrit words *upa* (near), *ni* (down) and sad (to sit)—so it means "sitting down near" a spiritual teacher to receive instruction. The relationship between Krishna and Arjuna in the *Bhagavad Gita* portion of the *Mahabharata*, and between Rama and Hanuman in the Ramayana are examples. In the Upanishads, gurus and shishya appear in a variety of settings (a husband answering questions about immortality, a teenage boy being taught by Yama, the Hindu Religion's Lord of Death, etc.) Sometimes the sages are women, and the instructions may be sought by kings. In the *Vedas,* the *brahmavidya* or knowledge of Brahman is communicated from guru to shishya by oral lore.

Within the broad spectrum of the Hindu religion, the guru-shishya relationship can be found in numerous variant forms including Tantra. Some common elements in this relationship include:

— The establishment of a teacher/student relationship.

— A formal recognition of this relationship, generally in a structured initiation ceremony where the guru accepts the initiate as a shishya and also accepts responsibility for the spiritual well-being and progress of the new shishya.

— Sometimes this initiation process will include the conveying of specific esoteric wisdom and/or meditation techniques.

— Gurudakshina, where the shishya gives a gift to the guru as a token of gratitude, often the only monetary or otherwise fee that the student ever gives. Such tokens can be as simple as a piece of fruit or as serious as a thumb, as in the case of Ekalavya and his guru Dronacharya.

Traditionally word used for a succession of teachers and disciples in ancient Indian culture is *parampara* (*parampara*in IAST). In the *parampara* system, knowledge is believed to be passed down through successive generations. The Sanskrit word literally means *an uninterrupted series or succession.* Sometimes defined as *"the passing down of Vedic knowledge"* its believed to be always entrusted to the *ācāryas*. An established parampara is often called *sampradaya*, or school of thought. For example in Vaishnavism a number of *sampradayas* are developed following a single teacher, or an acharya. While some argue for freedom of interpretation others maintain that "[a]lthough an *ācārya* speaks according to the time and circumstance in which he appears, he upholds the original conclusion, or *siddhānta*, of the Vedic literature."

## Types of Guru-shishya Relationship

There is a variation in the level of authority that may be granted to the guru. The highest is that found in bhakti yoga such as that in the Sai Baba movement, and the lowest is in the Pranayama forms of yoga such as the Sankara Saranam movement. Between these two there are many variations in degree and form of authority.

### *Advaita vedanta*

Advaita vedanta requires anyone seeking to study advaita vedanta to do so from a Guru (*teacher*). The Guru must have the following qualities:

1. *Srotriya*—must be learned in the Vedic scriptures and sampradaya.
2. *Brahmanistha*—literally meaning established in Brahman; must have realised the oneness of Brahman in everything and in himself.

The seeker must serve the Guru and submit his questions with all humility so that doubt may be removed. According to Advaita, the seeker will be able to attain moksha.

***Śruti tradition***

The Guru-shishya tradition plays an important part in the Shruti tradition of Vaidika dharma. The Hindus believe that the Vedas have been handed down through the ages from Guru to shishya. The Vedas themselves prescribe for a young brahmachari to be sent to a Gurukul where the Guru teaches the pupil the Vedas and Vedangas. The pupil is also taught the prayoga to perform yajnas. The term of stay varies. After the stay at the Gurukul the brahmachari returns home after performing a ceremony called samavartana. The word S .rauta is derived from the word Sruti meaning that which is heard. The S .rauta tradition is a purely oral handing down of the Vedas, but many modern Vedic scholars make use of books as a teaching tool.

***Shaktipat tradition***

The guru passes his knowledge to his disciples by virtue of the fact that his purified consciousness enters into the selves of his disciples and communicates its particular characteristic. In this process the disciple is made part of the spiritual family (kula)—a family which is not based on blood relations but on people of the same knowledge.

***Bhakti yoga***

The best known form of the Guru-shishya relationship is that of bhakti. Bhakti (Sanskrit = Devotion) means surrender to God or guru. Bhakti extends from the simplest expression of devotion to the ego-destroying principle of prapati, which is total surrender. The bhakti form of the guru-shishya relationship generally incorporates three primary beliefs or practices:

1. Devotion to the guru as a divine figure or avatar.
2. The belief that such a guru has transmitted, or will impart moksha, diksha or shaktipat to the (successful) shishya.
3. The belief that if the shishya's act of focusing his or her devotion (bhakti) upon the guru is sufficiently strong and worthy, then some form of spiritual merit will be gained by the shishya.

### *Prapatti*

In the ego-destroying principle of *prapatti* (Sanskrit, "Throwing oneself down"), the level of the submission of the will of the shishya to the will of God or the guru is sometimes extreme, and is often coupled with an attitude of personal helplessness, self-effacement and resignation. This doctrine is perhaps best expressed in the teachings of the four Samayacharya saints, who shared a profound and mystical love of Siva expressed by:

— Deep humility and self-effacement, admission of sin and weakness;

— Total surrender to God as the only true refuge; and

— A relationship of lover and beloved known as bridal mysticism, in which the devotee is the bride and Siva the bridegroom.

In its most extreme form it sometimes includes:

— The assignment of all or many of the material possessions of the shishya to the guru.

— The strict and unconditional adherence by the shishya to all of the commands of the guru. An example is the legend that *Karna* silently bore the pain of a *wasp* stinging his thigh so as not to disturb his guru *Parashurama*.

— A system of various titles of implied superiority or deification which the guru assumes, and often requires the shishya to use whenever addressing the guru.

— The requirement that the shishya engage in various forms of physical demonstrations of affection towards the guru, such as bowing, kissing the hands or feet of the guru, and sometimes agreeing to various physical punishments as may sometimes be ordered by the guru.

— Sometimes the authority of the guru will extend to all aspects of the shishya's life, including sexuality, livelihood, social life, etc.

Often a guru will assert that he or she is capable of leading a shishya directly to the highest possible state of spirituality or consciousness, sometimes referred to within Hinduism as moksha. In the bhakti guru-shishya relationship the guru is often believed to have supernatural powers, leading to the deification of the guru.

### *Buddhism*

In the Pali Buddhist tradition, the Bhikkus are also known as Sekha's. In the Theravada Buddhist tradition, the teacher is a valued and honoured mentor worthy of great respect and a source of inspiration on the path to Enlightenment. In the Tibetan tradition, however, the teacher is viewed as the very root of spiritual realisation and the basis of the entire path. Without the teacher, it is asserted, there can be no experience or insight. The guru is seen as Buddha. In Tibetan texts, emphasis is placed upon praising the virtues of the guru. Tantric teachings include generating visualisations of the guru and making offerings praising the guru. The guru becomes known as the *vajra* guru, the one who is the source of initiation into the tantric deity. The disciple is asked to enter into a series of vows and commitments that ensure the maintenance of the spiritual link with the understanding that to break this link is a serious downfall.

In Vajrayana as the guru is perceived as the way itself. The guru is not an individual who initiates a person, but the person's own Buddha-nature reflected in the personality of the guru. In return, the disciple is expected to shows great devotion to his or her guru, who he or she regards as one who possesses the qualities of a Bodhisattva. A guru is regarded as one which has not only mastered the words of the tradition, but one that with which the student has an intense personal relationship; thus, devotion is seen as the proper attitude toward the guru.

## References

Compayre, Gabriel; Payne, W. H., *History of Pedagogy (1899)*, translated by W. H. Payne, 2003, Kessinger Publishing.

Hailman, W. N. *Twelve lectures on the history of pedagogy, delivered before the Cincinnati teachers' association*, 1874, Wilson, Hinkle & Co.

Mookerji, Radha Kumud. *Ancient Indian Education: Brahmanical and Buddhist.* 1990.

Majumdar, Raychauduri and Datta. *An Advanced History of India*. London: Macmillan. p. 64.

# 4

# Education in Medieval India

Medieval period witnessed a radical transformation in the Indian subcontinent. The country was invaded by various foreign rulers and several traders from around the world came and settled in the country. The tradesmen and the invaders brought with them their own cultures and intermingled with the people of the each district of the state. Besides, religion, society and culture, Education in medieval India also experienced a new perspective. The Mughal rulers came to India and established their rule. In the 11th century the Muslims established elementary and secondary schools. Furthermore, this led to the commencement of universities at cities like Delhi, Lucknow and Allahabad. Education developed with a fresh aspect during that period as there was an excellent interaction between Indian and Islamic traditions in all fields of knowledge like theology, religion, philosophy, fine arts, painting, architecture, mathematics, medicine and astronomy.

However, before the advent of the Muslims in India, there was a developed system of education, but Education in medieval India was shaped with the founding of the institutions of learning. Muslim rulers promoted urban education by bestowing libraries and literary societies. They founded primary schools (*maktabs*) in which students learned reading, writing, and basic Islamic prayers, and secondary schools (*madrasas*) to teach advanced language skills in India. Several Madrasahs were set-up by Sultans, nobles, and their influential ladies. The main objective of these Madrasahs was to train and educate scholar who would become eligible for the civil service as well as performing duties as judge. Iltutmish was the first ruler to establish a Madrasahs at Delhi during the medieval rule. Gradually many Madrasahs came into being.

The system of Education in medieval India was under the control of Ulama who were in favour of curriculum as laid down by Akbar. During those days education was related to religious training. However, various subjects such as medicine, Arabic literature, grammar and philosophy were also taught. History states that Arab and Central Asian peoples brought Muslim educational models to the India in both the medieval and early modern periods. Women education in India during the medieval period was prevalent.

Muslim girls of affluent families studied at home and moreover, as Persian was the court language of the period, elite boys could attend Persian schools to learn literature, history, ethics, law, administration.

Education in medieval India flourished mostly during the Mughal rule from the beginning of 1526 until the end of Mughal political presence in 1848. In the later medieval era, the British came to India and introduced English education. With the coming of the European missionaries, Western education made firm advances in the country. Various universities and thousands of colleges got affiliated and popularity of education increased in the medieval period.

Education in Medieval India was influenced mostly by foreign invasions. Various traders and rulers came to India during the medieval period and brought their own culture and tradition as well as learning process. Indian society imbibed those knowledge and introduced it among the people of the country. However, these foreign conquests resulted in the decline in women's status in the medieval period. The female literacy rate in India was lower than the male literacy rate. Women Education in Medieval India suffered a lot.

Women were described in Ancient Indian texts as weaker sections of the society. They were considered as frail physically and both socially. Thus, though women were given equal rights in the Vedic period, their situation deteriorated with time. The medieval societies were subjected to inequalities and they were oppressed too. Historically, the medieval period is attributed as the 'dark age' for women in India. In the medieval India, women were introduced to

'Purdah', (a veil) system. Moreover, several evils started in the society. Social evil practices such as Child Marriage, Sati, Jauhar were restriction on Women Education in Medieval India.

Nevertheless, the status of women in Southern India was far better than the North India. Women Education in Medieval India was seen in the south India. Several thinkers emerged at that time such as: Priyaketaladevi, queen of Chalukya Vikramaditya and Jakkiabbe. Furthermore, the evil practices of the societies existed only among the Hindu community. Other religions such as Hinduism and Buddhism gave freedom to women. They were given the freedom of education and were offered a more liberal approach. The plight of Indian women during the middle Ages was very intense.

The coming of the Muslims aggravated the troubles of the women in India in the medieval period. The women were forced to practice 'zenana'. In addition to that Muslim women were prevents them from getting equal access to education. Women Education in Medieval India was restricted among the Muslim women due to religion. Muslim women were illiterate; however, certain sections of the women were better off and were given higher levels of education.

During the Muslim rule, Women Education in Medieval India was constrained because Muslim men were also subjected to low educational attainment in general. On the other hand many women excelled in arts, literature, music in the medieval period. Women also served as rulers in the medieval period. Razia Sultan was the only woman monarch to rule the throne of Delhi in the middle ages. The Gond queen Durgavati ruled for fifteen years, before she lost the battle to Mughal emperor Akbar's general Asaf Ali.

## Aims of Education

The most important point to bear in mind about the British educational experiment in India is that it was conducted on a people which had already been exposed to educational experience for over two thousand five hundred years. The elaborate ritualistic religion developed during the Vedic period naturally called for a system of instruction for the continuous production of Vedic scholars and specialists in various aspects of the sacrificial literature.

At a time when the art of writing and writing materials were still in their infancy and memory and mnemonic devices the only methods available for the transmission and propagation of knowledge, the Vedic masters developed the concept of teacher, the ideal relationship between the teacher and the pupil, and a system of training in conformity with this relationship and the new life the pupils had to live in the modest household of the teacher. About the institution of this relationship, known as *upanayana,* Mookerji says: 'It is not like the admission of a pupil to the register of a school on his payment of the prescribed fee'. It is a spiritual initiation into a new life, for the pupil is now a twice-born *{dvija),* inasmuch as the teacher 'impregnates him with his spirit'. Das explains *upanayana* as literally meaning 'taking near', that is, the act of handing over one's ward to the teacher. The teacher-pupil relationship attained a great perfection and characterised the educational experience in ancient and medieval India.

The original emphasis on Vedic literature gradually lent itself to a process of acquiring knowledge in all branches of learning, including arts and sciences, as the Vedic corpus itself became diversified and the Upanisadic and other philosophical writings made their headway. Thus the term *svadhyaya,* used in several places of the *Satapatha Brahmana,* originally meant Vedic study, or the study of the three *Vedas*, *Rk*, *Yajus* and *Saman*. Gradually the study included the six *Vedangas*,—the *Kalpasutras*, *Siksa*, *Vyakarana*, *Chanda*, *Nirukta*, and *Jyotisa*, as proficiency in these auxiliary sciences was indispensable for the mastery of the Vedas.

This early realisation of the all-embracing character of education is a remarkable feature of ancient India. Despite its overall concern for the religion of the land, the education did not remain confined to priestly class although the latter was the most important single source of supply of teachers. In view of this secular character, education came to be regarded quite early in its history as a source of illumination, and an agency for improvement and for giving the correct lead in life. Thus the *Mahabharata* declares unhesitatingly that there is nothing like education which gives one such unfailing insight. The Rgveda also realised that 'if one human being was superior to another it was not because the person had an extra hand or eye, but because education had sharpened his mind and intellect and rendered him more efficient'.

Apart from sharpening intellect, the *Mahabharata,* moreover, characterised education as an agent for ensuring good character and behaviour in anticipation of Froebel's wellknown remark: "To give firmness to the will, to quicken it and to make it pure and strong and enduring is the chief concern in education." The above objectives relate to the development of the individual. But transcending the individual is the society. Therefore, another primary aim of education should be the development of the individual in the service of the society, a point which has not failed to be emphasised in some of the Upanisads. Thus *Chandogya Upanisad* emphasises the social role of the educated when it says: "Infinity is bliss, and only one who obtains bliss performs social duties." Interestingly enough this echoes a similar idea met with in the Rgveda—*atma iva sevapy.* The social responsibilities of the educated and the enlightened have been more clearly stated along with other qualities generated by education, in a passage in the *Taittirìya Upanisad,* which reads like a modern convocation address.

The primary duty of a person who has completed his education under a teacher is to propagate education to others in order that the continuity of the educational process from one generation to the next remains uninterrupted *(prajatantum ma vyacchetsiti).* Equally important is the advice to always strive for greatness (as a scholar) through continuous study and teaching.

In other words, the process of acquisition of knowledge is an open-ended endeavour, and the ideal teacher must always be engaged in it in order to remain at the vanguard of knowledge. A high standard of scholarship and a life of study and research were prescribed for a teacher in order that he can command the highest respect and veneration from his pupils and the society at large. An acid test for a teacher's reputation was his ability to attract students. Instances of teachers failing to attract pupils in the face of more competent rival teachers and as a consequence being obliged to close their schools were not wanting. Now, this competence does not always depend upon scholarship alone but calls for the development of other qualities such as the fluency of speech, ability for graphic description, ready wit and presence of mind, lucid explanation of difficult passages etc. These and several other qualities of ideal teacher are discussed in the *Mahabharata* and by Kalidasa.

## EDUCATIONAL INSTITUTIONS

The early development of the teacher-student relationship, the *upanyayana* ceremony, and the very concept of knowledge being directly impregnated by the teacher into the plastic mind of the pupil, confined the school to the modest household of the teacher, or to his hermitage when he was living as a sage in his forest resort. The epics are full of descriptions of such forest hermitage schools such as Valmiki's at Citrakuta hill, Bharadvaja's at the confluence of the Ganges and the Yamuna, Rajarsi Trnavindu's by the side of the mountain Sumeru, Visvamitra's on the banks of the Kausika, and so on." Similar descriptions of forest schools were still popular with the poets of the classical age, as for example, Kalidasa's picturisation of Atri's hermitage in his *Raghuvamsa* and Vana's description of Jabali's hermitage in his *Kadambari,* clearly indicating the continuance of the time-honoured system. The same system was also sometimes followed by Buddhist saints, like Jayasena, as we have it from Hiuen Tsang's travels in India. This preference for a private-teacher-oriented system, as opposed to the collective, has been explained away by the Brahminical abhorrence for mechanisation of education.

Education, like religion, was a spiritual experience involving the control and development of mental faculties, which did not call for any mechanical institutionalisation. As in education, so in a more marked degree in the sphere of religion and spiritual life, India did not believe in the external and mechanical methods of organisation and did not develop any ecclesiastical institutions like the churches' Yet organised efforts in religious and educational matters were not unknown in Vedic times. The words *samgha, paridad,* and *caraka* frequently appearing in the Samhitas, Brahmanas and Upanisads refer to a body of Brahmanas or learned men who from time to time assembled for a specific intellectual or religious purpose. There was a similar assembly in the time of the Rgveda for giving a direction to the philosophy and the language of the Veda. The Upanisads speak of a gathering of wandering scholars, namely the *carakas.* The Pancala Parisat is reported to have rendered signal service to the development of philosophy. But none of these references throws any light as to whether there was any effort at organising a number of teachers into a school or an institution collectively responsible for the teaching of a number of pupils. In India the Buddhists and the Jainas must be credited with such institutionalisation of education with far-reaching cultural and international consequences to which we shall presently return in what follows.

The ancient private-teacher system and the Buddhist monastic organisation combined to encourage the development among the Hindus of three distinct types of educational institutions, e.g., (a) the Gurukula schools, (b) Temple colleges, and (e) the Agrahara village institutions.

## Gurukul Schools

The system owed its inspiration to the private-teacher-system and was based on the direct personal relationship between the teacher and his pupils. The imperative necessity of the pupil's character and ideals being formed by the teacher's constant presence, his practical life-style and precepts required them to take residence with the teacher. Unlike the old hermitage concept, the Gurukula schools were established in villages and cities like Banaras in a more or less secluded place away from the main settlements. A close parallel to the system was the schools maintained by the Bishops in Europe during the sixth century A.D.

A modern variation of the ancient private-teacher-system is the *toi* for Sanskrit learning. The *toh* had a flourishing career in medieval times, due largely to liberal land-grants from the landlords and local rulers. This type of institutions prospered, particularly in Bengal, Bihar and the United Provinces, and survived into the British period upon receiving some encouragement. In this type of schools some of which function even today the enrolment is usually limited to 20 or 25 students, classes are held

in thatched mud huts and subjects of instruction include grammar, literature (poetry), philosophy, (Samkhya, Nyaya etc.) and astronomy (Jyotisa). The *toh* of Nadia in Bengal which became famous in the medieval times for original studies offered courses in logic, smrti, jyotisa, grammar, kavya and tantra. Gowell who saw some of these schools in action in the middle of the last century observed as follows : "I could not help looking at these unpretending lecture-halls with a deep interest, as I thought of the Pandits lecturing there to generation after generation of eager, inquisitive minds. Seated on the floor with the "corona" of listening pupils round him, the teacher expatiates on these refinements of infinitesimal logic which make a European's brain dizzy *to think* of, but whose labyrinth a trained Nadia student will thread with unfaltering precision."

**Temple Colleges**

South India with its profusion of temples, big and small, led the way in the development of temple colleges in the medieval times. These were no doubt inspired by the example of the Buddhist monastic colleges and universities. Although their early history is difficult to trace inscriptional records indicate that this type of colleges started becoming important from the tenth century A.D. These were generally supported by land-grants and other forms of endowments.

The temple college at Salotgi, a village in the Bijapur district, established by Narayana, minister of the Rastrakuta king Krisca III in the tenth-century is an important example. It was associated with the temple of Trayi-purusa and functioned in a spacious hall specifically built for the purpose and good for accommodating a large number of students. According to the inscriptional records which provide some information about this college, the college used to attract students from different parts of the country. It was a residential college comprising of twenty-seven houses designed for providing free boarding and lodging to about two hundred students.

The temple authorities received an endowment of five hundred *nivartanas* for the construction of the buildings and twelve *nivartanas* for their lighting. To meet other expenses, the villagers had agreed to contribute five coins for each marriage, two-and-half coins for each *upanayana* and one- and one-fourth coins for each *cudakarana* ceremony.

The Vedic college at Ennayiram in South Arcot district was established in the eleventh century during the reign of king Rajendra Cola I out of a land-grant of 300 acres made by the villagers of the place. The college offered free lodging, boarding and tuition to 340 students and maintained sixteen teachers. The various branches of Vedic studies and the fixed number of students for each branch were as follows: Rgveda-75; Yajurveda-75; Chandogya-Saman-20;

Talavakara-Saman-20; Vajasaneya-(White Yajurveda)-20; Atharvaveda-10; Baudhayana Dharmasutra (Grhya, Kalpa and Gana)-10; Rupavatara (probably a grammatical work21)-40; Vyakarana-25; Prabhakara Mimamsa-35; Vedanta-10. A teacher's daily allowance was fixed at 1 *kalam* of paddy equivalent to the cost of food for sixteen persons a day. For an average family of five, this income meant three times the food budget and ensured a standard of living far above the poverty line. Each Vedic scholar received a ration of one seer of rice per day for his meals and half *kalanju* of gold per year for meeting other expenses. For scholars of grammar and philosophy the allowance was 66 percent more.

The whole arrangement is equivalent to a modern maintenance scholarship designed to attract meritorious students from all over the country. The Venkatesh Perumal Temple College at Tirumukkudal, established in the eleventh century, was a much smaller institution than that at Enrtayirarn, being able to provide instructions to 60 students at a time. Its special feature was a hospital in addition to the usual students' hostel. The college offered only Vedic courses including grammar, and it is not clear if Ayurvedic studies were included as the provision of a hospital in the college campus appears strongly to suggest.

In the thirteenth century the temple at Tiruvorriyur in Chingleput district came into prominence as a centre for linguistic studies. The college was dedicated specially to the study of Panini's grammar for which a separate hal. For this college about 400 acres of land were donated, which, by analogy with the Ennayiram establishment, implies that the college was intended for about 450 students. The same century records another temple college at Malkapuram in the Guntur taluk, which had a hospital in addition to a hostel. It accommodated 150 students and offered courses in Vedic as well as secular studies (grammar, literature, logic and Agamas).

The inscriptional records, particularly of South India, are rich in references to such temple colleges during medieval times, from which only a few have been noticed in the foregoing paragraphs. About several others of which information is scanty, Altekar has mentioned the Macha College at Hebbal in Dharwar district (10$^{th}$ century), Managoli College in Bijapur (12$^{th}$ century), Belgame College in Karnataka (12$^{th}$ century), Grammar College at Punnavayil in Tanjore district, and a few others. Some places such as Nagai in Nizam's territory and a temple college in Tinevelli district witnessed the establishment of libraries or Sarasvati Bhavanas or Bhandaras, as such institutions were then called, for the collection and preservation of manuscripts.

The extant materials, though not abundant, are sufficient to indicate a resurgence of Sanskrit learning centring round temples in medieval India. By contrast with the South, Northern India almost draws a blank with respect to temple colleges due to their systematic destruction by the invaders. From the general patterns of temple organisation and management it appears reasonable to conclude that North Indian temples were equally engaged in the promotion and dissemination of knowledge.

**Agrahara Institutions**

South Indian inscriptions, specially those from Mysore, have revealed another kind of educational institutions variously called Agrahara, Ghatika and Brahmapuri. All these institutions represent colonies of scholarly Brahmins specialised in different branches of study and free to impart education to willing pupils. Such colonies of teachers had their own revenue sources, generally from land-grants, and were empowered to administer their villages.

Typical examples of agrahara institutions are provided by Kadiyur, Sarvajnapura, Sthanagunduru and Belgame. Kadiyur, in Dharwar district in Karnataka, became an agrahara village during the rule of the Rasfrakutas (tenth century) when about two hundred Brahmins versed in the various branches of the Vedic studies, and also in logic and Puranas were settled there by the king. Provision was made for one or more endowments from which to pay the salaries of teachers, meet the cost of a free feeding house, and provide for the students.

At the Sarvajnapura agrahara, the Brahmin teachers not only held classes with their pupils, they used to spend a good part of their time chanting the Vedas in the streets and debating the six philosophical systems. At the Sthanagunduru agrahara, the teachers were 'skilled in medicine, in sorcery (or magic), in logic, in poetry, in the art of distorting people by incantation, in poetry, in the use of weapons, in sacrificing and in the art of cookery to prepare the meals such was the glory of that great agrahara that all the surrounding country prayed to be taught in the four Vedas, the six Vedangis, the three rival divisions of Mimamsa, the *tarka* and other connected sciences, the eighteen great Puranas, the making of numerous verses of praise, the art of architecture, the arts of music and dancing and in the knowledge of all the four divisions of learning which were possessed by the Brahmanas of the Sthanagunduru agrahara.'

As an agrahara centre for learning Belgame surpassed all such institutions. This capital city, during the early Satavahanas, experienced the first settlement of the Brahmanas; in the third century a Kadamba king invited thirty-two Brahmana families to develop Talgunda near Belgame as an agrahara village; by the time of the king Mayuravarman, the colony owned 144 villages. Its sizable organisation is also reflected in a variety of studies which included the sacred literature of the Hindus and the Bauddhas, the Lokayata, Samkhya, Vaisesika and other branches of philosophy, the Puranas, poetry and drama. One of the inscriptions mentions the name of an agrahara teacher, Vamasakti, who is described as 'a Panini in Grammar, Bharata in Drama and Music, Subandhu or Magha in Poetry, and Nakuliavara in Siddhanta'. Belgame had scores of Agraharas, seven Brabmapuris and five Machas or temples as centres of education.

The ghatika mentioned in the inscriptions is a smaller version of the agrahara. According to the Talagunda Pillar inscription of Kakusthavarman, the Western Ksatrapas patronised at Kancipura a number of ghaṭikas. A pupil intending to master the *Pravacana,* we are told, spent some time in turn in all the ghatikas in Kanci and soon attained mastery.

The archaeological labours of Sir John Marshall established the existence of three separate cities,—the Bhir Mound which was in occupation from 1500 B.c. to 180 B.C., the Sirkap probably founded by the Greeks in the second century B.c. and occupied in succession by the Scythians and Parthians upto the first century A.D., and Sirsukh, founded by the Kusanas. Politically dominated by the Hindus, the Persians, the Macedonians, the Mauryans, the Bactrian Greeks, the Parthians and the Kusanas, Taxila served as the capital of a number of dominions, was exposed to many cultural influences and inevitably assumed a cosmopolitan character.

The references in the epics and the Jatakas leave no doubt as to Taxila's great reputation as a centre of learning. The Mahavagga speaks of its 'world renowned' teachers to whom students flocked from all over the country for acquiring mastery in various arts and sciences and also relates the story of Jivaka learning medical science.

The Jatakas mention Banaras, Rajagrha, Mithila, Lalya country, Ujjayini, Koaala, Sivi and Kuru kingdoms as the places sending students for study at Taxila. These students comprised princes as well as sons of commoners. In the Achaemenian period Kharosthi script became popular and the Taxila teachers played an important part in its teaching and dissemination. In the time of the Bactrian Greeks, the Greek language and arts such as coinage and sculpture received encouragement. Until the advent of Buddhist monasteries Taxila did not probably possess any college or university and followed the private-teacher system. During the first few centuries of the Christian era, the Buddhist monasteries endeavoured to maintain and further develop the educational reputation of Taxila until these were swept away by the depredations of the Huns in the fifth century A.D. When Hiuen Tsang visited Taxila in the first half of the seventh century most of its old monasteries were already in ruins. But at some distance from the city he still noticed an old monastery in a dilapidated state still being used by some monks; here lived and worked the celebrated Sautrantika scholar Kumaralabdha, often bracketed in scholarship with Nagarjuna, Asvaghosa and Deva. The city was once noted for Mahayana Buddhism.

## Buddhist Universities

The word 'university' was used in medieval Europe as a collective noun to indicate the association of men, including businessmen, teachers, students, scholars, people engaged in municipal work, and so on. The expression 'studium generale' was used to indicate what we today understand by 'university'. To be designated a 'studiumgenerale', the organisation must form an assembly of many teachers and students, the students must be drawn from many places and not merely locally, and any of the three branches of higher learning,—theology, law and medicine, should form the subject of instruction and discourse. The oldest 'studia generale' in Europi date from the beginning of the twelfth century,—

Bologna and Reggio in Italy, Montpellier and Paris in France, Oxford in England, although the medical school at Salerno in South Italy functioning from the tenth century is sometimes regarded as the oldest university. Bologna specialised in law, Montpellier in medicine and Paris in theology.

In India the Buddhists developed similar 'studia generale' or university institutions several centuries before their appearance in Europe. The starting point may be fixed at the concept of *viharas* as places for the residence of monks. Originally implying a private apartment of a single Bhikkhu, a *vihara* later on came to mean a large and complex structure for the accommodation of a community of monks, where they can peacefully meditate and be engaged in canonical studies.

**Nalanda**

Situated 40 miles south of Patna and 7 miles north of Rajgir in Bihar, Nalanda is traditionally believed to be the place of birth and death of *aariputta*. Originally the place was a seat of Brahmanic learning. From Taraiiatha's account of the association of Nagarjuna (4th century A.D.) and his pupil Arya Deva with this place and the famous debate here between the Buddhist logician Dinnaga and Sudurjaya, a Brahmin, Nalanda appsara to have retained its importance as a Brahmanic centre of learning till the beginning of the fifth century A.D. Its rise as a Buddhist university may be put down to the middle of the same century.

Under the patronage of the Gupta emperors a number of high-rise *viharas* changed the sky-line of the place, and this building activity continued well into the eleventh century. According to the report of archaeological excavations, the University covered an area of one mile long by half a mile broad. The central college was provided with 7 large halls and 300 rooms presumably for the holding of classes. Other monastery buildings were arranged in a row according to plan, and some of them, as the Yaaovarman inscription tells us, towered to such great heights that they appeared to lick the clouds. According to Hwui Lun, a Korean pilgrim, the building of Nalanda stood four square like a city precinct, the gates were of three storeys rising to a height of thirtysix feet, outside the great hall of the temple there were a large *stupa* and various *cailyas* adorned with precious substance, and a water-clock kept time.

The number of scholars studying at any time at Nalanda was of the order of several thousand. In Hiuen Tsang's time the monastery's population of monks and students stood at 10,000 and Tsang noticed the number of students to exceed 3,000. Of these between 1,000 to 1,500 monks used to be engaged in teaching students four to six times their number. The teachers were well-versed in their respective subjects.

According to the biographer of Huen Tsang, there were 1,000 men who could explain twenty collections of Sutras and Sastras, 500 who could explain thirty collections and 10 (of whom Hiuen Tsang was one) who could teach fifty collections. To maintain the intellectual activity at a high standard, Nalanda organised a fine library in a special quarter comprising three buildings called Ratna-sagara, Ratnodadhi and Ratnaranjaka, the entire library quarter being appropriately designated as Dharmaganja. These facilities enabled Tsang to copy 400 Sanskrit texts comprising 500,000 verses.

Although Nalanda specialised in the study of the Mahayana school, particularly the works of Vasubandhu, Nagarjuna, Asaftga and Dharmakirti, it also taught Hinayana works and many secular subjects popular with the Brahmanas, such as the Vedas, the Hetuvidya, Sabdavidya and the Ayurveda. In fact, almost every branch of knowledge then known in India was included as a subject of study. A wide range of subjects and a galaxy of unrivalled teachers explain why scholars used to seek admission to this university from such distant places as China, Korea, Tibet and Tokhara. For the same reason the teachers and scholars trained at Nalanda were in great demand outside India. Near at home this demand was insistent from Tibet, which led Nalanda to organise Tibetan studies and cultivate Tibetan language under Candragomin, who himself wrote over sixty books, aantaraksita, Padmasambhava, Kamalasana and Sthiramati were some of the Nalanda scholars to have visited Tibet upon special invitations from the king for preaching Buddhism and translating Sanskrit and Pali into Tibetan. Of Nalanda scholars who taught and worked in China mention may be made of aubhakara Simha (eighth century) and Dharmadeva (tenth century A.D.).

### Valabhi

As a Buddhist university, valabhi, near Wala in Kathiawar in Western

India, played the same important role as did Nalanda in the east. Its development was due to the munificent grant of the Maitraka kings who flourished from the fifth to the eight century A.D. Hiuen Tsang visited Valabhi and found there about hundred Sarngha-ramas and some 6000 monks. Tsang was also full of praise for this university and noticed that Nalanda and Valabhi were the two places where students from all parts of India went to complete their education. These two universities were, therefore, the Oxford and Cambridge of ancient India. Unlike Nalanda, Valabhi specialised in the study of the Hinayana school of Buddhism. Secular subjects like *Ntti, Varita* and *Cikil-savidya* were encouraged.

**Vikramashila, Odantapuri, Jagaddala**

The university of Vikramashila (also called Sri Vikramashila Vihara) was founded by King Dharmapala in the eighth century A.D. The place has been variously identified with the village Silao near Baragaon, with Sultanganj in Bhagalpur district, with Patharaghata hill in Bhagalpur district, and with Keur near Hulsaganj 15 miles from Nalanda.

Vikramasila is known to us mainly from Tibetan sources and from the great service the scholars of this university rendered to Tibet in the propagation and consolidation of Buddhism. The university had six colleges and a central hall, called the House of Science, with which each college communicated. The entrance of each college in this central hall was guarded by a Dvara-Pandita (scholar gate-keeper), implying that admission to the university was restricted to the really capable student as he had to satisfy the Dvara-Pandita.

The names of the six scholar gate-keepers have come down to us as follows: (1) East gate—Ratnakarasanti; (2) West gate—Vagisvarakirti of Banaras; (3) North gate—Naropa; (4) South gate—Prajfiakaramati; (5) First central gate—Ratnavajra of Kasmira; and (6) Second gate—Jnanasrimitra of Gauda. We have very little information about the courses of study, their duration etc. Grammar, logic, metaphysics, tantras and ritual literature were some of the subjects popular at the university. It also organised Tibetan studies to a high standard inasmuch as a large number of Vikramasila scholars worked in Tibet as teachers and translators of sacred books. The institution of some kind of degrees or diplomas was another speciality of Vikramasila, as some of its graduates such as Jetari and Ratnavajra are recorded in Tibetan sources to have received certificates from the reigning kings of Bengal, the patrons of the university.

The Vikramasila University has been immortalised by the great Dipankara Srijnana Ausa (b. A.D. 980), versatile scholar and master of both the Vehicles and President of the university (1034-38) who, at the invitation of the Tibetan king, spent the last thirteen years of his life in that Himalayan country, composing several works on Tibetan Buddhism (Vajrayana) and translating Sanskrit works into Tibetan. Other Vikramasila scholars who worked and wrote in Tibet included Vairocana Raksita (c. A.D. 750), Jetari, Ratnakarasanti, Janasrimitra, Ratnavajra and Vagisvarakirti, each of whom was a scholar gate-keeper at Vikramasila at one time or another. During his travels in India Huen Tsang noticed similar Buddhist centres of learning in North and Western India.

Kashmir was littered with them, of which Jayendra Vihara had some reputation as the great pilgrim stayed there for some time for his studies and collection of manuscripts. The Punjab had Chinapati and Jallandar monasteries, the United Provinces the Matipur monastery in Bijnor district, and Kanauj and Bhadra monastery. All these monasteries in the north and northwest of the country were then in a declining state. Only in the east, particularly in Bengal, where Buddhism was active until the advent of the Muhammadan rule, did the monasteries carry on then-usual educational work with some enthusiasm. Special mention may be made of two such places, namely the Odantapuri and Jagaddala Viharas.

The Odantapuri monastery and university was founded by Gopala, of the Pala dynasty in the middle of the eighth century A.D This centre of learning attained celebrity in view of its association with noted Buddhist scholars like Ratnakarasanti, Dipankara Srijnana Atisa, Sila Raksita and others. The first-named who rose to be a scholar gate-keeper at Vikramasila was ordained here in the Sarvastivada school. Here Dipankara took the sacred vow at the age of nineteen from the presiding Acharya. Then, Odantapuri which developed into a famous centre for Tantric Buddhism was accepted as a model when the King of Tibet decided to build a Vihara at Samye with the help of Santaraksita. During the eleventh-twelfth century, the university had about one thousand monks as against one thousand at Mahabodhi and three thousand at Vikramasila, and a splendid library.

The university, the clerics, the library collections every thing perished before the advancing Turks towards the end of the twelfth century, of which some graphic account is recorded by Taranatha and in *Tabakat-i-Nasari.* The Jagaddala Vihara was established in the beginning of the twelfth century by king Rama Pala of Bengal on the banks of the Ganges and the Karatoya in Varendra country. It was swept out of existence by Bukhtyar's hoards in A.D. 1203. Within this short period the university produced a number of well-known scholars such as Vibhuticandra, Danasila, aubhakara and Moksakaragupta, some of whom were also good Tibetan scholars.

## Science and Technology Education

Temple colleges, *tolls,* and Buddhist universities, we have seen, uniformly encouraged secular studies including the sciences, medicine and technical subjects. Mathematics and astronomy occupied a pride of place in Vedic studies, the former being compared to the proverbial jewel on the hood of the snake and the latter being of such central importance that without a knowledge of it one cannot perform the sacrifices.

The construction of sacrificial altars of various sizes and shapes involved the knowledge of geometry of rational triangles, rectilinear figures, trapeziums and circles, transformation of figures from one type into another, irrational numbers and their operations, the determination of the ratio of the circumference of a circle to its diameter, and so on. As all these mensurational works used to be carried out with the help of a measuring cord, the *iulb,* the geometer was called the *sulbavid* and his science the *sulba-Sastra.* The subject formed part of the more comprehensive *Srautasûtras* concerned; with rituals and sacrifices. As mathematics and astronomy separated out as secular subjects of study and became more and more specialised and sophisticated it came to be associated with individuals and families taking a special interest in, and developing aptitude for, the subject. The large number of commentaries on mathematical and astronomical works of a few masters, produced in ancient and medieval periods, bear testimony to their popularity.

Physical sciences as we know them today did not then have separate existence, but formed part of philosophical studies. These envisaged the six systems, of which the Nyaya-Vaisesika and the Samkhya were noted for their many physical concepts, such as the concept of matter, its physical properties, its atomic character, explanation of physico-chemical changes on atomic and molecular theories, the concept of motion, sound, and light, of gravity and fluidity, and of force and energy.

About many of these concepts, e.g. atomism, nature of motion, sound, to mention a few, there were sharp differences of opinion between the Brahmanic and the Buddhist schools which undoubtedly enlivened the teaching and discussions of these subjects in the Buddhist universities as well as in Hindu temple colleges, *tols* and agraharas. The method of mastering these sciences was by debate and discussion, an art perfected in Nyayaor Tarkasastra. These subjects received special encouragement for the sake of medical studies upon which some of the philosophical systems, particularly the Samkhya, and the Nyaya-Vaisesika, had a deep impact.

## Medical Education

While our information on the teaching of mathematics, astronomy and physical sciences needs must be scrappy it is fortunately not so with regard to medical education. This is because medical works took particular care to preserve for us what, in the opinion of ancient medical authorities, constituted the most effective teaching methods for the training of competent physicians.

Both Caraka and Susruta stressed in various ways the characteristics of a good physician, the marks of a quack, the service the former can render to the society and the disaster the latter may bring about. Susruta defines a physician as one 'who is well versed in the science of medicine and has attended to the demonstrations of surgery and medicine, and who himself practises the healing art, and is lean, courageous, light-handed, fully equipped with supplies of medicine, surgical instruments and appliances, and who is intelligent, well read, and is a man of ready resources, and who commands a decent practice, and is further endowed with all moral virtues.

Caraka makes a similar but longer statement about the qualifications of a good physician. Such a physician must be well acquainted with the anatomy and physiology of the entire body, manifestation and growth of the body and origin and evolution of the universe. He must understand the eight sections of the Ayurveda and apply his knowledge so acquired for the treatment of diseases. A bad physician or a quack, on the other hand, has qualities quite the opposite of those given above. Instead of curing diseases he may cause death and torture people like thorns. Quacks are traitors moving about in the guise of physicians because administrative vigilance is lacking. Susruta is equally furious with them when he equates them with 'killers of men out of cupidity'.

Thus, the production of good physicians depends both on the qualities and qualifications of the teachers as well as the pupils, and therefore utmost care should be exercised in the selection of both the teachers and the taught. Let us first consider the selection of students. For learning medicine caste was no bar.

Caraka first directs that Ayurveda can be mastered by any member of the three castes Brahmana, Kshatriya and Vaisya, but immediately corrects himself by saying that, in general, the science of life can be studied by all for the attainment of virtues, wealth and pleasure. Right *to* study medicine by any body regardless of caste has also been recognised by Suaruta with the subtle distinction that a sudra student at the time of initiation should omit to recite the *mantras* required on such occasions. More important than caste are the faculties of body and mind,—thin lips, teeth and tongue, straight nose, large, honest and intelligent eyes, a contented frame of mind, good character, pleasant speech and good dealings with others, a good retentive memory, clear comprehension and insight into the subject of study.

A student deficient in these qualities of faculty and character may not be regarded suitable for admission to a medical course. About the initial education of the entrant, Visweswara Sastry says that a preliminary knowledge of saddaraana or at least of Samkhya and Nyaya-Vaisesika was considered necessary. The normal age of entrance for medical studies appears to be sixteen. By this age he is sufficiently grown up, educated and mature to decide whether he intends to be a physician.

Just as the teacher should decide the suitability of his would-be pupil for a medical course so the onus of selecting a proper teacher must rest with the pupil. Caraka lays down the qualifications of a good teacher of medicine as follows: "An ideal preceptor is he who is well grounded in scriptures; equipped with practical knowledge, wise, skilful, whose prescriptions are infallible, who is pious, who has all the necessary equipment for treatment, who is not deficient in respect of any of the sense organs, who is acquainted with human nature, and the rationals of treatment, whose knowledge is not overshadowed (by the knowledge of other scriptures), who is free from vanity, envy and anger, who is hard working, who is affectionately disposed towards his disciples and is capable of expressing his views with clarity. A preceptor possessed of such qualities infuses medical knowledge to a good disciple as the seasonal cloud helps bring about good crop in a fertile land.

After his selection the pupil is introduced to his studies by the usual consecration ceremony. Here the advice and oath-taking are, however, much more elaborate as medical ethics are involved, and remind us of the Hippocratic oath. Thus, in the presence of fire, Brahmanas and physicians, the teacher initiates his pupil, by saying that he should observe *brahmacarya* and truthfulness, and take a vegetable diet to sharpen his intellect; that he should obey the teacher's instructions, respect him and remain devoted and pleasant to him like his son, servant or supplicant; and that he should act without ego and jealously, but with care, affection, modesty, vigilance and undisturbed mind.

The medical instruction and practice usually took six years. According to the original classification of the subject, as taught to Bharadvaja in Vedic times, the course comprised the principles of health and ill-health, the aetiology, symptomatology and the treatment of diseases. Later on, Ayurveda was divided into eight *angas* or branches for the convenience of teaching. Susruta mentions these eight branches as follows: *Salyatantra* (surgery, general principles), *salakyatantra* (surgery of regions above the clavicles), *kayaakitsa* (treatment of diseases), *bhutavidya* (demoniacal diseases), *kaumarabhriya* (children diseases), *agadatantra* (toxicology), *rasayanatantra* (science of rejuvenation), and *vajikaratantra* (science of aphrodisiacs). In many texts, the subject matter was arranged not in accordance with the above eight *angas,* but into broad areas, e.g. *sutrasthana,* dealing with fundamental principles of Ayurveda; *sarirasthana,* discussing anatomy and physiology, including embryology; *nidanasthana,* dealing with pathology, *cikitsasthana,* devoted to treatment of diseases, etc.

In Caraka's time several textbooks were available but all of them did not obviously attain a good standard, as we can infer from his advice regarding the selection of a good textbook so essential for the successful mastery of the science. Criteria given by him not only apply to medical texts but to all textbooks concerning science and technology, and are, therefore, of general interest. A good textbook is one which is used by reputed physicians and teachers, and is full of ideas calculated to contribute to the intellectual growth of the students. Such a book must be free from the faults of tautology and contradictions as also from vulgar, difficult and ambiguous expressions. A good book gives clear definitions (of aetiology, symptomatology and therapeutics) and illustrations and deals with ideas and concepts which can be grasped quickly and without confusion.

In the daily learning exercise, the teacher selected one full verse or one-half or one-fourth of it, according to the capacity of the student, and recited, paraphrased and explained the same to him. The student then repeated the whole process. The passages or verses were not to be recited too hastily, nor in a timid or faltering voice, nor even with a nasal intonation. According to Caraka, the pupil should repeat his recitation with a view to removing his own deficiencies, and this practice should continue in the noon, in the afternoon and at night without any break. Memorisation was clearly insisted upon as was the practice in the case of all sciences, but not learning by rote. Susruta strongly discouraged learning by rote and without understanding and stated that it was like the ass carrying a load of sandalwood.

For a proper understanding of medical science, Caraka advised the holding of regular seminars and friendly discussions. Physicians should always hold professional discussions among themselves with a view to developing their powers of application, clarity of knowledge, the gift of the gab, resolving doubts and confirming what was understood before. To derive the fullest possible benefit out of such seminars, the discussions must be friendly and free from a hostile spirit.

The emphasis on practical training is clearly underlined by Susruta in his instructions on the development of surgical skills among the pupils. A pupil who is well read in the textbook and grounded in the principles of Ayurveda, but not initiated in surgical skills and practice of medicine is not competent to undertake either the medical or the surgical treatment of a disease. For the attainment of surgical skills the pupil must learn specific forms of incision by making cuts in the body of a fruit—watermelon, cucumber etc. The art of making excisions should be demonstrated by performing neat openings in the body of a full water-bag, or in the bladder of a dead animal or in the side of a leather pouch filled with slime or water. Scrapping should be practised on a piece of skin from which hairs were not removed. The vein of a dead animal or the stem of a lotus should be used for acquiring the skill of venesection (vedhya). Cauterisation or application of alkaline preparations should be demonstrated on a piece of soft flesh. There are several other surgical operations of which practical learning methods have been described. A physician who thus becomes well versed in the principles of surgery as well as experienced in the practice of medicine is alone capable of curing distempers ; just as a two wheeled cart is of service in a battlefield so is such a physician expected to achieve victory in his fight against disease.

After having mastered the science of medicine, both theoretically and by practical experience of surgery and medicine, the young physician should now seek the permission of the king of the country for commencing his medical and surgical practice. Susruta's clear statement in this regard shows that there was something like the licensing and registration of practitioners in order to distinguish between licensed qualified practitioners and unlicensed quacks. In the same section, Susruta even advises as to the dress and demeanour of the physician. The physician, he says, should wear white garments, put on a pair of shoes, carry a stick and an umbrella in his hands, and walk about with a mild and benignant look as a friend of all created things, ready to help all, and frank and friendly in his talk and demeanour.

Both Caraka and Susruta laid emphasis on the need for nursing in the successful treatment of the patient. According to Caraka, there are four aspects of treatment or therapeutics, namely, the physician, the medicament, the attendant and the patient himself. A good attendant's qualifications should be knowledge of nursing, dexterity, affection and purity. Susruta holds the same opinion that the physician, the patient, the medicines and attendants are the four essential factors in medical treatment. If the physician be qualified, the patient self-controlled, medicines genuine and the attendants intelligently watchful, even a serious case is readily cured. About the attendant he further says that a person who is coolheaded and pleasant in demeanour, does not speak ill of others, attends readily and willingly to the needs of the patient, and strictly follows the instructions of the physician, is alone fit to attend the bedside of a patient.

The Mahavagga prescribes that, to be a good nurse, he should possess five qualities, that is, (1) he should be capable of prescribing medicines (as directed by the physician), (2) he should know the diet which is good for the patient and accordingly serve him with such diet, (3) he should wait upon the sick out of love and not out of greed, (4) he should not revolt from removing the evacuation, saliva and vomited matter, and (5) he should be capable of teaching, inciting, arousing and gladdening the patient with religious discourses.

The medical texts are silent on the question of training of nurses, but the qualifications detailed clearly envisage some form of training. We also find interesting statements about the duties and responsibilities of a physician in the service of the king. Such a physician must be responsible for the protection of the life of the king and also of the royal army particularly during war. There were always the dangers of secret poisoning when a king mobilised his armies to attack a neighbouring ruler. In such cases the enemy usually had recourse to the common practice of poisoning roadside wells, articles of food, cattle fodder, and shady resting places.

## Technical Education

With regard to the various schools at Taxila eighteen silpas or industrial and technical arts and crafts are often mentioned. From scraps of information contained in the Jatakas, the Mahavagga, Milinda-pañha and other sources, Altekar suggested the following to constitute the traditional eighteen silpas: 1. vocal music, 2. instrumental music, 3. dancing, 4. painting, 5. mathematics, 6. accountancy, 7. engineering, 8. sculpture, 9. agriculture, 10. cattle breeding, 11. commerce, 12. medicine, 13. conveyancing and law, 14.

administrative training, 15. archery and military art, 16. magic, 17. snake charming, and 18. the art of finding hidden treasures. 63 Persons engaged in these arts and crafts formed themselves into guilds for purposes of professional safeguards as also for organising the training and education of the new entrants to the trade. The Müga-Pakkha Jataka mentions eighteen guilds, but as no list is given it is not possible to ascertain whether they conformed to the list constructed by Altekar.

On the basis of literary and inscriptional information, Das worked out a list of 27 guilds representing the following arts and crafts :-1. cultivators, 2. traders, including caravan traders, 3. herdsmen, 4. money-lenders, 5. workers in wood, 6. workers in metal including gold and silver, 7. leather workers, 8. workers fabricating hydraulic engines (udqyantrika), 9. bamboo-workers (vasakara), 10. braziers (kasakara), 11. weavers, 12. potters, 13. oil-millers, 14. painters, 15. corn-dealers {dharrMika), 16. garlandmakers and flower-sellers, 17. mariners, 18. robbers and free booters, 19. forest-police who guard the caravans, 20. workers in stone, 21. ivory-workers, 22. jewellers, 23. rush-workers and basket-makers, 24. dyers, 25. fisher folk, 26. butchers, and 27. barbers and shampooners. While the list includes many important industrial or technical arts and crafts it is baffling to understand why items like money-lenders, corn-dealers, butchers have been included, and important crafts like architecture, engineering and medicine omitted. Finally we have Vatsyayana's list of sixty-four traditional kalas (arts) which are expected to contribute to the cultural and technical development of a lady. For technical education in the above-mentioned arts and crafts an apprentice system was developed and perfected. The system in all its essential details is given in the Naradasmrti.

When a young man intends to be trained in his own (hereditary) craft, he should first have the approval of his relations and friends, approach a master, and live with him after making sure the period of his apprenticeship. It shall be the duty of the master to teach him at his own house, feed him (at his own cost), treat him as his son and not to engage him for any other work. If the master teaches him well, the apprentice must not leave him, but if he does so, the master has the right to compel him by force to stay with him and inflict such punishment and confinement as necessary. After the completion of the training the apprentice is still required to stay with his master till the contract period expires.

During this period whatever the apprentice earns belongs to his master. Upon completion of the training and the contract period, the apprentice is free to leave his master with the latter's permission. If the master offers him a salary in keeping with his technical skill, the apprentice should accept it in preference to an offer from another craftsman. The apprentice system emphasises the teacher-student relationship perfected in other spheres of learning. Here it has certain contractual obligations binding on both sides, as for example, the master craftsman must teach the apprentice his trade secrets honestly, shall treat him as his son and must use him only in work concerning the trade for which he is apprenticed. The apprentice, on his part, cannot run away before the expiry of the contract, nor claim any part of his earnings during this period which to a certain extent account for his free food and lodging, the fees etc. The central feature of the system was that the apprentice was brought up and trained in the actual workshop of the master craftsman. In hereditary craft the father himself was the master craftsman and the filial relationship guaranteed the unwritten contract. The system worked with equal, if not more, efficiency with the congenital defect that it was bound to lapse into stereotype and mediocrity.

## References

Bhattacharya, Sabyasachi, ed. (1998). *The Contested Terrain: Perspectives on Education in India.* New Delhi: Orient Longmans.

Ghosh, Suresh Chandra. (2001). *The History of Education in Ancient India*, c. 3000 B.C. to A.D. 1192. New Delhi: Munshiram Manoharlal.

Hasan, Mushirul, ed. (1998). *Knowledge, Power and Politics: Educational Institutions in India*. New Delhi: Lotus.

Kumar, Nita. (1999). *Lessons from Schools: The History of Education in Banaras.* New Delhi and Thousand Oaks, Calif.: Sage.

# 5

# Education During Mughal Period

The Mughal Empire in India lasted from 1526 to roughly 1761. Generally the Mughal Empire is thought of as a prosperous time period. Even though the Mughal Empire existed 300-500 years ago, its influence still exists in current day India. The social aspects of the Mughal Empire and India today especially relate including family life, religion art, music, and literature, education.

During the Mughal Empire, women had a significant role in family life. Women had an active role in Mughal tribal society, especially apparent when women fought on the battlefield. This is important and unique to this society because during the same time, in other parts of the world, women were oppressed. Some women could not even go to war with their husbands let alone fight. Women were also allowed to voice their political opinions, and were relied on for political advice. In the United States for instance, women were not even allowed to vote until the 1800s. In some regards, India's social standards were more advanced than other countries. Women also received salaries, owned land, participated in business transactions, and literary activities. Aristocratic women painted, wrote poetry, and played music because they received a higher education.

The Mughal Empire was run by Muslim emporers, however India was and still is Hindu dominated. Hindus, specifically of the upper class, adopted the Muslim practice of isolating women, called *purda.* This is an example of Muslim influence in a Hindu dominant culture. The Hindu practice of cremation of widows, called *suttee*, continued even though the Mughals tried to abolish it. The Mughal rulers sometimes forced Islam upon the Hindus, but many times the

Hindus resisted. Hindu men would marry Islam women and convert them to Hinduism in order to keep their religion prominent. Families looked down upon Hindus if one converted to Islam. Specifically, the family member would loose their inheritance rights. Child marriage also remained common. There was religious acceptance and tolerance, but religious segregation still existed. This time also promoted spread of wealth. There was a very prosperous merchant class and nobility. Many Indians established trading ties with foreigners, specifically Europeans. This seemed a benefit in the beginning, but resulted in European domination.

During the time of the Mughal Empire, there was a lot of mixed culture. There was combined Islamic, Persian, and native Indian themes. Art especially thrived during this time because it was a very rich and important part of their culture, and to the emperors of this time. The Akbar style describes the style of paintings that combine Persian and Indian motifs. Some examples of this would be painting humans in action because that had never been explored as a possibility before. Akbar encouraged the imitation of European art, such as use of perspective and realism. Emperor Humayun was interested in the making of Persian miniatures so he started a workshop to make many Persian miniatures. An excellent example of architecture during this time is the Taj Mahal, now located in Agra. Shah Jahan, built the Taj Mahal in the 17th century as a burial chamber for his wife. The Taj Mahal is a symbol of Indian architecture because it is very famous and is equally as beautiful as today. Many painters, poets, and artisans had a dream to one-day work in India because it had such an art enriched cultural environment. Poetry was also a big accomplishment in Indian culture during the Mughal Empire. Most poetry was written in Persia because it was the official language until the sack of Delhi in 1739, and Urdu became the new language after that. These are examples of the arts and literature that flourished during the Mughal Empire rule.

In current day India three fourths of the population lives in villages and the other one forth lives in cities and urban areas. The caste system still exists in India. People are unequal in India due to the caste system; in the villages there is segregation. The higher and more powerful castes live towards the centre of the village. The lower class and Muslims live on the outskirt. This is an example of Muslim exclusion in a Hindu dominating population. This is similar to the

Mughal Empire when Hindus resisted the Muslim influence. In the villages, people live in small huts usually made out of mud. There is not much furniture, there is no real plumbing, and electricity is uncommon in villages. Water is accessible by wells, and stored in clay jars. Households usually have more than one married couple. India has the second population and because of this many people are homeless and there is a high rate of malnutrition. There is usually a senior male, the guy that is in charge, and senior female, usually related to the senior male, assigns chores to the women. Girls usually marry outside of their village, when they are teenagers. People look down upon remarried widows. Couples, when expecting, usually prefer male children because they not only make them more money but also participate in cremation of his parents. Couples dread having girls because they usually have to pay a large dowry, which can cause financial difficulties. Boys are expected to help in the fields and girls in the home.

The art in India today is made up of many different cultures and influences, as during the Mughal Empire time. The art of the past especially influences and makes up the art of today, including the art of the Mughal Empire. Art is still a big part of Indian culture today. Each group of people has created a diverse kind of art. Art is respected as a tradition in India, and will continue to thrive. A free sense of expression along with strong characterisation would describe Indian art. Along with art, architecture and sculpture also thrive. Some prime examples of sculpture can be found in Hindu temples.

Classical Indian music, dance, and drama are closely related because they have the same origination, beginning over 2,000 years ago. They all require great discipline and practice. Of course, regional styles have developed. Indian instruments can be classified as either an instrument that carries the melody or an instrument that accompanies another. In Indian music, the voice is considered an instrument, a melody carrier.

There are many apparent similarities and influences of Mughal in the culture and social aspects of India today. More specifically, the family life, religion, art, music, and literature are all re-occurring themes in history but especially linking to the Mughal Empire which helps make up India today.

## EDUCATION SYSTEM

Under the Mughal rule special attention was given to education. During the Akbar's reign important changes were introduced in the syllabus of education through the efforts of Shah Fathullah Shirazi. Islamic schools were attached to mosques, Khanqah of the Sufis and tombs. Special buildings were also constructed for imparting education. Their expenses were met from endowments.

During the Mughal period the principal centres of learning were at Lahore, Delhi, Ajmer, Sialkot, Multan, Ahmedabad, Allahabad, Lucknow, Murshidabad, Dacca. Many scholars were attracted to these institutions from Persia and Central Asia. Students received education free of cost. Famous scholars received fixed stipends from the royal treasury.

Provisions were made for the teaching of Persian; the official language of the government in the Maktabs. Nizamiyah system of education became popular during the later days of the Mughals. The aim of this system was to create such ability in the scholar so that he is able to acquire perfection in any branch of learning through self-study and personal efforts. While Muslims received education in Maktabs, Hindus had their pathsalas for imparting religious instructions

Before turning to the arts themselves, something must be said of the vigorous educational activity at the capitals—both Delhi and Agra—and in such great provincial cities as Sialkot, Lahore, Ahmedabad, and Burhanpur. Without these centres, the cultural achievements of the Mughal period would scarcely have been possible. During Akbar's reign the "mental sciences"—logic, philosophy, and scholastic theology-had taken on new importance. About the same time, we notice a very considerable improvement in the teaching of the religious sciences. Akbar's conquest of Gujarat opened up ports like Cambay and Surat to those scholars from northern India who wished to go to the great religious centre of Hejaz for further study. That the standard of learning in these subjects rose as a consequence is evidenced by the career of scholars like Shaikh Abdul Haq Muhaddis. The extensive study of hadith, in which Indian scholars were to distinguish themselves in the eighteenth century, began because of this contact with Arabia.

Bernier, the French traveller who was in India during Aurangzeb's reign, deplored the deficiencies of the educational system. To prove his point, he quoted Aurangzeb's reproaches against his tutor for having wasted time on grammar and metaphysics, while ignoring geography, history, and politics. No attempt was made to control education, even though the state gave large grants of rent-free lands to uleama for setting up madrasas. There were no regular examinations, and no organisation for maintaining standards. Yet Mughal education had its special values, for Muslim education did not decay in the eighteenth century with the decline of Muslim political authority. The reduced calls made by the state employment on Muslim manpower left more men free to devote themselves to academic and literary work. A number of educational institutions and foundations, including the colleges established by Ghazi-ud-din Khan Firuz Jang, Sharaf-ud-daulah, and Raushan-ud-daulah in Delhi belong to this period.

The standardisation of the educational curriculum was accomplished in the eighteenth century. The Dars-i-Nizamiya, named after Mulla Nizam-ud-din provided instruction in grammar, rhetoric, philosophy, logic, scholasticism, *tafsir*, *fiqh*, *hadith*, and mathematics. This curriculum has been criticised for containing too many books on grammar and logic and in general for devoting too much attention to formal subjects, and too little to useful secular subjects like history and natural sciences or even religious subjects like *tafsir* and *hadith*. But it provided good mental discipline, and its general adoption was responsible for the widespread interest in intellectual and philosophical matters. In the period in which it was systematised it was perhaps reasonably adequate for the average student. Those wishing to specialise or pursue a particular branch of knowledge went to the experts in that subject. The needs of the students specially interested in religious subjects were better served at institutions like Madrasa-i-Rahimiya, the forerunner of the modern seminary of Deoband, where *tafsir* and *hadith* were the principal subjects of study, but for those needing a general education to qualify for the posts of munshis, qazis, or religious preachers, Dars-i-Nizamiya provided a satisfactory basis until modern times.

Bernier, despite his criticism of the educational system, has left evidence that at least two intellectuals of the Mughal court tried to learn about Western philosophy. One of them was Fazil Khan, the prime minister, whom Bernier taught "the principal languages of Europe, after he had translated for him the whole philosophy of Gassendi in Latin, and whose leave [to depart] he could not obtain, until he had copied for him a select number of best European books, thereby to supply the loss he should suffer of his person." The other was Danishmand Khan, who supported Bernier for a number of years. "My Nawab, Agha Danishmand Khan, expects my arrival with much impatience," Bernier wrote. "He can no more dispense with his philosophical studies in the afternoon than avoid devoting the morning to his weighty duties as Secretary of State for Foreign Affairs and Grand Master of the Horse. Astronomy, geography, and anatomy are his favourite pursuits, and he reads with avidity the works of Gassendy and Descartes." Colonel Sleeman, who knew India in the first half of the nineteenth century better than almost any other Englishman, paid high tribute to the quality of Muslim education in India. He wrote:

> Perhaps there are few communities in the world among whom education is more generally diffused than among Mohammadans in India. He who holds an office worth twenty rupees a month commonly gives his sons an education equal to that of a Prime Minister. They learn, through the medium of Arabic and Persian languages, what young men in our colleges learn through those of Greek and Latin—that is, grammar, rhetoric, and logic. After his seven years of study, the young Mohammadan binds his turban upon a head almost as well filled with the things which appertain to these branches of knowledge as the young man raw from Oxford-he will talk as fluently about Socrates and Aristotle, Plato and Hippocrates, Galen, and Avicenna.

Nor was education confined only to men. Many Muslim women were patrons of literature and themselves writers. The memoirs of Gulbadan Begum, Akbar's aunt, are well known, and his foster-mother, Maham Anga, endowed a college at Delhi. Akbar's wife Salima Sultana, the famous Empress Mumtaz Mahal, and Aurangzeb's sister, the Princess Jahan Aarra Begum, were poetesses of note, as was his daughter, Zeb-un-Nissa.

The spread of knowledge and intellectual development is linked up with the growth of libraries. Printing was not introduced in northern India till after the end of the Muslim rule, but hundreds of katibs were available in every big city, and no Muslim noble would be considered cultured, unless he possessed a good library. The royal palaces contained immense libraries. According to Father Manrique, the library of Agra in 1641 contained 24,000 volumes, valued at six and a half million rupees.

## LITERATURE

Persian was the language of Mughal intellectual life. Since the Ghaznavid occupation of Lahore in the beginning of the eleventh century, Persian had been the official language of the Muslim government and the literary language of the higher classes, but with the advent of the Mughals it entered a new era. Hitherto Persian had reached India mainly from Afghanistan, Turkistan, and Khorasan, and had many common features with Tajik. With the establishment of closer relations between India and Iran after Humayun's visit to that country, and the arrival of a large number of distinguished Iranis in the reign of Jahangir and later Mughal rulers, the linguistic and literary currents began to flow from Iran itself. Shiraz and Isfahan now replaced Ghazni and Bukhara in literary inspiration, with considerable refining of the language as a result.

A large number of prominent Irani poets, including Urfi, Naziri, Talib, and Kalim, migrated to India, and at times the level of Persian literature was higher in Mughal India than in Iran. Unluckily the style of poetry, which was popular in both countries at that time, was the subtle and involved type made popular by Fighani of Shiraz. This school of poetry culminated in Bedil, the best known poet of Aurangzeb's reign. His similes and metaphors are often obscure, but his poetry is marked by great originality and profundity of thought. From love, the traditional preoccupation of Persian poets, he turned to the problems of life and human behaviour, and in certain circles (particularly in Afghanistan and Tajikistan) he ranks high as a philosophical poet. But the two poets who outshone all others in a distinguished group were Faizi and Ghalib. Faizi, whose genius matured before the large-scale immigration of poets from Iran and the introduction of the "new" school of poetry, was the brother of Abul Fazl. As Akbar's poet—laureate, his poetry mirrors a triumphant age. Ghalib, who was attached to the court of the last Mughal emperor, Bahadur Shah, began in the style of *Bedil*, but soon outgrew it and came under the spell of the immigrant Irani poets-Urfi, Naziri, Zahuri, and Hazin. His maturer work epitomises all that is best in the different schools of Mughal poetry-the profundity and originality of Bedil's thought, combined with the polished diction of Urfi and Naziri. He wrote largely of love and life, but the deep, melancholy note in his poetry reflects the sad end to which the Mughal empire was drawing in his day.

Next to poetry, history and biography were most extensively cultivated during the Mughal period. Historians include Abul Fazl, whose comprehensive Akbar Nama is one of the most important historical works produced in India; Badauni, who wrote with bias and even venom, yet who was a consummate artist, a master of the telling phrase, and capable of evoking a living picture with a few deft strokes; the intelligent and orderly Firishta; Khafi Khan; and the author of Siyar-ul-Mutakhkhirin, the last of the great Mughal historical works. Among biographical works, Babur's autobiography, originally written in Turkish, but soon translated into elegant Persian by Abdul Rahim Khan-i-Khanan, is the best. There were, however, other biographical works, including the comprehensive Ma'asir'ul-umara dealing with the Mughal nobility, and numerous biographies of saints, poets, and statesmen. A very interesting historical work written during Aurangzeb's reign is Dabistan-i-Mazahib, which has been translated into English under the misleading title "School of Manners," but which is really a "History of Religions." The author, who belonged to the band of the writers and thinkers around Dara Shukoh, gives considerable first-hand information about non-Muslim sects.

The Persian literature produced in India is of interest not only for its intrinsic worth, but also for the influence it exercised on the formation and shaping of regional literatures, especially those cultivated by the Muslims. In addition to vocabulary and general influence on thought, it contributed a number of literary genres to the regional languages, provided models for the writers, and supplied themes for many major literary works. Indeed, apart from Islam itself, the Persian literary heritage has been the most important basis of the cultural unity of Muslim India.

It is characteristic of the Mughals that, next to Persian, the language which received the greatest patronage at court was Hindi. The practice started in Akbar's day of having a Hindi *kavi rai* (poet-laureate) along with the Persian *malik-ul-shuara*. Already Muslim poets such as Jaisi and Kabir had enriched the Hindi language. Among Hindus, the greatest Hindi poet of Akbar's days was the famous Tulasidas, whose career was spent far from the worldly courts. There were, however, well-known Hindi poets amongst Akbar's courtiers. Raja Birbal (1528-1583) was the *kavi rai*, but the works of Akbar's famous general Abdul Rahim have been better preserved. A skilful writer in Hindi, Abdul Rahim furthered the development of the language by extending his patronage to a number of other poets who used it. The title of *kavi rai* continued to be conferred even in Aurangzeb's time, and two of his sons, Azam and Muazzam, who ascended the throne as Bahadur Shah, were known to be patrons of Hindi literature. It is interesting to observe that during the later Mughal period Hindi poets like Bihari followed the same ornate style which was popular with the contemporary Persian poets.

Until the decline of the empire Urdu literature received scarcely any encouragement at the Mughal courts, but it was systematically nourished in the south by the Sufi saints and the Deccani kings. Nusrati, a poet attached to the court of Bijapur, wrote masnavis in a language remote from modern Urdu but within its tradition. The first collection of Urdu lyrics was written by Sultan Mohammed Quli Qutab Shah, the king of Golkunda and founder of the city of Hyderabad. Modern Urdu poetry really began, however, with Wali, who came in contact with the spoken Urdu of the Mughal camp during the long campaigns of Aurangzeb in the Deccan. He blended the Deccani and Gujarati idioms with the polite and more sophisticated language of the north, and following the traditions of standard Persian literature, he produced poetry which set a literary fashion in Delhi. He transferred to Urdu poetry ideas and images with which readers of Persian poetry were familiar; and thus enriched, Urdu could replace Persian poetry. Although a proportion of Wali's verse is in Deccani idiom, a good proportion is in polished Urdu.

Once Urdu was adopted as the medium of literary expression by the writers of the metropolis, its development was rapid, and it soon replaced Persian as the court language and principal literary language of Muslim India. The process of change-over to the new literary language was facilitated by certain other factors. The invasion of Delhi by the Persian monarch Nadir Shah in 1739 and the massacres perpetrated by his army must have led to a revulsion of feeling against everything Persian-including the language. An acute literary controversy of the period further hastened the process. Hazin, a major Persian poet who came to India to escape Nadir Shah, was subjected to great hardship in the unsettled conditions prevailing at that time, and in a controversy with Arzu, the foremost local writer of Persian verses, expressed his contempt for the Persian poetry written in India. Some local writers sided with him, but the general effect of the controversy must have been to set people thinking about the advisability of writing in Persian.

Thus the ground was prepared for literary change-over. What was needed was the appearance of talented writers in the new language to give it a literary status. This was provided by Mazhar, Sauda, the Sufi poet Dard, and above all Mir-popularly known as the four pillars of classical Urdu poetry. Both Sauda and Mir had been trained by Arzu to write in Urdu rather than in Persian.

The encouragement which the growth of regional languages and literatures received in the regional Muslim kingdoms has already been outlined. Muslim rulers, unhampered by any religious devotion to Sanskrit, freely patronised Bengali, Kashmiri, Hindi, Deccani, and other languages of the people. This trend was most powerful in the regional kingdoms which grew up after the weakening of the Delhi Sultanate. Persian continued as the court language in these kingdoms; but local languages were freely patronised, and became respectable vehicles of literary expression.

The literary trend under Mughal rule was not exactly in the same direction. The establishment of a well-organised central government at Delhi, with cohesive control over the outlying regions, resulted in greater linguistic unification, and the influence of Persian became far more dominant. Mughal rule, however, indirectly assisted the regional literatures. Apart from the direct patronage of Hindi at the Delhi court, the conditions in the country helped the regional literatures. The general peace and tranquillity; greater prosperity, particularly in urban areas; the more general diffusion of education; and the patronage of literature by the Mughal emperors and the nobility, led to extensive literary activity, from which the regional literatures benefited. By now they had developed so much that they could not wither away by want of direct court patronage, and the general prosperity in the country was enough to sustain them. The result was that a marked literary activity in the regional languages continued along with the cultivation of Persian, and particularly in the later part of Mughal rule there was a great outburst of literary activity in Bengali, Deccani, Hindi, Sindhi, Pushto, Kashmiri, and other regional languages.

## ORGANISATION OF EDUCATION

The credit for organising education on a systematic basis goes to Akbar, a contemporary of Queen Elizabeth I of England and undoubtedly the greatest of Mughal emperors. He treated all his subjects alike and opened a large number of schools and colleges for Muslims as well as for Hindus throughout his empire. He also introduced a few curricular changes, based on students' individual needs and the practical necessities of life. The scope of the curriculum was so widened as to enable every student to receive education according to his religion and views of life. The adoption of Persian as the court language gave further encouragement to the Hindus and the Muslims to study Persian.

Akbar's policy was continued by his successors Jahangir and Shah Jahan. But his great-grandson Aurangzeb changed his policy with regard to the education of the Hindus. In April 1669, for instance, he ordered the provincial governors to destroy Hindu schools and temples within their jurisdiction; and, at the same time, he supported Muslim education with a certain religious fanaticism. After his death, the glory of the Mughal empire began gradually to vanish, and the whole country was overrun by warlords.

During the Mughal period, girls received their education at home or in the house of some teacher living in close proximity. There were special arrangements for the education of the ladies of the royal household, and some of the princesses were distinguished scholars. Vocational education was imparted through a system of apprenticeship either in the house of ustads (teachers) or in karkhanahs (manufacturing centres).

Muslim rulers of India were also great patrons of literature and gave considerable impetus to its development. Akbar ordered various Hindu classics and histories translated into Persian. In addition, a number of Greek and Arabic works were translated into Persian.

Literary activities did not entirely cease even in the troubled days of later rulers. Men of letters were patronised by such emperors as Bahadur Shah and Muhammad Shah and by various regional officials and landlords.

Such is the history of Muslim education in India. It resembles ancient Indian education to a great extent: instruction was free; the relation between the teachers and the taught was cordial; there were great centres of learning; the monitorial system was used; and people were preoccupied with theology and the conduct of life. There were, however, several distinctive features of Muslim education. First, education was democratised. As in mosques, so in a maktab or madrasah, all were equal, and the principle was established that the poor should also be educated. Second, Muslim rule influenced the system of elementary education of the Hindus, which had to accommodate itself to changed circumstances by adopting a new method of teaching and by using textbooks full of Persian terms and references to Muslim usages. Third, the Muslim period brought in many cultural influences from abroad. The courses of studies were both widened and brought under a humanistic influence. Finally, Muslim rule produced a cross-cultural influence in the country through the establishment of an educational system in which Hindus and Muslims could study side by side and in which there would be compulsory education in Persian, cultivation of Sanskrit and Hindi, and translation of great classics of literature into different languages. Ultimately, it led to the development of a common medium of expression, Urdu.

Education in the Muslim era was not a concerted and planned activity but a voluntary and spontaneous growth. There was no separate administration of education, and state aid was sporadic and unsteady. Education was supported by charitable endowments and by lavish provision for the students in a madrasah or in a monastery.

The Muslim system, however, proved ultimately harmful. In the early stages genuine love of learning attracted students to the cultural centres, but later on "the bees that flocked there were pre-eminently drones." The whole system became stagnant and stereotyped as soon as cultural communication was cut off from the outside world because of political disturbances and internecine wars. The Indian teachers were reduced to dependence on their own resources, and a hardening tradition that became increasingly unreceptive to new ideas reduced the whole process to mere routine.

## Science and Technology Education

With the consolidation of Muhammadan power in India a new pattern was woven slowly but surely in the educational fabric of India. Educational inspiration and models, it hardly goes without saying, were derived from leading Islamic cultural centres in West Asia. The ancient college of Nizamia at Bagdad where philosopher al-Ghazzali was at one time the head professor offered a course widely known as Silsilai Nazamia.'' The main subjects taught according to that system included grammar, rhetoric, logic, dialectic literature, philosophy, mathematics, theology, and law. Philosophy embraced two important branches of knowledge, e.g., physics and metaphysics, based upon Aristotelian principles, and mathematics included astronomy, particularly the geocentric system of Ptolemy, besides Algebra, Geometry and Arithmetic. These subjects were taken up at the secondary and higher stages of education, while at the primary stage instruction, as universally everywhere, was confined to reading, writing and elementary arithmetic. This system was generally adopted in madrassas and maktabs in India in Conformity with the general practice obtaining throughout the Islamic world. The striking feature of this general curriculum was the balance between scientific and humanistic studies, and in practice, Jaffar thinks, science seems to have received greater attention than philosophy.

The schools and colleges were not generally concerned with technical education in arts and crafts, which was the prerogative of special institutions and industrial workshops (karkhanas). For general education we meet with three broad types of institutions; *(a)* private houses for giving elementary knowledge or primary education, *(b)* mosques and other religious places for imparting secondary education, and *(c)* maktabs and madrassas for providing higher education. In the house schools the beginners learnt the alphabet, pronunciation, punctuation, reading and writing on his takhti (writing board or slate) and also doing figures and sums. The secondary education which received considerable attention usually centred round mosques, anqahs, and dargahs. Qutabuddin established hundreds of mosques for the promotion of Muhammadan education, and his example was emulated by subsequent rulers. The hanqahs were analogous to medieval European monasteries and were established by saint scholars like Shah Nizam-ud-Din Auliya and Muin-ud-Din Chisti. The dargahs were tombs of noted saints, and many of them developed into educational centres due to their natural power of attracting people. The maktabs and madrassas were also attached to mosques; or established separately and generally supported by the State, noblemen or private liberality in the form of land-grants or cash. Gopamau and Khairabad in Oudh and Jaunpur in Agra province had such institutions which attracted students from Afghanistan and Bokhara; renowned professors lectured in these places on grammar, rhetoric, logic, theology, metaphysics, literature, jurisprudence and science.

There was yet another system, namely, the domestic system of teaching under a learned expert. The house of such a learned expert often developed into a centre of instruction, where pupils were afforded free boarding and lodging. 'Such educational centres, small but numerous', writes Law, 'not only provided a field for post-collegiate studies, but were also in many cases the only means by which instruction in some subjects was imparted. This type of instruction with which institutional schools could not compete became popular in the case of arts, crafts and various technics.

The most notable among the pre-Mughal emperor-sultans was Firuz Shah Tughluq (1351-1388) who patronised learning, established a large number of educational institutions, and surrounded his court with distinguished men of learning such as Maulana Jalal-ud-Din Rumi, Siraj Arif, Zia-ud-Din Barai, Maulana Kjnvajgi, Qazi Abdul Qadir and Aziz-ud-Din Khalid Khani. In the list of public works initiated by Firuz and recorded by Ferishta, colleges with mosques attached figure prominently. Thirty such colleges provided with paid professors of merit were founded by him whereas, according to the evidence of Abdul Baqi, he opened as many as fifty madrassas. The most magnificent of them all was the college at Firozabad called the Firuz-Shahl Madrassa, of which Barra has left a detailed description. Here taught Maulana. Jalalud-Din Rumi and several renowned professors some of whom were invited from Samarqand. Special mention should also be made of another college, the Qadam Sharif, found near the tomb of his son Fath Khaq, about a mile and half to the south of the Lahore Gate in Delhi.

Sikandar Lodhi (1458-1518) was a patron of learning and converted temples and shrines he destroyed into caravansaries and colleges. During his reign, Ferishta records, the Hindus for the first time applied themselves to the study of Persian and Muhammadan literature. It did not take them a century before their mastery of the new language in point of literary merits compared favourably with that of the Muhammadan scholars. About his promotion of scientific learning, Sikandar must be given credit for arranging the translation of an Ayurvedic work on the science of medicine and treatment of diseases. Miyan Bhowa, Lord Chamberlain of Sikandar Lodhi, under orders from the sultan, assembled competent Hakims and Vaids and made them compile an authoritative treatise of medicine on the basis of a dozen important Ayurvedic works. Siddiqi gives the name of this work as Madanush-Shijai-Sikandan, whereas according to the Waqiati-Mushtaqi, 'the book so compiled received the name of Tibb-i-Sikandari, and there is no work of greater authority in India. We learn from the same source that five caligraphists and learned men were procured from Khurasan and other places for 'writing books on every science'.

The Mughals maintained and extended the educational activities of the Sultanate periods. Humayun was a bibliophile with a special interest in sciences. During Akbar's reign educational activities made such a headway that Abul Fazl unhesitatingly declared : "All civilised nations have schools for the education of youths; but Hindustan is particularly famous for its seminaries". Akbar's educational reforms benefited all communities equally, and for the first time the Hindus and the Muhammadans were seen studying in the same schools and colleges. In the revised system of teaching pupils were given four exercises daily, viz., the alphabet, the combinations, a new hemistich or distich, and repetition of what they had learnt before. By this procedure the students were reported to master their lessons in months instead of years as was normal before. At a higher stage sciences were taught in the following order—morality, arithmetic, accounts, agriculture, geometry, longimetry, astronomy, geomancy, economics, the art of government, physics, logic, natural philosophy, abstract mathematics, divinity and history. Akbar founded a large number of madrassas, including a big college at Fathepur Sikri.

## Technical Education

The excellence of manufactured articles of medieval India, e.g. fine fabrics of cotton and silk, embroidered caps, painted and enamelled wares, cups and basins, steel guns, knives, scissors, white paper, gold and silver ornaments is well known. This excellence could not have been achieved and maintained for centuries without a dependable system of technical education. In the domestic or private system of education already referred to the ustad was the pivotal figure, and, depending upon his reputation, he used to attract apprentices from far and near. In most cases the apprentice had to live in the house of the ustad as one of the inmates, and the system was more or less the same as we have found in ancient Indian law-books. In hereditary craft the father himself was the ustad and teacher of his son, while the mother took charge of her daughter. The natural advantage of a filial relationship between the father and the son, the spontaneous desire of the father to train his son in all the secrets of the trade and of the son to become as skilled as his father, cannot be denied, and the system was adhered to despite its disadvantages such as tendency to stereotype, loss of innovation, and progressive decline in competitiveness. In the highly specialised trade of instrumentation, we hear of a family of astrolable-makers in Lahor, Zia'ud-Din Muhammad, son of Qa'im Muhammad, son of Mulla Isa, son of Sheykh Allah-Dad, who for four generations continued to produce excellent astrolabes in great demand in astronomical circles both in India and abroad.

Alongside with the old master artisan-cum-apprentice system, the manufacturing establishments, called karkhanas, themselves gradually undertook to impart technical education in the types of manufacture in which they specialised. The Muslim rulers usually maintained a Public Works Department or the Shwat-i-Am, and one of its duties was to look after and assist such workshops as were engaged in industrial training activity. Each workshop had a number of sections with which several mechanics and artisans skilled in various types of job were associated.

Bernier saw a number of workshops and left a vivid account of these establishments in working order. These were large halls generally called karkanays (karkhanas), possibly divided or partitioned into several smaller halls. 'In one hall embroiderers are busily employed, superintended by a master. In another, you see the goldsmiths; in a third, painters; in a fourth, varnishers in lacquer-work; in a fifth, joiners, turners, tailors, and shoemakers; in a sixth, manufacturers of silk, brocade, and those fine muslins of which are made turbans, girgles with golden flowers, and drawers, worn by females, so delicately fine as frequently to wear out in one night. This article of dress, which lasts only a few hours, may cost ten or twelve crowns and even more, when beautifully embroidered with needle work.

The apprentice had a wide choice in such a place. He started his training at an early age, doing such menial work as cleaning the tools and watching the artisans in their daily work. Soon he was permitted to handle ordinary tools and perform the simplest operations of the trade. As the apprentice picked up some skill and experience and was in a position to render some small service to the establishment, he was given some allowance, and the whole affair proceeded like this till his training at the workshop was complete. "To the poor artisans this system had an advantage in this that their sons began to earn their livelihood at an early age and ceased to be a burden on their parents.

The early Sultans and the great Mughals enthusiastically supported the karkhanas and their associated system of technical education. Firuz organised a regular department of industry and showed personal interest in the technical education of his slaves. There were about one hundred and eighty thousand slaves at his disposal, and he arranged to place them under master craftsmen in order to enable them to learn one or more arts and crafts. Such interest in technical education, on the part of the ruling authorities, Hindu as well as Muslim, produced an abundance of technical hands in India which Babar, in the course of his experiences in India, did not fail to notice. "Another convenience of Hindustan", he wrote in his Memoirs, "is that the workmen of every profession and trade are innumerable and without end. For any work, or any employment, there is always a set ready, to whom the same employment and trade have descended from father to son for ages. In Agra alone, and of stone-cutters belonging to that place only, I everyday employed on my palaces six hundred and eighty persons; and in Agra, Sikri, Biana, Dholpur, Gwalior and Koel (Aligarh), there were everyday employed on my works one thousand four hundred and ninetynine stonecutters. In the same way men of every trade and occupation are numberless and without stint in Hindustan.

## Medical Education

Reference has already been made to the interest in medicine of Firuz Shah Tughluq. Delhi Sultàns, provincial rulers and the great Mughals were all uniformly interested in the development of medical sciences and in the organisation of hospitals and clinics. In this area they willingly and freely invited the cooperation of Ayurvedic practitioners in the further development of a system which had already been based on the Greek one. The Unani Tibb, as the system is known, started taking shape in the middle of the ninth century A.D. when Ali B. Rabban composed his Firdausul-Hikmat (Paradise of Wisdom), on the basis of the Greek medicine of Hippocrates and Galen as well as on the Ayurvedic system represented by Caraka, Susruta, Vagbhata, Madhavakara and others. A more comprehensive and thorough work was produced by al-Razito be again superseded by Ibn Sina's (980-1036) Canon. Van Sina's magnum opus which dominated European medical schools for over five hundred years was also accepted as the most authoritative medical work in India. Still Firuz's example of updating medical treatises in the light of current experiences of both Hakims and Vaids was emulated by subsequent rulers. During the fourteenth and fifteenth centuries in Gujarat, Hakim Shahabuddin compiled two works, Tibbi-Shifaul-Khani and Tibbe Shihabi on the basis of Arabic, Persian and Ayurvedic works and Hakim Muhammad, court physician of Mahmud Shah (1458-1510) translated Vagbhata into Persian. Similar efforts were made by the Hakims under Bahamanid rulers in the Deccan. Unani medicine received liberal encouragement from the Mughal rulers.

According to Abul Fazl's gazetteer, the capital was well served by 39 Hakims, and then number exceeded thousand when the whole country was considered. For reputed Hakims major cities and capitals and central and provincial governments such as Lahore, Delhi, Lucknow, Patna, Murshidabad, Hyderabad and Madras were famous. Most of these practitioners were involved in the teaching of the Unani system of medicine, and included a good number of specialists from Iran. Jaul notes that medical education during the Mughal rule was largely tutor-oriented. The medical students generally attended the clinics of physicians where they spent several years.

Many of the hospitals, including the large ones built by Akbar at Sikri and Jahangir at Delhi near Jami's Mosque, had attached to them active medical schools. Many of these schools languished with the fall of the empire, and quite a few survived, as in the Deccan, under the patronage of the Asaf Jahi Kings (Nizam). Siddiqi and Subba Reddy mention five well known Hakims serving the Nizam's court between 1761 and 1803, six physicians between 1803 to 1829, and notice their number to increase steadily as efforts were being made to revive the old system. The political disintegration of the country during the eighteenth century adversely affected the entire educational system. In the absence of royal support and encouragement the institutions languished and teachers and learned men became impoverished.

## References

John F Richards. (1996). *The Mughal Empire*, Vol I.5, *New Cambridge History of India*, Cambridge University Press.

Ganeri, Anita. (1999). *Looking Back: India Under the Mughal Empire 1526-1858*. Austin, Texas: Raintree Steck-Vaughn.

Savage-Smith, Emilie (1985), *Islamicate Celestial Globes: Their history, Construction, and Use*, Smithsonian Institution Press, Washington, D.C.

Baber, Zaheer (1996), *The Science of Empire: Scientific Knowledge, Civilization, and Colonial Rule in India*, State University of New York Press.

# 6

# Education in Colonial India

The ideas and pedagogical methods of education during the colonial period, from 1757 to 1947, were contested terrain. The commercial British East India Company ruled parts of India from 1764 to 1858. A few eighteenth-century company officials became scholars of Sanskrit, Persian, and Tamil and promoted "Oriental" learning, which was classical, demotic learning in indigenous languages. However, they were outnumbered by "Anglicists," those who denigrated "Oriental" learning and advocated the introduction of institutions for Western learning based upon the British curriculum with English as the medium of instruction.

By the early nineteenth century, when English was made the official language of government business, British policy promoted a cheap, trickle-down model for colonial education. When the British crown abolished company rule in 1858, government universities existed at Bombay (contemporary Mumbai), Calcutta (Kolkata), and Madras (Chennai); about two thousand students studied at thirteen government colleges in all of British India, and another 30,000 students were in government secondary schools. Direct rule did not change the decision to de-emphasise primary education to provide occupational training for young Indian men who took jobs both in the lower tiers of the government and in urban, Western-style legal and medical services.

Non-government schools established by Western Christian missions and Indian social and religious reform organisations provided the only opportunities for elementary education in the nineteenth century. American and English missionaries founded men's colleges, and by the twentieth century, Lucknow, Lahore, and Madras all had Christian women's colleges as well. Foreign teachers staffed these institutions, offering a Western curriculum in English with financial support for the children of Christian converts.

Reformist societies also started schools, partly to provide Western education without the threat of Christian conversion. The curricula in private girls' schools ranged from the Urdu, Persian, writing, arithmetic, needlework, and Islamic studies of the Punjabi. Anjuman-i-Himayat-i-Islam primary schools in northwestern India to the Western-style liberal arts curriculum of Bethune College, founded by liberal Brahmo Samajists (Hindu reformers) in Calcutta. Even voluntary societies' members who wanted to provide educational alternatives for their children disagreed about the advantages and disadvantages of the colonial educational model for both content and the language of instruction.

When British officials who represented direct rule by the crown introduced modest self-government in the 1860s, they shifted financial responsibility for education to a growing Indian middle class. Educating urban sons for professions dominated local educational spending, to the detriment of rural and women's education. Families of respectable middle class usually chose to send their daughters to gender-segregated educational institutions once there were schools taught in vernacular languages with general curricula. While older historians narrated the "insidious, total and transparent" domination of the educational system by the colonial state, more recent scholarship delineates the "creative resistance" to state agency and suggests that there was a "combat" between "consciously opposed sides".

As the nationalist movement gained supporters in the twentieth century, Indian leaders developed several nationalist educational paradigms to challenge the colonial model. Mahatma Gandhi wanted the state to teach basic literacy in vernacular languages to the majority of the population. Rabindranath Tagore, India's first recipient of the Nobel Prize for literature, believed that the English language provided Indians access to the sharing of knowledge across international borders and that education should include the teaching of India's cultural traditions. The fight for freedom from colonialism pre-empted decisions about educational ideologies until after 1947.

## British Education in India

From the early decades of British rule, deliberate attempts were made to introduce and propagate Western educational system in India. Education in India under the British government was first ignored, then violently opposed, then conducted on a system now universally admitted to be erroneous and finally placed on its present footing.

The East India Company was a mere trading company. It had no interest in the education of people whose language is neither understood, nor appreciated. According to the policy of Cornvallis, Indians were not appointed to responsible posts. However, during this period East India Company had encouraged missionaries to come and work in this country.

In 1813, in order to import Christianity and European culture from the west, the parliament inserted a clause No.43 in the charter of the East India Company, which for the first time made an annual provision for the promotion of the learning. To the effect that after defraying all civil and military expenses a sum of not less than one lakh of rupees in each year shall be set apart and applied to the revival and improvement of literature and the encouragement of learned natives of India and for the introduction and promotion of knowledge of the science among the inhabitants of the British territories in India." This is the foundation stone of British educational system in India.

Ram Mohun Roy, Radhakant Dev and others were feeling the need for a new type of education. Ram Mohun Roy was of the view that the introduction of English education in this country would lead to renaissance. So Hindu College was established for the education of the children of the upper and middle classes of the Indian society in European sciences and English literature.

In 1823, the general committee of public instruction was set-up to give shape to the educational policy of the government. The committee was guided by two principles:

*(a)* It wanted to win the confidence of the educated and influential classes, by encouraging and learning the literature that they respected.

*(b)* As the funds at the disposal of the committee were quite inadequate, it would be best to apply the funds to the higher

education of the upper class as distinguished from the general elementary education of the masses.

In 1824, it was proposed to open a Sanskrit college in Calcutta. Raja Ram Mohun Roy vehemently opposed the proposal.

In 1835, Lord William Bentick outlined the policy of the British clearly. While endorsing the views of Macaulay, he issued a proclamation which stated. "The great of the British government would henceforth be the promotion of European literature and science through the medium of English and that government funds appropriated for the purpose of education would be best employed on English education alone."

The primary aim of Macaulay was to produce Indian "Babus" who are well versed in English, so that they will work for the British. As a result English language became a cause for Indian nationalism.

In 1844, Lord Hardinge proclaimed that for services in public offices, preference would be given to those who were educated in English schools. The emphasis was on producing good clerks who will serve the British raj. In addition they had the aim of converting the whole India into Christianity. A letter, which Macaulay wrote to his parents, clearly shows this. Our English Schools are flourishing wonderfully."

The effect of this education on the Hindus is prodigious. No Hindu, who has received an English education, ever remains sincerely attached to his religion. Some continue to profess it as a matter of policy, others profess themselves as pure deists and some embrace Christianity.

## Wood's Despatch

In 1854, Sir Charles Wood, then president of the board of control to Government of India, gave his official report, popularly known as the Woods despatch. It is said to be the Magna Carta of Indian history education. The chief provisions were as follows.

1. Education, which we desire to extent, is that which has for its object, the diffusion of the improved arts, philosophy and literature of Europe.

2. A separate department of public instruction was created in Bengal, Madras, Bombay, Punjab and the northwest province.
3. Universities on the model of London universities should be established to hold examinations and confer degrees.
4. Teacher training institutions should be opened.
5. A network of graded schools should be set-up.
6. A system of grants-in-aid to be set-up.

Woods despatch is known as the cornerstone of Indian education, for it has laid the foundation of our present system of education. The establishment of universities in the year 1857 had far reaching consequences, especially on the range of secondary education.

The universities in India suffered from a series of defects. Majority of the ills could be traced to the act of Incorporation passed by the Governor-General and Viceroy, Lord Canning in 1857. The acts defined the objects of the universities as "ascertaining by means of examination the persons who have acquired proficiency in different branches of literature, science and art and of rewarding them by academic degrees as evidence of their respective attainments".

In 1882, Punjab University was established by a special act of Incorporation and in 1887, another special act of incorporation established the fifth Indian University at Allahabad.

**Allahabad University**

The most glaring defects of the Acts of incorporation was in the appointment of fellows to the senates of the universities. These fellows were appointed for life, not for a specific period. These universities were affiliating universities from the distant geographic area. These affiliated universities were nothing but collections of lecture rooms, classrooms and laboratories.

While an education department could exercise control over the government and aided colleges, it has no control over the private colleges, which had the chief part in the education of undergraduates. The education departments were unable to banish politics from the unaided colleges especially those imparting legal education. The politics was mainly antagonistic to the British rule. So the government thought it has done a mistake to let the control of legal education go entirely out of his hands. Since there was no separate education department for the Government of India, the universities could not be expected to maintain a uniform and high academic standard.

## Curzon's Minute on University Reform on 23 Feb., 1901

The main thrust of his arguments in the minute was that:

*a)* Extend the functions of the Indian universities from examination to teaching.

*b)* Regulate the number, tenure and classifications of the fellows.

*c)* Reconstitute the electorate by adding residential qualifications among the graduates.

*d)* Provide a statutory status to the syndicates.

*e)* Narrow the geographical limits of each university.

*f)* Strengthen the law relating to the recognition and affiliation of colleges.

*g)* Curtain power of the board of studies.

Curzon summoned a conference at Simla to look for the light at the end of the tunnel. The first-educated conference in India started on 2 September 1901 was attended by Vice-chancellors of the universities of Calcutta, Bombay, Madras, Punjab and Northwestern provinces. The character of the conference was both official and private and did not include any representative from Indian people.

The proceedings of the conference were never published and the secrecy with which Curzon enveloped the conference at Simla earned for it such names as Secret Conclave or Star Chamber. As Surendranath Banerjee later remarked rather sarcastically, " The conference met in secret, deliberated in secret, resolved in secret and it presume dispersed in secret".

## Appointment of Indian Universities Commission

In a telegram to Hamilton on 13 January 1902 Curzon proposed to appoint six persons as permanent members of the commission. There was only one Indian among the six members—Syed H. Bilgrami. The absence of a Hindu among the six commissioners created a great stir since the Hindus had the largest interest in the educational problems that were to be considered. So Curzon had no other alternative, but to nominate Gurudas Banerjee, a former vice-chancellor of the Calcutta University as the commissioner. Curzon also made appointment to the newly created post of Director General of Education. Orange who was working in the Department of Education as examiner in the Whitehall was appointed to the post.

The Indian University Commission submitted its recommendations on 9 June to Curzon. The commissions' recommendations faithfully reflected Curzon's viewpoints on university reform. Sri Gurudas Banerjee disagreed on many points with them. Curzon tried to keep these recommendations also in secret. However, a local newspaper got hold of a copy of the report and began in his words "Publishing a series of daily recommendations of the government or rather of myself, for having rung the death-knell of higher education in India". There was fierce agitation put up by the Indian people. But inspite of all this, the Indian University bill was passed on 21 March 1904, despite stiff resistance by G. K. Gokhale and Asutosh Mukhopadhyaya.

The Indian universities act introduced radical changes into the five existing universities at Calcutta, Bombay, Madras, Lahore and Ahmedbad. Among these were the enlargement of the functions of the university and reduction in the size of the university senates. The act, which had not found any favour with the educated Indians, created problems when the government set about to carry it out.

## Genesis of National Education

However, the idea of a national system of education, more appropriately Indian education in spirit and substance did not emerge suddenly as a reaction to the passing of Indian Universities Act in 1905-06. In 1890-92, in his convocation address as the vice-chancellor of the Calcutta university, Gurudas Banerjee has drawn attention to some of the most glaring defects from the point of view of intellectual training and of the discipline of the system set-up by the education despatch of 1854. He suggested the urgent introduction of mother tongue as the medium of instruction. About the same time Rabindranath Tagore in his paper on 'shiksher her fer' published in December 1892 issue of 'Sadhana' pointed out clearly the inadequacy of the prevailing system of education under the British raj and pleaded for acceptance of Bengali as the medium of instruction.

In the wake of the Indian Universities Act, which reflected the recommendations of the Indian University commission, came the partition of Bengal in 1905. The British raj felt "Bengal united is a power. Bengal divided will pull several ways". The people of Bengal rose like one man to resist, to suffer and to sacrifice. Spearheaded by the students who represented youth and dream, vigour and selfless dedication and joined by the workers and peasants, the clerks and the teachers who had been affected most by the rising prices and since 1904, the antipartition movement soon broke away from traditional moorings and after transcending its rather limited and immediate objective broadened into a struggle for 'Swaraj'.

G. K. Gokhale believed that "an illiterate and ignorant nation can never make any solid progress and must fall back in the race for life". He moved a bill in the Imperial Legislative Council which suggested free and compulsory education for boys between the ages of 6 and 10 especially in those areas where 33% of the male population was already at school. But the Government of India was not willing to accept the bill. However, as Gokhale has observed in his concluding speech in the council "We of the present generation in India, can only hope to serve our country with our failures". Primary education began to receive attention from the Government of India, and how sanctioned a grant of Rs 50 lakhs and a non-recurring grant of Rs 84 lakhs for the purpose.

While Gokhale's bill was pending with the legislative council, King George V and his queen Mary visited India. He announced an additional grant of 50 lakhs for primary education and expressed a desire that "there may be spread over the land a network of schools and colleges". This coupled with administrative charges brought about by the Government of India Act of 1909, led the government to review the whole field of education and to issue its resolution on Indian education policy on 21 Feb., 1913.

The Government of India Act of 1919. It introduced dyarchy in the provinces where departments with less political weight and little funds like education, health and agriculture were transferred to Indian ministers and vital departments like law and order and finance were given to British officials.

The non co-operative resolution passed by the Nagpur Congress in 1920 advised the gradual withdrawal of children from schools and colleges owned, aided or controlled by the government, and, in place of such schools and colleges, the establishment of national schools and colleges in the various provinces. Within a short period of time, national schools and colleges were established throughout the country.

In 1921, Tagore found the Viswa-Bharati without any financial support from the government, the object of understanding the diverse cultures of the east and the west and building up a platform for world fellowship, peace and harmony.

The Government of India Act of 1935. This act divided the educational administration into two categories only. Federal or Central and state or provincial. They included the following subjects. Imperial library, Indian museums, Imperial war museum and Victoria memorial—all in Calcutta and any similar institution controlled or financed by the Federal government. In the state or provincial subjects, the act included all matters regarding education other than those included in the Federal or Central list.

Gandhiji wrote a series of an article in the *Harijan* about his ideas on educational reconstruction in India. He suggested universal compulsory education for all children under the age group 13-16 through the medium of mother tongue, which would be self-supporting leading to all-round development of pupils. First conference on National Education was held at Wardha on 22 and 2 October 1937 with Gandhi the Chair person. The conference adopted Gandhiji's views and came upon some resolutions.

1. That in the opinion of this conference free and compulsory education will be provided for seven years on a nation wide scale.
2. That medium of instruction is mother tongue.
3. That the process of education throughout this period should centre on some form of manual productive work.

Gandhi's scheme on basic education aroused considerable interest in the provinces of British India and the central board of education and decided to go through the Zakir Hussain Committee's report, on Gandhi's scheme. In 1938 it appointed B. G. Kher then prime minister of Bombay state who went through it and made the following observations: the scheme should be first introduced in rural areas while the medium of instruction should be mother tongue, there should be no external examinations.

By 1943 the Government of India asked all provincial governments to check out plans of post-war developments in India and as a part of the general scheme, Sir John Sergent, the then education advisor of Government of India, was also asked to prepare as memorandum post-war educational development in India. On the basis of Sargent plan in 1945, a separate education department was established at the centre and in 1946 University Grants Commission was established. By the time India got independence in 1947 there were many schools and colleges in India There were 1.72 lakhs primary schools in 1946-7, 17,258 institutions for secondary education, 17 universities, 297 arts and science colleges.

## WOMEN EDUCATION

The lives of Indian women began to change significantly in the late nineteenth century when the colonial government, critical of the treatment of both Hindu and Muslim women, found allies among Indian reformers. Keen to reform their own society, these men agreed that women should be educated and play some role in public life." Indeed, reformist stalwarts like Raja Rammohun Roy formed a coalition power with the British to abolish the social abuse, Sati. Again, Pundit Ishwarchandra Vidyasagar consolidated the way for the remarriage of socially forsaken widows through the Widow Remarriage Act no XV of 1856.

The air of reformation held high the urgency for casting the enlightenment of education on women. The sea or sagar of Vidya, i.e. Knowledge, the erudite and social-activist, Vidyasagar inundated the nation with the deluge of education. He opened 30 schools for girls in Bengal to promote the betterment of the feminine community. Similar to him was the Telegu feminism-enthusiast, Kandukuri Virasalingam Pantulu of Andhra Pradesh. In fact, the Bengal Renaissance of Consciousness, Intellectuality and Cultural pursuits, ushered in a phenomenal rebirth or Renaissance of the Consciousness of Women's well-being amidst the prevalent tyrannical society.

The British government eager to prove their liberal, ethical and pro-modernity attitude resorted to the "woman question". This is the fundamental feminist question concerned with the rights and progress of women. British denounced the existing insignificance of Indian womanhood, and tried to initiate some feminist welfare activities to show their socio-cultural advancement and Western nobility. They took help of the native indigenous modern minds like Raja Rammohun Roy, Ishwarchandra Vidyasagar, Keshubchandra Sen and other eminent Indians. What began as a more or less contest for moral supremacy among the oriental tradition and the Western civilisation, was turned into a beneficial move by the benevolent Indian priests of humanism, like Rammohun Roy.

The ancient Indian system of learning involved the accretion of the knowledge of the sacred Vedas and Puranic Sastras. The biased caste-system made Vidya available for the Brahmin or the priestly class, the Kshatriya or the warrior class and the Vaishya or the businessman's class. The Shudras or the non-Aryan class were the socially marginal section, barred from accessing education. Early Vedic society, allowed girls to acquire knowledge and grow into prominence. We can boast of women poets like Lopamudra and Gargi but in the later Vedic society, the orthodox Brahmins introduced blind superstitions, rituals, and rigid customs, which forbade Girls from learning. Only some women hailing from the upper class Vaisnavite families could study the precious Puranas. Islam wanted girls to be knowledgeable about the Quran and accounting tactics. However the austere confinement of girls within the four wall of the interiors of house-prison, minimised the possibilities.

We recognise a severe disappointment of the Western educational entrepreneurs with the oppressive social norms. In his Report on the Condition of Education in Bengal, the annoyed William Adam informed with condescension: "A superstitious feeling is alleged to exist in the majority of Hindu families, principally cherished by the women and not discouraged by the men, that a girl taught to read and write will soon after marriage become a widow." Adam was disgusted with the disgraceful fear, that loomed large over the Hindu and Muslim social arena. The overriding tension was that "knowledge of letters" would teach female to oppose the meaningless coercion. The terrible situation made Hindu women absolutely dependent on fathers in childhood, then on husbands in marital life, and ultimately on the sons during the old age. All her life, a woman observed religious practices wishing for the long and safe life of the male members of her family, as per as the custom. So, it was easy to impose the demeaning superstition that a woman's contact with learning was harmful. She would welcome the curse of her husband's death, and thereby would turn her into hell.

It was obvious that women were so intellectually and emotionally blind, under the cover of false definition of femininity tied on their vision, that one woman was prejudiced against the efforts of the other to attain freedom. On the contrary, true womanhood is only understood and adhered to, when illuminated by education. It is education which makes a female competent enough to handle the issues of her life, to be self-sufficient, to become an able daughter who can have economic independence and support her family, to stand by her husband in difficult times, and to rear up her children with the right education. Certainly, the strength of today's global woman lies in the truth that she is a multi-tasker, invested with such outstanding calibre.

Indian society thus deliberately practiced conspicuous gender-equality. There sprouted a lot of hostility from the conservative lawmakers of society against the new innovations, like advent of education for women. And hence it was really tough for the colonial government as well as the interested reformers, to give a concrete shape to their dreams.

The Calcutta School Society was built in 1816 to improve the status of female education. Radha Kanta Deb, the secretary of this society, was committed towards the cause and helped the coming up of the Calcutta Female Juvenile Society. In 1821, the School Society asked Miss Mary Anne Cooke, who came down to Calcutta to manage the task. The Church Missionary Society appointed Miss Cooke for the purpose. The resultant was the establishment of thirty schools for "respectable" Hindu girls. The schools expanded their work under the finances funded by the Hindu aristocracy. However, the endeavour, did not bear fruits, as the elite class intentionally distanced themselves from the institutions where the poor crowded tempted by gifts of clothing and other articles.

The Church Missionary Society tasted greater success in South India. The first boarding school for girls came up in Tirunelveli in 1821. By 1840 the Scottish Church Society constructed six schools with roll strength of 200 Hindu girls. When it was mid-century, the missionaries in Madras had included under its banner, 8,000 girls.

Initially the Indian social-correctors and the British supervisors went into a dispute over the course of operations. The Indian intelligentsia did not approve of the first girls' school, founded by the Missionaries. It was unfortunate that until the grants were afforded by the government and the Wood's Despatch, 1854, in the second half of the nineteenth century. The Wood's Despatch, launched in July 1854, drew the government 'to the importance of placing the means of acquiring useful and practical knowledge within reach of the great mass of the people'.

Women's education started spreading its wings. The outcome was the evolution of the nineteenth century generation of the "new woman". The latter half of the 19th century started seeing the rise of Indian womanhood to freedom and assertion. Women used to attend schools and colleges, though in limited numbers, receive education and assume the respectable professional roles of teachers and doctors. The new women voiced their feelings on contemporary affairs, penned their arguments in instruments of expression, such as the journals or magasines, and even participated in mainstream nationalist politics, to represent the Indian womanhood. Women established their presence in almost all the areas, which were previously the monopoly of men.

## REFERENCES

Bandyopadhyay, Sekhar (2004), *From Plassey to Partition: A History of Modern India*, New Delhi and London: Orient Longmans. Pp. xx, 548.

Bose, Sugata; Jalal, Ayesha (2003), *Modern South Asia: History, Culture, Political Economy*, London and New York: Routledge, 2nd edition. Pp. xiii, 304.

Judd, Dennis (2004), *The Lion and the Tiger: The Rise and Fall of the British Raj, 1600-1947*, Oxford and New York: Oxford University Press.

Kulke, Hermann; Rothermund, Dietmar (2004), *A History of India*, 4th edition. Routledge, Pp. xii, 448.

Markovits, Claude (ed) (2005), *A History of Modern India 1480-1950 (Anthem South Asian Studies)*, Anthem Press.

Metcalf, Barbara; Metcalf, Thomas R. (2006), *A Concise History of Modern India (Cambridge Concise Histories)*, Cambridge and New York: Cambridge University Press.

# 7

# Role of Christian Missionaries

India's first major contact with Christianity began when Vasco da Gama, from Portugal, landed with gunboat and priests in 1498. The Christian missionaries helped to spread education in India and other parts of the subcontinent. It was emperor Akbar who dreamt of creating a secular state in India, and accordingly he received the Christian missionaries with utmost honour in his court. A look at Akbar's religious policy indicates that, he formulated the concept of Suhl-i-Kul, and created an Ibadaat Khanna, where different religious groups met together and discussed various precepts. This term has been at times translated as 'hall of worship'; but it might be more accurately be rendered, 'debating hall'. The Christian missionaries even thought that Akbar might be converted to Christianity, but Akbar created 'Din-e-elahi' instead.

In the attempt to penetrate the obscurity which at many points rests on the story of the first coming of Christianity in India, Stephen Neil in his book, *The History of Christianity in India, The Beginnings to ad 1707*, examines the contemporary developments in politics, literature and religion which form the background of the later penetration of the Indian world by the Christian gospel. Don Francisco de Jassu Xavier, better known to the English-speaking world as Francis Xavier, was born on 7 April 1506 at the castle of Xavier. In 1525 he left his home to study at the University of Paris. Stephen Neil clearly understands the conditions under which Xavier went to India, who had been commissioned by the King of Portugal, who had a personal regard for Xavier. At all times he had access to the king, and was able to write to him on a number of occasions with considerable freedom. He had been appointed by the Pope as legate to all the countries of the east of the Cape of Good Hope.

The society was very new. The constitution of the society was not clearly drawn up until 1555, and Xavier had already been dead before these rules reached India. But organisation was not his greatest talent, and it is at least possible that the stability of Jesuit work in the East would have been greater, if he had spent more time at headquarters and less on his bold wanderings about the western world.

Voyages from Lisbon to India at that time were always terrible. That on which Xavier sailed was worse than most; it was not till 6 May 1542 that he finally landed at Goa. The voyage gave him and his companions every opportunity to manifest themselves as true servants of the Christ in their ceaseless care for the sick and the dying. According to Neil, it is easy both to sympathise with the first enthusiasm of Xavier and to admit that he had to learn in many respects his first impression had been mistaken. Even in the city of Goa itself, there were many Hindus and Muslims. And he was to learn that the level of Christian life among both the Portuguese and recent converts was very low.

The Christians came to India mainly as merchants, as officers working in the English East India Company. However, they first made their presence felt in different coastal areas of Gujarat, west and south India, and Bengal. They circumscribed Africa and entered Indian coasts as traders, and often they went into some trading relations with the Mughal emperors and received 'Farman's as trading rights. The 'Farman' of emperor Farrukh Shiyar has a distinct place in Indian history, as well as the history of Bengal. The English East India Company also received the Dewani in 1765, so that they may enjoy some special privileges in the Bengal 'subah'. However, the most important contribution of the English East India Company, was the Permanent Settlement of 1793, that has been much criticised by Dr. Ranajit Guha in his book, *A Rule of Property for Bengal: An essay on the Idea of Permanent Settlement.*

The Portuguese had been able to settle at Chittagong in the 16th century under the auspices of the King of Arakan. The Augustinians established themselves there in 1621, and baptised thousands who had been captured in the piratical raids in the Ganges delta area. Later in the

17th century Nagari became an important center, following the conversion of about 20,000 mainly low-caste Hindus by Antonio de Rozario, son of the raja of Bhushna (Jessore), who himself was converted to Christianity.

By the 1690s there were 13 Augustinian Churches in Bengal, but the majority of Christians received only rudimentary instruction and tended to migrate to new centers as they rose in importance – including the English settlement at Calcutta from 1690, where the Augustinians built a chapel. In 1696 the French appointed a Jesuit to serve the Christians at Chandannagar.

Apart from textbooks, the Baplist missionaries made other contributions to the development of the Bengali language. These included a dictionary and grammar; a translation of the *Bible*, subsequently improved upon by others; and the periodicals *Digdarshan* and *Samachar Darpan*, which represent the beginnings of the Bangla press. They also founded *The Friend of India*, ancestor of *The Statesman*.

Another area in which William Carey of Christian missionary made a lasting contribution was Botany and agriculture. He created a botanical garden at Serampore, obtained seeds from abroad and acclimatised new plants. He also took a leading part in the establishment (1820) of what became the Agri-Horticultural Society of India. The Serampore Baptist missionary also sought to influence public opinion and government against the cruel practices which existed in contemporary Hinduism, such as infanticide at Sagar island and 'sati', on which they undertook a survey which indicated its frequency.

Other Protestant missionary societies followed the Baptist Missionary Society to Bengal after 1813, notably the London Missionary Society, the Church Missionary Society and the Church of Scottland. The Christian Missionary Society, an Anglican Society, provided the initial support, from 1821, for Mary Anne Cooke, a pioneer in the establishment of girls' schools. Then in 1830 the Church of Scotland missionary Alexander Duff arrived in Kolkata and proceeded to set a new standard for Christian education. He founded a school, that achieved a rapid and lasting success, developing eventually into Scottish Church College. Duff stressed the vital role of the teacher in evoking the interest and understanding of the pupil. He also believed in developing the whole person and made provisions for exercises and games. His insistence on English as the medium of instruction left a more debatable legacy. His example was one factor in causing the government in 1835 to decide to devote its funds to western education through the medium of English.

So far as the thought-process is concerned, the Christians left a definite mark on the young Derosians in the nineteenth century, and they transformed the religious culture of the English-educated Bengali intelligentsia. It is a well-known story that Krishna Kumar Mitra greeted Godess Kali as, 'Good Morning madam'. Ramtanu Lahiri of Tatkalin Bangashamaj, written by Shibnath Shastri, gives the story of the forsaking of sacred thread by a 'Brahmin'. Therefore, the Christian influence on the Bengali youth had a definite landmark in the conservative Bengali society.

The missionaries' linguistic and educational work represents their main contribution to the development of the major work was modern Bengal. Other than the missionaries, the British administrators in the colonial rulers were successful bureaucrats, one of whose major work was the foundation of the Asiatic Society in Calcutta, by William Jones. When the Asiatic Society was established on 15 January 1784, its founder Sir William Jones (1786–94), began his work with a dream, that visualised a centre for Asian studies, including almost everything concerning man and nature within the geographical limits of the continent. Most of the mysteries of this vast land, like its old inscriptions in Brahmi, were still undeciphered.

Sir William Jones, an outstanding scholar from Oxford, arrived in Calcutta on 25 September 1738 as a Puisne Judge of the Old Supreme Court. He prepared a memorandum detailing his plan of study. A history of Asiatic Society points out that, while others were thinking in terms of individual study and research, Sir William Jones was the first man to think in terms of a permanent organisation for Oriental Studies and researches on a grand scalein this country. He took the initiative and in January 1784 sent out a circular letter to selected persons of the elite, with a view to establishing a society for this purpose.

## Missionary Involvement in Education

Prior to 1793 there was very little European or Protestant missionary involvement in education in India. Native education took place in *pathsalas*, Indian village schools. Their purpose was to produce pupils who were literate so that they could obtain jobs. Secondary education consisted of either private tutors or Persian schools. Standards were often poor. The early Catholic missionaries had had some involvement in education, but this had declined by the end of the eighteenth century. The first non-Catholic missionaries to go to India from Europe were the pietists Bartholomew Ziegenbalg and Henry Plutschau. Neil cites five principles that stood out in the strategy of these pioneers; the first was:

> Church and school are to go together. Christians must be able to read the Word of God, and therefore all Christian children must be educated.

It is these pioneers that influenced William Carey. Carey arrived in India in 1793 and by 1794 he had set up his first school. By 1795 he had outlined ambitious plans for a College. For William Carey schools were 'one of the most effectual means of spreading the light of the gospel through the world'.

In 1800 he moved to Serampore and became one of the Serampore trio. The trio's long-term goal was to reach India with native preachers. To facilitate this meant a threefold strategy: the translation of the Scriptures into native languages; preaching; and the establishment of schools and a college to train up Christian Indians to be missionaries. Joshua Marshman was the 'chief architect' of the trio's educational policy. The development of Baptist educational undertakings in India, according to Potts, is 'largely the story of the Marshmans'. Marshman had been influenced by Lancaster's monitorial system. In 1811 he was utilising the system in their 'Benevolent Institution', which had been set up in 1809 for 'the education of the neglected and poor Anglo-Indians'. By 1818 they had established 92 schools with about 10,000 pupils. However, by 1824, a lack of finance meant that the elementary schools had to be closed.

Serampore College was opened in 1818. The College's original aim was the training of Christian Indians to be missionaries to their own people. Thus the curriculum was broad, it included Western science and the study of Oriental languages. The College included non-Christians as well as Christians among its pupils. When it opened it had 18 non-Christians and 19 Christians. It is the only tangible aspect of the trio's educational work that remains.

The Scottish Presbyterian Alexander Duff landed in India on 27 May 1830 after twice enduring shipwrecks. His initial visits to other missionaries in the area, led him to the conclusion that contemporary missionary strategies were failing. He saw that direct attacks on Hinduism through street preaching were largely ineffective. A decade later he recalled his original strategy:

> we shall, with the blessing of God, devote our time and strength to the preparing of a mine, and the setting of a train which shall one day explode and tear up the whole from its lowest depths.

He used Christian education through the medium of English, rather than native languages, targeted at the high-caste Brahmins. His justification:

> ... in the very act of acquiring English, the mind, in grasping the import of new terms, is perpetually brought in contact with the new ideas, the new truths,... so that, by the time the language has been mastered, the student must be tenfold less the child of Pantheism, idolatry and superstition than before.

Duff's 'trickle down' policy aimed at educating the high class Brahmins, in the hope that the minority would eventually effect the majority.

Duff viewed Christian education through the medium of English as a 'large and effectual door opened for immediate exertion'. Immediate because other branches of missionary labour such as preaching 'before any profitable intercourse could be maintained with the mass of the people, much time must necessarily be expended in acquiring such an idiomatic form of speech, and in gaining such an intimate acquaintance with the habits of thought and long cherished opinions, as would enable you to address them with effect.'

Duff opened his school on 12 July 1830, with the help of the Hindu liberal reformer Ram Mohan Roy. He started with five and by the end of the week he had 200 boys wanting to attend. The support of Ram Mohun Roy, who was not a Christian, was invaluable in attracting many pupils whose parents were sceptical of Duff's missionary motives; he was able to remove the prejudice against reading the Bible he told them: 'Read and judge for yourself'.

Duff charged for textbooks and made the parents and guardians formally sign an agreement 'to secure punctual and regular attendance'. Thus he overcame two problems that contemporary missionary schools in Calcutta were facing. Taking the free textbooks and leaving, and hopping from one new school to another.

One of Duff's strengths was that he did not overstretch himself. He opened a second school at Taki in 1833 and by 1836 there were 130 pupils. A third school was opened at Fort Gloucester. He concentrated his efforts on education, and even then he concentrated his efforts on one main school. This school then became a model for other schools. Although Duff's ideas were never original, he was a better at implementing them than many others.

The educational debate in India was for a time centred around what language to use for education. However, there was not the polarisation of views which is often supposed. And this thirty years before the arrival of Duff also used the vernacular in his elementary schools. In March 1839 he said:

> The acquisition of [Bengali] as the medium of instructing the mass of the population is indispensable.... it is acknowledged that the Bengali language alone is available for imparting an elementary education to the people at large....

The Anglicists included Duff, Charles E. Trevelyan, Lord Macaulay and Lord William Bentinck. Their main arguments were:

*i)* The success of English medium schools such as the Hindu College and Duff's school.

*ii)* The inappropriateness of native languages to convey European learning, according to Duff, Bengali was insufficiently developed as a medium:

> This language does not afford any adequate means for communicating a knowledge of the higher departments of literature,

> science or theology. It is no more fit for such a purpose, than the whole range of Grecian literature and philosophy. And if it had the requisite vocabulary, it has not the necessary books.

*iii)* The Indians themselves wanted English education.

The Orientalists were concerned that if English was adopted as the language of education many students would remain ignorant of their national language which would help to denationalise them, and that they would stop their studies too soon to gain employment as English copyists. They were also dubious of the trickle down theory of education; as J. S. Mill stated: 'It is through the vernacular languages only that instruction can be diffused among the people'.

The adoption of the Anglicist policy was a mixed blessing. The use of English meant that there was a common language for the transmission of information and ideas, and it can be said to have contributed, ironically, to an increasing awareness of a national consciousness and integration, because it could unite the country. On the other hand it meant that the vernacular languages remained largely undeveloped.

The influence of Duff on the government's educational policy could also be seen in the 1854 grant-in-aid policy. Grants were made available to those who undertook to run schools and colleges. There was much debate as to whether the missions should accept 'government funding'. It was felt that in doing so the autonomy of the missions in running the schools could be usurped by the paymasters. However, the majority eventually did accept them.

**Higher Education**

The missions' first higher education establishments were Serampore and Bishop's College, Calcutta. The latter was opened in 1824 as an Anglican training college. After the deaths of the Serampore trio the success of Serampore college was mixed. In 1883 Alfred Baynes, who had been asked to report on training provision, recommended that the college should become a 'Native Training Institution'. The BMS concurred with this. In 1890 Baynes recommended that the BMS should abandon the College. However, E. B. Underhill took up the Serampore cause, and obtained a reprieve for the College. Underhill published: *Principles and Methods of Missionary Labour* which presented the case for the retention of the college.

At root this issue was about the aims of education: Baynes emphasised the need to train leaders, hence his emphasis on vernacular theology. Underhill saw it as a preparation for evangelism. Both could appeal to Carey's original vision.

George Howells, impressed by Underhill's work, did much to improve the standing of the college and it later became a Christian University. He resurrected the Danish charter of 1827 which enabled the college to confer degrees. It was re-affiliated with Calcutta University in 1911, as they had done in 1857. However:

> The nature of the dissatisfaction with the College had changed little since the 1880s: it was said that the College was impossibly expensive, wrongly located, and largely irrelevant to the life of the churches.

It never really fulfilled Carey's original vision.

Higher education was more successful in the South of India. This can be primarily attributed to the larger Christian population in that area compared with the North. This meant that they had a larger number of potential students and teachers. The other striking fact is the impact of the Scots.

John Wilson was a contemporary of Duff. He served the Scottish Missionary Society for 47 years. Wilson had a remarkable linguistic ability: he learnt Marathi, Gujarati, Hindustani, Persian and the ancient language of the Parsis scriptures. He also studied the Parsi and in 1843 published *The Parsi Religion*. He was responsible for establishing Bombay College of the General Assembly of the Church of Scotland in 1835. Like Duff he felt that Western methods required Western knowledge and came to see that English would establish itself as the 'second vernacular'.

Madras College's origins can be traced back to John Anderson, who opened a school in Madras in April 1837. Anderson had two Scottish colleagues, Robert Johnston and John Braidwood. One of Anderson's successors was William Miller. Miller did much to establish the high reputation of Madras College.

Other influential Scots were Dr Andrew Bell, who while at a school in Madras pioneered the monitorial system, and Hislop. Hislop was the first missionary to work in Nagpur, Central India, an area that was outside of British control and ruled by Raja Raghoji Bhonsle III. In May 1846 he set-up a school in Nagpur, he was convinced that he was 'preparing the way for a great moral revolution in a future age, and that no distant one'.

Despite coming relatively late to the scene the Scots were soon at the forefront of missionary education in India. At least two factors contributed to this: the example and influence of Duff and the Scottish educational system.

The Scottish educational system, which has always been separate from the English and Welsh, was also more advanced and recognised more fully with the role of religion and education. The Reformers had stressed the importance of education and it was in Scotland that their ambitions were best realised. All prospective teachers had to sign the Confession and Faith Formula of the Church of Scotland. Education certainly up to 1861 was under the control of the presbytery of the Kirk. Whether or not this explains the strong Scottish influence it is difficult to say. More obvious is the influence of Duff. He was directly responsible for the involvement of Wilson, Anderson and Hislop.

At the beginning of the twentieth century there were increasing misgivings about the role of higher education in the rapidly changing context of India. In July 1929 the International Missionary Conference set-up a commission chaired by A. D. Lindsay to 'review the field of service open to the Christian colleges in India'. They noted the Christian colleges' increasing dissatisfaction with the University system. The alliance between Christian colleges, Government and the Universities which at first was so promising had changed and now proved to be too great a price to pay. The colleges had lost control of the curriculum and were straight-jacketed by the examination system. They had also become too remote from the rest of the Church.

The Lindsay Commission considered four alternatives:

*i)* to withdraw from higher education;

*ii)* business as usual;

*iii)* to cut loose from the Government and establish a Christian University; and

*iv)* a rethinking of the task, and the creation of a Central Educational Committee.

To adopt either of the first two was regarded as renouncing the idea that Christian scholarship does not have a contribution to Indian life and thought. The third might result in a 'guild' for the benefit of Christians only. The only viable option was *(iv)*. The impact of the report was lessened by the onset of World War II which once again changed the conditions in India and thus rendered many of the report's conclusions out of date.

## Aims of Missionary Education

There has always been a strong relationship between Christianity and education. People need to be literate to read the Bible. 'Some degree of education must be added to enable believers to read the Word of God for themselves in their native tongue'. Though for many missionaries education was subservient to the preaching of the gospel. Typical is the view of C. B. Leupolt, a CMS missionary who arrived in Banares in 1832:

> Another means which we think of the greatest importance, next to preaching of the Gospel, are Schools, or the training up of the young in the fear and admonition of the Lord.

And of Revd J. Oswald Sykes:

> ... the Missionary college supplements the preaching of the Gospel in its simplest form; it does not and cannot supersede it.

Education was seen as a 'powerful instrument' to expose the 'fallacy of idolatry'. It was not primarily a philanthropic venture; it 'was not merely to educate'. It was to uproot Hinduism.

The early emphasis of Marshman and Duff was upon the training of indigenous leaders and as a preparation for evangelisation. William Miller of Madras similarly saw a twofold aim for education: 'a strengthening, training, developing agency' and a 'preparatory agency'. He saw the latter as being primary; the former, aimed at

Christians, being secondary and a by-product of its work for non-Christians.

The World Missionary Conference (WMC) of 1910 noted these four aims present in missionary education:

*(a)* Education may be conducted primarily with an evangelistic purpose, being viewed either as an attractive force to bring the youth under the influence of Christianity or as itself an evangelistic agency.

*(b)* Education may be primarily edificatory, in so far as the school has for its object the development of the Christian community through the enlightenment and training of its members.

*(c)* Education may be leavening, in so far as through it the life of the nation is gradually permeated with the principle of truth. ...

*(d)* The motive for missionary education may include the philanthropic desire to promote the general welfare of the people.

Most missionaries would have concurred with those aims, the argument was over the ordering of the priorities. Though the philanthropic aspect was not a primary motivation for missionaries in India. How successful were these aims?

**Evangelistic**

If this was solely the role and purpose of missionary schools then they can be regarded as a failure. The number of direct conversions through schools were small. Maurice Phillips in 1889 wrote:

> Changed conditions have taken away the value of Mission high schools and colleges as converting agencies.... That they are barren is well known.... I think I am within the truth when I say, that not more than one or two conversions have taken place in them during the last twenty-five years.

The lack of a large number of conversions was often countered by claiming that the conversions that did take place were 'generally of a far higher type, intellectually, morally, and spiritually, than the men of a lower grade'. Education was at least able to reach some of the higher castes.

## Edificatory

The aim of a self-governing indigenous church meant that education was required to train native leaders. This was one of the aims that inspired Serampore College, and CMS policy for schools was as training establishments for native leaders and teachers. This was also the view of the missionary strategist Rufus Anderson:

> Without education, it is not possible for mission churches to be in any proper sense self-government; nor, without will they be self-supported, and much less self-propagating. For the church-members there must be common schools.

Here again the schools were only partially successful. Smith notes:

> Baptist missionaries in nineteenth century Bengal rarely found that their educational schemes did much more for their converts' than provide them with the literacy for reading the Bible.

The colleges and schools were more successful at providing men 'who are influential in Government service, at the Bar, in trade, commerce, and in politics, but not leaders of the Church'. The problem was one of the differential in the rates of pay. Though:

> It is significant that in 1970 the four newly consecrated bishops of the Church of North India had all received their theological education at Serampore.

## Leavening

Education as a praeparito evangelica was exemplified by Duff and Miller. And to an extent it became the majority view in the nineteenth century. Miller felt that 'inadequate recognition' had been given to this third aim by the WMC report. As E. S. Summers noted 'these colleges are leavening society with Christian thought and developing Christian feeling, and so preparing for a great harvest of conversions in the future'. Of all the aims this has been the most successful aspect of missionary education, certainly up until the turn of the century.

Education was open to a wider stratum of society; it thus exposed many to Christian ethics and principles. Perhaps one of the greatest successes was education for females and the corresponding raising of the status of women. The WMC report summed up the importance of female education for the missionaries:

> The Christianisation of life in India depends in a very real sense on the Christianisation of the women of India. 'The stronghold of Hinduism is in the home, among the women. The men lord it over the women in material things, and the women lord it over the men in the spiritual or religious things.'

William Adam had maintained that the education of Indian girls was impracticable. Indians held the belief that literate girls would be widowed soon after marriage; they also thought that they would become corrupted by contact with male teachers. The missionaries had shown education of females was possible and worthwhile. The WMC 1910 report states:

> Missionaries led the way in the education of girls in India, and set an example which has widely influenced the aspirations of the India of today.

Hinduism had undergone a change under the onslaught of the first missionaries. It had become more syncretistic it had an 'undiscriminating comprehensiveness', it maintained that the 'truth embodied in all other religions is contained in Hinduism'. It is this syncretism that now needed to be exposed, 'and not the far easier one of exposing the absurdities of the Hinduism of 1830'.

## EXPENSE OF MISSIONARY EDUCATION

Missionary education was expensive for the missionary supporting bodies. This often led them to question the validity of it. Particularly at the turn of the century when it was recognised that Duff's 'trickle down' theory was not working.

A deputation on behalf of the LMS was sent in 1913 to reduce missionary expenditure. However, they concluded that only minor economies were possible in education and that:

> Christian education is no appendage but belongs to the central fibre of a mission's life.

In 1933 the LMS board of directors setup an enquiry on 'Education in Relation to Evangelism'. Two questions were asked of the 292 missionaries asking: (1) if they were satisfied that '... the educational work of the Society so far as you know it is making a contribution to the spreading abroad of the Gospel ...'; and (2) if '...through excessive devotion to education we are neglecting other methods...'?

A total of 167 replied, a response of 57%. Those who had strong opinions about education would certainly have responded thus slightly biasing the results. 155 answered in the affirmative to (1) and 149 negatively to (2). The committee reported:

> We have reached the conclusion that the Society's educational policy in the past has been in the main justified. We are convinced that the expenditure in men and money on its educational work is not out of balance with the expenditure on what may be described as its more directly evangelistic work. There can be no doubt that the former has greatly strengthened the latter, and that without it the Fundamental Principle and main objective of the Society to preach the glorious Gospel of the blessed God to the heathen could not have been efficiently realised.

Missionary education was thus once again vindicated; although not all would have agreed with the reports prioritisation of education. The missionaries always felt that education in India was a necessary expense - even if their supporters did not.

## Advantages and Disadvantages

Comparing the education offered by the missionaries with that in England, shows that the missionary education was not as backward as one might suppose. There are many parallels with what was happening at home. Lancaster and Bell's monitorial system, with all its weaknesses, was widely used at home and abroad. In India and England education was initially in the hands of individuals and voluntary organisations before the government increasingly took control. Much of the impetus for education was in the hands of Christians. In India it was the missionaries, at home it was largely evangelical reformers such as Robert Raikes and Hannah More who were motivated to provide education so that people could read the Bible.

Williams has identified three distinct groups whose ideologies have influenced education: the industrial trainers, the old humanists and the public educators. The industrial trainers emphasised the utilitarian aspect they are concerned with the training of a suitable workforce. The old humanists stressed the transmission of a cultural heritage comprising of 'pure' knowledge. The radical reforming tradition is associated with the public educators.

Most missionary early education, as that at home, was in the old humanist tradition. Knowledge was seen as a body of structured knowledge. Children were seen as 'fallen angels' and as Lockean tabula rasa. Learning was by rote.

It would be easy to criticise the conservative old humanist tradition. However, it merely reflected the contemporary educational climate.

The one exception to the old humanist framework was that missionary education, unlike British education, was not elitist or class/ caste structured; although it did assume Western superiority.

Missionary education in India played its part in attempting to break the caste hierarchy. The purpose of missionary education was not one of social control but of social transformation. Duff and the other Scots used education in the 'struggle against caste and to affirm that a liberal and Christian education could not recognise or tolerate caste observances within its walls'. With an emphasis on 'education for all' - without caste or sex distinction - the missionaries were more allied to a 'public educator' tradition. They were prepared to admit those of low caste and of no caste even at the expense of losing many of their pupils. For example, John Anderson of Madras accepted three Pariah boys who had deceitfully entered the school; this meant that he lost 100 out of 270 boys. Anderson commented: 'This caste dispute...will prepare us for greater trials in the case of a conversion'. The examples could be multiplied. The one notable exception was Robert Noble, a CMS missionary in Andhra Pradesh, who refused to admit the 'outcastes' to his school.

The missionaries also offered a much wider curriculum than that at home. Science played an important role; this was because: The sacred books of the Hindus are 'inextricably committed to a collision with the truths of astronomy, chemistry, medicine, geography, and all the facts of modern science.' Instruction in the elements of physical science and or geography not only upsets the old notions on these subjects, but so far forth uproots the Hindu religious system.

'The incorporation of literature and science with the religion of India, true information on such themes lays a train which, when it explodes, must shatter the whole hideous fabric of Hinduism into atoms...'Science was an integral part of the missionary curriculum! It has been asserted that believers have nothing to do with Natural Science. Strange assertion! For what is natural science? If true, what is it but the record and interpretation of God's visible handiworks? And has the Great Creator deemed it worthy of his great name to produce aught, which is unworthy of any of his creatures, far less of any of his own adopted children, to know and understand? Believers, nothing to do with God's works! Why, we would exhort you to assume at once the highest ground, and demonstrate, in all your teachings, that believers alone are properly enabled, and alone are justly entitled to scan and enjoy these works.

## Problems Faced by Missionaries

The missionary educational enterprise was conducted on a very small budget and often in buildings that were inadequate. Consequently, many of the missionaries overstretched themselves. It is noticeable that those who had most educational influence were those, such as Duff, Robert May, J. D. Pearson Marshman and Miller, who devoted themselves predominantly to education.

Another associated problem was the lack of suitable teachers. Many schools had to rely upon non-Christian teachers. They had to do so for pragmatic reasons, without them 'Missionary education would be seriously restricted in its extent'. It was regarded as: a temporary expediency to meet a temporary necessity; no Educational Mission work can be regarded as satisfactory until it has been provided by full Christian staff.

This begs the question: Can a non-Christian deliver Christian education? The lack of Christian teachers was particularly prevalent in the North of India. Pupil attendance, especially of the agricultural population, was 'partial and irregular'. Many would attend for a few months only. The large number of religious festivals also interrupted schooling.

As the Lindsay Commission pointed out in the mid-nineteenth century there was a coincidence between government and missionary aims. The Western education which provided the best *praeparito evangelica* corresponded with the education the natives required for Government service. It was this that made the education so sought after by the natives; it was the passport to employment.

## References

Peers, Douglas M. (2006), *India under Colonial Rule 1700-1885*, Harlow and London: Pearson Longmans.

Robb, Peter (2004), *A History of India (Palgrave Essential Histories)*, Houndmills, Hampshire: Palgrave Macmillan.

Sarkar, Sumit (1983), *Modern India: 1885-1947*, Delhi: Macmillan India Ltd. Pp. xiv, 486.

Spear, Percival (1990), *A History of India, Volume 2*, New Delhi and London: Penguin Books.

Stein, Burton (2001), *A History of India*, New Delhi and Oxford: Oxford University Press.

Wolpert, Stanley (2003), *A New History of India*, Oxford and New York: Oxford University Press.

# 8

# Educational Developments in Post-independence Period

Education has always been accorded an honoured place in the Indian society. The great leaders of Indian freedom movement realised the fundamental role of education and throughout the national struggle for independence stressed its unique significance for national development. The development of education in India during the post-independence period has been guided by the national goals and aspirations as embodied in the Indian Constitution. Education being a powerful instrument of social, economic and political change, its broad principles and objectives are related to the long-term national goals, the programe of national development on which the country is engaged and the complex shortterm problems it is called upon to solve.

After India became independent the first governmental act to organise the educational system in the light of independence was the setting up of the University Education Commission, headed by Prof. S. Radhakrishnan to suggest improvements and extensions that may be desirable to suit the requirements of the country. The Commission covered the problems of admission, length and contact of courses, the relation between teaching and research, examination, student discipline, teachers' service conditions etc.

The First Five Year Plan visualised education as the vehicle for the successful achievement of planned development. The commencement of Ist Plan coincided with the appointment of Secondary Education Commission headed by A. Mudaliar. Mention may be made here, that the government constituted special commissions for university education and secondary education to go into the details of problems and hurdles and suggest ways and means to remove them but till nowno special Commission has been constituted to enquire the problems of elementary education which is the most important stage for the educational development in terms of both quality and quantity.

## Legacy of National Education

India became independent in 1947. This aroused great hopes about many things and especially about a radical reconstruction of Indian education. The Indian national leadership had always expressed great faith in the use of education for modernisation and development and had shown deep and continuing interest in a radical transformation of the colonial education system built-up by British Administrators. As early as 1906, the Indian National Congress adopted a Resolution on national education which said that the time had arrived "for the people all over the country earnestly to take up the question of national education for both boys and girls, and organise a system of education, literary, scientific and technical, suited to the requirements of the country, on national lines under national control and directed towards the realisation of national destiny." The movement thus started was kept up throughout the pre-independence period and made three major contributions to educational development.

(1) The first was to clarify the concept of national education and to indicate the broad lines on which educational reform should be attempted. Among the various ideas put forward from this point of view, the following deserve mention:

— Relating education to India's great cultural traditions of the past and to her present needs and future aspirations so that Indian education comes into its own, ceases to be a servile imitation of Britain, and aims at creating, not a lesser England, but a greater India;

— Liquidation of mass illiteracy which Mahatma Gandhi described as the sin and shame of India and the development of a programe of adult education which, according to him, must include political education;

- The provision of seven years of basic education to every child (age-group 7-4) whose content, according to Mahatma Gandhi, would be broadly equal to that of matriculation minus English plus craft;
- The reduction of the over-importance attached to English; the development of Hindi as the link language for the country and as the official language of the Union; and the use of regional languages as media of instruction at all stages;
- Work with the hands and social or national service to be an integral part of all education with a view to creating a work-based culture and to minimising the large traditional gap between the intelligentia and the people;
- Emphasis on the teaching of science and technology with a view to the creation of a scientific temper, modernisation and economic growth;
- Emphasis on vocational, technical and professional education; and
- Cultivation of patriotism and moral and social values

(2) The second contribution was to conduct a few institutions of national education at all levels (e.g. Gujarat Vidyapeeth, Tilak Maharashtra Vidyapeeth, Kashi Vidyapeeth and Jamia Millia Islamia) where these ideas of national education were tried out to gain practical experience. It was hoped that these institutions would provide the necessary leadership when, after the attainment of independence, the Government of India would initiate a large scale programe of transforming the existing system into a national system of education.

(3) The third major contribution was that it created a small but powerful band of social workers who had dedicated themselves to education and who would provide the core of the large group of educational thinkers, planners and administrators which the country would eventually need.

As is to be expected, the attainment of freedom created the hope that all this fundamental work of four decades of struggle would now be systematised, expanded and improved so that a national system of education suited to the traditions, life, needs and aspirations of the country would be created or so. Pandit Jawaharlal Nehru showed his awareness of these hopes and the urgency of working for their realisation when he addressed the first Conference of Education Ministers held in Free India and said:

> "Whenever conferences were called to form a plan for education in India, the tendency, as a rule, was to maintain the existing system with slight modifications. This must not happen now. Great changes have taken place in the country and the educational system must also be in keeping with them. The entire basis of education must be revolutionised."

For various reasons, this promised revolution in education never materialised. It is not that no educational reform was attempted; in fact, many good and useful things were done. But, in the final analysis, they did not amount to the revolution which Pandit Jawaharlal Nehru had promised. On the other hand, they only meant the one thing which Pandit Nehru wanted to avoid, viz., a linear expansion of the earlier educational system with minor modifications.

## Political Decisions

Two main reasons can be given for this failure to transform the educational system on radical lines. The first lies outside the educational system. As education is a sub-system of the society, it cannot be revolutionised unless a social revolution takes place first or unless at least a simultaneous effort is made to bring about a complementary revolution in society and in education. The basic problem before the national leadership in 1947, therefore, was not whether a revolution in education should or should not be carried out, but whether a revolution in the political, economic and social life of the country should or should not be carried out, and if so, the form that it should take. Here the decisions taken were based on the concept of stability with change and in an evolutionary and reformist perspective. For instance;

— In politics, Mahatma Gandhi had given a radical advice that the Indian National Congress should be disbanded and that all Congress workers should remain out of Government office and work among the people to organise and strengthen the under-privileged groups to fight for their rights. But this advice was ignored. The Congress decided to remain in power and also to continue the parliamentary model of government which the British had already introduced in the country with some modifications.

— In economic life also, no decision was taken to alter radically the existing highly skewed property structure or the arbitrary and in egalitarian wage pattern. On the other hand, it was decided to leave the property structure as it is (in fact, the constitution made property a fundamental right) with some minor modifications (e.g. a weak attempt at land reforms or a largely ineffective system of wealth tax and death duties). Similarly, the erstwhile wage pattern also continued and, if any thing, became even more arbitrary and unsuited to the economy of the country. The capitalist Organisation of the economy was also continued with the addition of a large public sector.

— Mahatma Gandhi had talked of a new model of development in his book, *Hind Swaraj*, and had said that India should strive to bring about this kind of development as soon as it becomes free. This advice was also ignored and it was decided to adopt the model of development evolved in the Western nations based on science and technology, industrialisation, modernisation of agriculture, and provision of modern basic services.

— In social life, too, the decisions taken were similar. No radical changes were decided upon and emphasis was laid on two programes which were the least controversial, though not minor, viz, improving the status of women through the reform of the Hindu Code and continuance of the programes designed earlier for the Scheduled Castes and Scheduled Tribes.

— In administration, it was decided to continue and consolidate the existing system rather than attempt a radical reform and to make only some minor changes such as the creation of the IAS to replace the ICS.

— In the field of languages also, all major decisions were postponed. English was to continue as Official Language of the Union till 1965 after Hindi was that to take over. English was also continued as medium of instruction at the university stage sine die.

In 1947, it was argued that the partition of the country had created a delicate situation in which the very survival of the country was at stake and that it was therefore essential to postpone all such issues to a later date and to concentrate all efforts on consolidation of freedom and nation- building. Of course, one could have accepted this argument in 1947. But these decisions were not re-opened for consideration even when the immediate problems of partition had been tackled and the conditions within the country had considerably stabilised. The truth is that these decisions were taken because they were in the interest of the ruling groups that came to power in 1947. The British had created a westernised class in India mainly to work as interpreters and intermediaries between them and the people. This class developed a national pride, had a brief honeymoon with the masses to secure their support in the struggle against imperialism and won independence. It was now fully in saddle and was determined to continue to rule with such attention to the welfare of the poor and underprivileged social groups which can be legitimately expected from enlightened rulers. With this basic decision, all revolutionary perspectives in society were ruled out and the country had to settle down to a reformist, evolutionary and gradual process of modernisation and development.

## EDUCATIONAL DECISIONS

If the policy adopted in political, economic and social life was thus evolutionary and reformist, and was trying to provide for stability and change in a proper balance, it would obviously be wrong to expect radical reforms in education. In fact, the best that could have been hoped for was a gradual, reformist and evolutionary Perspective in education also. It is, therefore, an idle exercise to blame the leadership of the day for not bringing about a revolution in education of which they talked so eloquently; and by now, we have all been fully conditioned to distinguish between the words and deeds of the political leadership.

The first reason for this failure is adhocism. To make the best use of the attainment of freedom even in an evolutionary and reformist perspective, we needed a good comprehensive plan of educational development which would help us to make the optimum use of all available opportunities and resources. Unfortunately, no such plan was available in 1947 although, as a matter of fact, the need for such a plan was foreseen as early as in 1937 when the National Planning Committee was appointed by the Indian National Congress under the Chairmanship of Pandit Jawaharlal Nehru. This Committee constituted two sub-committees one for general education under the Chairmanship of Dr. S. Radhakrishnan and the other for technical education and developmental research under the Chairmanship of Dr. M. N. Saha. Unfortunately, the work of the National Planning Committee and its sub-committees could not progress satisfactorily. Pandit Nehru was arrested in 1940 and, under the stress of political events, neither he nor the other members of the Committee could devote adequate attention to its work till 1947 when it was practically wound up. The sub-committee on General Education prepared a broad and a tentative report which was considered by the National Planning Committee; but the report of the sub-committee on Technical Education and Developmental Research could not even be considered.

The General Secretary of the Committee, however, brought out a volume on Education in 1948 containing a broad outline of whatever work had been done in planning educational development. But the document made practically no contribution to the formulation of national educational policies in the post-independence period. On the other hand, the official attempts to produce a long-term educational plan were more successful.

The Central Advisory Board of Education prepared, under the leadership of Sir John Sargent, the then Educational Adviser to the Government of India, a Post- War Plan of Educational Development in India (1944). It proposed to create, in a period of forty years, a national system of education for the country. This included the liquidation of illiteracy in a period of 25 years, the introduction of universal elementary education on the basic pattern for all children in the age-group 6-14, provision of secondary education for one child out of every five that completed elementary education and higher education for one young person out of every 15 that completed the secondary school, and a certain provision of vocational, technical and professional connection.

The only common element between this plan and the national ideas in the subject was the concept of basic education for all children in the age-group 6-14. On the other hand, its proposal of highly selective secondary and university education would never have been acceptable to the national leadership. What is even worse, the plan avoided all the issues such as language which had occupied public attention. Apart from this, the people would never have accepted the long period of 40 years for implementing the plan nor its basic approach of creating, in the India of 1984, an educational system that would be similar to that of England in 1939. This plan also was, therefore, side-tracked so that educational development in Free India had to be planned and implemented *ab initio*.

Obviously, this absence of a comprehensive and sufficiently detailed national plan to act upon was neither a difficult nor an insoluble problem. The Government of India could have appointed an Education Commission to advise it on the creation of a national system of education, as it ultimately did in 1964. But this decision was not taken and the development of education in the. country was attempted, for nearly two decades (1947- 65), without a clear cut national policy and a comprehensive long-term plan of educational development to guide all concerned. This adhocisim is certainly one of the important factors responsible for the inadequate and unsatisfactory progress of education in the country between 1947 and 1965.

The second reason for our failure to get even the best results possible in the reformist and evolutionary perspective was, that, in the absence of a clear-cut national policy on education, the, basic educational decisions tended to be taken under current social and political pressures. When this happens, educational policies tend to reproduce the status quo, to be geared to the demands of the groups in power rather, than to the needs of the deprived sections, and to emphasise stability rather than change. This is precisely what happened during this period.

The third reason was a weakening of the earlier commitment, to the creation of a national system of education, although this was not openly admitted for reasons of expediency. In the major educational decisions taken during this period, it was not possible to ignore the earlier attempts to create a national system of education and the significant commitments made to the people therein. While therefore the policy decisions taken did include some such concessions to earlier commitments, they were never given adequate emphasis in implementation. At best, they remained pious hopes.

The fourth reason for the failure was that the expectations entertained from the institutions of national education were belied. As was pointed out earlier, these institutions were expected to provide a leadership in the creation of a national system of education. While the patriotism and sacrifice of the people working in them was greatly, respected, especially as they had refused to lake grants-in-aid from the British Governments, their academic standing was never high and it is open to question whether one is or is not justified in expecting a stimulating leadership from them. They might perhaps have served a more useful purpose had they continued to work outside the formal system and developed their strengths further. But once they accepted grants from government and became a part of the formal system, they lost their earlier position of vantage and became a microscopic group of second-rate and ineffective institutions in a huge system.

The fifth and the final reason for failure was our inability to create a sufficiently critical mass of active and competent workers who could help to plan the transformation, improvement and expansion of the existing formal system of education and to gear it properly to the life, needs and aspirations of the people. The handful of workers trained in the national freedom struggle or in the earlier attempts to create a national system of education were no doubt available. But they could not obviously fill the bill and urgent and fairly large scale efforts should have been made to select competent individuals from different disciplines, and especially from the social sciences, and to train them through an interdisciplinary study of education. Simultaneously, efforts should have been made to develop a large-scale and high quality programe of interdisciplinary research on education partly to train such workers and partly to deepen an understanding of the education-society relationship. But this was not done and the universities and training colleges continued to equate education, as in the past, with the training of secondary school teachers or teacher-educators. There has consequently been an acute shortage of competent personnel to deal comprehensively and competently with the complex problems of educational reform; and this has made no small contribution to our failure to optimise the opportunities available to reconstruct the educational system.

With this explanation about the background, let us see what decisions about educational development were actually taken during this period, mostly in the process of educational planning which became an integral part of the technique of planned development adopted in 1950. In this context, the first three five-year plans are relevant; and a careful study of the proposals of educational development included in them shows that the major educational decisions of the period (1947-65) may be briefly summarised as shown below:

(1) One of the earliest issues that called for a decision was the role of the Government of India in education; this issue had to be decided by 1950 when the Constitution was adopted. In keeping with the general policy of not making a radical break with the past it was decided that education should continue to be essentially a State responsibility, as it actually was between 1921 and 1947, with some special responsibilities assigned to the Government of India. Both the radical issues viz. (1) inclusion of education in the concurrent list or (2) decentralisation of authority to the local level were carefully avoided.

(2) The next issue related to the priority to be accorded to education *vis-a-vis* other sections of development. If the statements of the national leadership were any guide, education ought to have received the highest priority as an instrument of human resource development. But the actual decisions taken were different; education came way down in the list of priorities after industry, agriculture, power, transport and family planning. If investment policies are an idea of priority, education must certainly be regarded to have been a low priority item in the first three five year plans because the total allocation to education was comparatively low and the axe of retrenchment always fell heavily on education. This may not have been a wrong decision. But it does indicate the serious limitations within which educational development had to be attempted.

(3) The priority between different categories of programes within education was decided that the highest priority should be given to expansion of educational facilities which were most in demand. Programes of qualitative improvement would follow to the extent possible. Programes of transformation of the educational system were, by and large, shelved especially in view of the reformist and evolutionary approach adopted.

(4) In the case of *inter-se* priorities between different sections of education, personal and social factors came into play. Pandit Jawaharlal Nehru had a great faith in universities and in higher education and believed that higher education must be developed on a priority basis in the larger interest of the country. His all too well-known a statement on the subject may still bear a quotation: "A university stands for humanism, for tolerance, for reason, for the adventure of ideas and for the search of truth. It stands for the onward march of the human race towards even higher objectives. If the universities discharge their duties adequately, then it is well with the nation and the people." This philosophical and cultural view was also supported by economists who argued that universities were the grandmother machine which produced teachers for themselves, the colleges and the secondary schools and that secondary education was the mother machine that produced the teachers for elementary schools. It was therefore necessary to develop university and secondary education even in the interests of the development of elementary education itself. Moreover, there was a strong demand for the development of secondary and higher education from all sections of society and especially from the upper middle classes who were its principal beneficiaries. What is equally important, Pandit Jawaharlal Nehru never showed any deep commitment either to elementary or to adult education. Consequently, it was decided to accord the highest priority to university and secondary education. A University Education Commission was, therefore, first appointed (1948-49) and was followed by a Secondary Education Commission (1952). Universal, elementary and adult education ought to have really been accorded the highest priority because, along with adult franchise which had been adopted, they would have helped to transfer real power to the people.

(5) It was decided to promote engineering and technical education on the basis of the highest priority because it was necessary for the newly adopted policies of industrialisation and import substitution. The same decision was taken about medical education which was necessary for the extension of modern health services and about agricultural education which was equally essential for increased food production. It should not also

be forgotten that the ruling classes were the principal beneficiaries of these programes.

(6) Science education and research were emphasised with a view to creating an indigenous capability in modern science and technology so essential for agricultural and industrial growth and for modernisation.

(7) The usual pedagogic issues were considerably emphasised with a view to giving, as it were, a face lift to the educational system we inherited at independence. Improvement in the remuneration of teachers, expansion and improvement of teacher education, improvement of curricula, teaching and learning materials, and methods of teaching, examination reform, improvement of supervision, provision of extension services, and such other programes received a good deal of attention. It was of course recognised that, these bad a significance of their own, they cannot be equated with 'radical' educational reforms that were needed.

It was these ad hoc policies of expediency and class interests, setup in an evolutionary and reformist perspective, that dominated the scene between 1947 and 1965. They could not be expected create a national system of education; and they did not. They merely led to a linear expansion of the educational system which had been evolved during the British period under a similar perspective with some minor modifications to suit the new situation created after independence.

## EDUCATIONAL DEVELOPMENTS

Let us now briefly review the educational developments of this period which can best be described as one of adhocism. The discussion may well begin with universal elementary education—a programe in which objectives and targets were definitely and clearly laid down; quantitatively free and compulsory education had to be provided to all children in the age-group 6-14 within a period of ten years (1950-60); and qualitatively, it had been decided to convert all schools to the basic pattern.

### Universal Elementary Education

The programe of universal elementary education is implemented in three distinct but concurrent stages; (1) universal provision of schools, (2) universal enrolment of children' in the concerned age-group; and (3) universal retention of the children 'enrolled until they complete the elementary course or reach the age of 14 years. Each of these stages needs to be discussed separately.

***Universal provision of schools***

The objective of the programe was to establish an elementary school within easy walking distance from the home of every child. In practical terms, the target was to establish a primary school teaching classes I-V within a distance of one mile and a middle school teaching classes VI-VIll within a distance of about two miles. To assist in the implementation of the programe, educational surveys were organised, for all parts of the country, in 1957 and in 1965. The targets are also comparatively easy to fulfil if the necessary funds are available and the Education Departments are efficiently organised to plan the location of primary and middle schools. But even by 1965-66 we had not been able to reach the target of providing a primary school within easy walking distance from the home of every child and we were far behind in making a similar provision for middle schools.

***Universal enrolment***

The mere establishment of a school in a given locality does not imply that it is availed of by all the children therein. In fact, the school is generally availed of by the children from the educated and well-to do families only in the first instance. It takes a long time, and needs many special measures, for the school to reach the poor and deprived sections of the community. This is why enrolment must be considered as a separate issue and we must try to carol all children in the age-group 6-11 in primary schools (classes I-V) and all children in the age-groups 11-14 in middle schools (classes VI-VIII).

The actual enrolment of children in classes I-V was 19.160 millions in 1950-51, and that in classes VI-VIII was 3.120 millions. it is, therefore, obvious that if we wanted to provide, universal elementary education by 1960-61, we should have enrolled 37.057 million additional children in classes I-V and 26.709 million additional children in classes VI-VIII. If, on the other hand, we had to reach this objective by

(1) It is necessary to point out that a fairly large proportion of the children actually enrolled in classes I-VIII is outside the usual age-limits (6-14); they are either below six or above fourteen. To (his extent, the number of non-enrolled children is larger than that indicated by the above, data. This factor is, however. ignored in this discussion because it is possible to argue It we can refuse admission to all such children below and above the prescribe ages and admit an equivalent number of children from within the age group 6-14.

(2) The above data gives no indication of adequacy of buildings equipment or teachers. In some cases we may have surplus teachers and partially filled classroom. In others, the situation may be just the opposite. These factors do not however cancel each other out. On the whole, the inadequacies are very large and are increasing with time.

In other words, our achievement was only about 30 percent of the expected if we had to reach the goal by 1960-61 and only about 50 percent of the expected if we had to reach the goal by 1965-66.

***Universal retention***

This failure was due, not so much to the non-enrolment of children in Class I but mainly to the failure to retain children in schools till they complete elementary education. More than sixty percent of the children enrolled left the schools prematurely, mainly because they had to work for or within the family. Since the economic conditions of the poor did not improve materially and since no special educational measures were also adopted to meet the needs of economically handicapped children, the wastage rates in elementary education continued to be high throughout the period under review; and these constituted the most difficult hurdle in the progress of universal elementary education.

## Basic Education

On the qualitative side, the target-in elementary education was equally clear; to convert every elementary school to the basic pattern. This was also a very major commitment of the pre-independence period. But for various reasons, it was not possible to realise this target also which, it must be admitted, was even more difficult than the quantitative targets.

The scheme of basic education as originally conceived by Mahatma Gandhi visualised an education of seven years (age-group 7-14) to be provided to every child. The scheme made socially useful productive work the medium of education so that children learnt as they worked and the work became, not a mere subject in the curriculum, but the very medium round which every other item in the curriculum was closely integrated.

Gandhiji also did not want any English to be taught at this stage and was therefore of the view that it should be possible to provide, during this period of seven years, a level of education equal to that of the matriculation, minus English plus craft. He also felt that the articles produced by the children should be able to make a profit which should meet all the expenses of the school including the salaries of the teachers; and he was sure that this would be possible if the State took over the entire produce of the school. In fact, he attached the highest significance to this self-sufficiency aspect of the scheme which he described as its acid test. It was only this financial independence, said Gandhiji, that would give education its autonomy and free it from State control or interference.

The scheme of basic education as it came to be finally accepted by the country was a very different cup of tea and compromised with many fundamental features of the programe. For instance, the scheme as visualised by Mahatma Gandhi was a non-formal system unconnected with the State. The scheme as accepted by the country was equivalent only to the introduction of socially useful productive work as an integral part of the formal school system supported by the State.

Gandhiji's scheme was to be financially self- sufficient. But in the scheme as adopted, this aspect of self- sufficiency was totally abandoned. All that was expected was that the children would either produce some articles for their own use or the receipts from the sales of articles produced by the children would be able to meet the cost of raw-materials and leave some profit which could be given to the students or used for their welfare.

While enough time was allotted to the learning of the craft, it was no longer necessary to correlate all items of the curriculum with it; correlation was desirable, wherever possible, but not mandatory. Each basic school, however, was expected to function as a community and engage itself in some meaningful programes of service to the local people. It was also decided that English could be taught in basic schools. In fact, a luminary of basic education observed that the principles of basic education were best practised in some of the English-medium special schools.

In implementation, the programe ran into many difficulties. The experiment did not become popular in urban areas or with the upper and middle classes who did not want their children to work with their hands and who felt that the standards of education would suffer because of the heavy time reserved for craft work. It did not have much relevance to the life of the children from poor families because it was tried out only in full-time schools which these working children could not and did not attend.

The attitudes of the State Government showed great variations; some evinced a firm commitment and many were almost totally indifferent. The top leadership paid lip sympathy to the programe but preferred to send their own children to English-medium schools so that basic education came to be defined as the best education for other people's children. The Government of Uttar Pradesh converted all its primary schools to the basic pattern overnight. But in other States where space, equipment and materials, trained teachers, etc. were considered essential, the progress of the experiment was very slow.

On the one hand, the State Governments; could not or did not provide the needed trends. On the other, it was, found that, while good work was done in schools where competent and; dedicated teachers were available, any large scale expansion of the programe did not work satisfactorily. It was also found that basic education would not help the programe of universalisation of elementary education. For one thing, the basic schools proved to be costlier than the non-basic schools and not cheaper as was originally expected. Besides, the basic schools were not popular with the parents and did not show that they had any greater power, to attract and hold children than the non-basic schools. As time passed, there was also an increasing opposition to the idea that elementary schools should be divided into two types-the basic and the non-basic and a demand was put forward that all elementary schools should provide a uniform education to all children-an education which would be- the best the country can afford. Two main lines of thought thus emerged in the light of the experience of nearly 30 years of the working of the scheme (1937-66); (1) the first was that a reformulation of the scheme itself was called for; and (2) secondly whatever the formulation of the scheme, its implementation had to be much better.

There were three principal gains on the pedagogic side. The salaries of the elementary school teachers were considerably improved; more extensive arrangements were made for the training of teachers whose quality was also improved and there was a general improvement in curricula and text-books. But even these were counterbalanced by two main losses.

In 1950-51, the expenditure on teachers' salaries formed 80.3 percent of the total direct expenditure on primary schools and the corresponding figure for middle school was 75.8 percent. In 1965-66, however, these proportions rose to 90.7 percent for primary schools and 89.2 percent for middle schools, thus showing that other qualitative inputs in elementary education was considerably declining. Secondly, because of the comparative neglect of elementary education, its share in total educational expenditure declined from 38.7 percent in 1950-51 to 34.4 percent in, 1965-66.

Throughout the period under review, the political leadership at the national, State and district levels laid great emphasis on the largest possible expansion of elementary education that could be secured within the resources available which, of course is quite different from a commitment to the goal of providing universal education. Incidentally, it may be pointed out that the policy of the British administrators was very similar; they also wanted the largest possible expansion of elementary education but ruled out the provision of compulsory education on administrative and financial grounds of decisive weight.

The way in which we are developing the programe of elementary education since 1950 implies that we strive for the-largest possible expansion of elementary education and only 'endeavour' to provide free and compulsory education at some distant and undefined date. Comments on the 'distinction' between these two policies, if any, are needless. But it is necessary to understand why even this emphasis on the largest possible expansion of elementary education was so consistently laid by the leadership at all levels.

The political leadership welcomed the expansion of elementary education for two main reasons; (1) it boosted their political capital if they opened schools in schools areas; and (2) the expansion of elementary education Save them the largest single avenue to provide employment to secondary school teachers. Let us not forget that between 1950-51 and 1965-66, the enrolment in elementary education increased roughly at 25.84 lakhs a year and that this implied the appointment of about 100,000 teachers a year. With the large expansion that was taking place, the system of secondary education would have collapsed if these employment opportunities were not available.

## ADULT EDUCATION

The cause of adult education or of liquidating mass illiteracy fared far worse and, as stated earlier, the problem was shelved altogether. The main argument was that, in the long run, the provision of universal elementary education was the surest way to liquidate illiteracy and that, if we were to achieve the goal of universal education for children in the age-group 6-14 within ten years, it would be unnecessary to mount up a massive programe of adult education in addition.

The programe of adult education, which was designated as social education to emphasise the fundamental and social aspects of the programe, was kept going in a small way, mainly in relation to the community development programe in which the integral role of social education was recognised. The following data speak for themselves:

*Table 1. Adult (Social Education 1950-51 to 1965-66)*

| *Year* | *No. of institutions* | *Enrolment* | *Expenditure (Rs.)* |
|---|---|---|---|
| 1950-51 | 48,556 | 1,256,011 | 7,218,126 |
| 1955-56 | 46,091 | 1,282,710 | 7,196,186 |
| 1960-61 | 62,815 | 1,494,794 | 7,927,765 |
| 1965-66 | 2,17,912 | 1,637,541 | 5,548,466 |

It appears that, throughout this period, we ran about 50,000 centres a year and made about 500,000 adults literate at a small cost, the total investment in the programe being less than one percent of the total educational expenditure.

It was explained earlier why, in spite of all the arguments to the contrary, the programes of universal elementary and adult education were so largely neglected during the period under review. It may also be mentioned that there was no strong social and political demand from any quarter to reverse these policies. The people themselves were poor and unorganised and the type of education we provided id, the elementary schools or literacy classes could not be seen by them as a felt need or as an acquisition of value. The opposition parties, not excluding the leftist ones, could hardly make an impact and unfortunately they were also not keen to make these programes basic issues in political struggles. The only group that fought for these ideas consistently were a few committed academics and social workers and a group of Gandhians. For a time, they bad some pull and did succeed in getting some support for these programes. But even before the period under 'review was over, their 'pull' had begun to wane very materially.

## Qualitative Improvement of Education

This expansion of educational facilities at all levels, i.e. the expansion of elementary education as well as in secondary and higher education, formed the most important programe of educational development between 1947 and 1965. It naturally absorbed the bulk of the finances available and left very limited resources for developing the programes of qualitative improvement. Inspite of all that could be done therefore through pedagogic inputs like improving teacher quality and competence, curricula, teaching and learning materials, methods of teaching and evaluation, or supervision, the standards did continue to deteriorate in the vast majority of educational institutions. Since no one was prepared to curtail expansion or to provide the additional resources needed, some method to solve the qualitative crisis had to be found.

Ultimately the method evolved was in keeping with the divided character of the Indian society, viz., to maintain a dual educational system in which a small core of high quality institutions is surrounded by a large penumbra of poor quality institutions. But even this was not a new invention; it was merely a continuation and further expansion of a system which had already come to exist during the British period.

At the school stage, the British model of public schools had already been introduced with various objectives, e.g. the training of the children of the Princes and the aristocracy, the early training of would be officers for the army, provision of special residential schools for the children of the modernised rich, and so on. There were also a few English-medium schools originally meant for Anglo- Indians and others who used or desired the use of English as mother- tongue. But the total number of such institutions was, on the whole, comparatively small before 1947. In the post-independence period, the ruling super elite decided that this core sector of good schools which used English a medium of instruction would be utilised by them for the education of their own children for the prestige and other obvious advantages it conferred. The ruling elite also followed suit and began to use good quality private schools for their children. The number of schools of both these categories increased by leaps and bounds in the post-independence period. Very soon, therefore, we created a dual system at the school stage ill which:

— a small group of fee-charging, good, high quality schools, mostly run by private agencies or minorities served the needs of the rich and the well-to-do, while

— the vast majority of publicly supported schools which were generally of poor quality were utilised by the common man for the education of his children. This solved the 'quality' problem for the ruling elite. Since resources were limited and it was not possible to improve all schools, it was decided that the best policy would be to maintain a core sector of good quality schools while the rest of the schools meant for the common man were allowed to be of poor quality. There was also no objection if even this low quality of the vast majority of schools continued to deteriorate further so long as the small core sector of good schools maintained standards and continued to raise them. This dualism therefore assured the ruling elite that their children would receive good education; and what does it then matter if other people's children got only bad education ?

The same dual policy was continued at the university stage also. Here a number of prestigious, good quality and useful institutions were created. They included the Indian Institutes of Technology (IITS), the and several institutions of general education. They had selective admissions Indian Institutes of Managements (IIMS), engineering and medical colleges, because the applicants for admissions far outnumbered the places available; and even when their methods of selections were academically fair, their admissions went largely to students who had received their school education through the English medium, to the children of the rich and well-to-do, of professionals and of senior employees in the private and the public sector, or, in short, to the top echelons of the ruling elite for the simple reason that there is a close correlation between the 'talent' of children as we now measure it and their socio-economic backgrounds. This core sector of good quality institutions was surrounded by a large number of colleges and other institutions of higher education whose standards were poor and which admitted the sons and daughters of the common people. The elite were thus assured of a good education for their children. The other people's children were assured of an open-door access to higher education; but this only meant that they would be admitted in some institution, however poor, and in some course however useless.

There was of course a continuous demand, especially from the left parties, that this dualism should go and that all public and special schools should be abolished. But they were too well entrenched to be affected. Government, however, responded by saying that they would also make good education, of the type given in public schools, available to talented children of the poor as well. It was from this point of view that the Government of India started its scheme of scholarships in public and special schools. The establishment of the Sainik schools had a similar objective. Some State Governments established public schools admissions to which were made on merits. Of course, the total number of students so admitted to education in public or special schools formed only a very small part of the total enrolment of these institutions.

Of course this does not mean that no attempts were made to improve quality in the general run of educational institutions meant for the common man. In fact, these attempts were almost continuous and included such measures as improving the remuneration of teachers and their general and professional education, improvement of text- books and teaching and learning materials, adoption of better, methods of teaching and evaluation, improvement of supervision, provision of buildings and equipment, and so on. But they did not produce any tangible effect for two main reasons. The first was that the resources available for all such programes were very limited; and secondly, the good results obtained through them were often negatived by deterioration in discipline and quality of administration by weakening of the motivation of students due mainly to the growing distance between a degree and a job, by the large influx of students from deprived backgrounds for whom no proper facilities of individual guidance were provided and by the far too frequent disturbances due to strikes, etc., especially at the university stage.

## VOCATIONALISATION OF SECONDARY EDUCATION

We have so far dealt with the attempts made to secure expansion of secondary and higher education, the problems it created in the maintenance of standards, and the manner in which these were broadly tackled. We shall now proceed to discuss some other major developments in secondary and higher education.

The vocationalisation of secondary education with a view to diverting a proportion of the enrolment at the secondary stage in terminal vocational courses of a practical character and reducing pressures on university admission was an accepted policy of long standing and was being pursued since 1882. But it made little progress in the pre-independence period partly because Government did not follow it with sufficient zest and partly because industry had not developed and other opportunities of employment to young persons who had received second level education were also very few. In the post- independence period, the attempts to vocationalise secondary education continued to be made more vigorously and the students were also attracted to these courses in increasing numbers because the economic and other policies of government were also more favourable to employment after the second level of education.

A major attempt for reform in Secondary education made during this period was the adoption of the concept of multipurpose secondary schools recommended by the Secondary Education Commission (1952) and accepted by the Government of India. Under this proposal, secondary education was divided into a number of streams to suit the varying interests, aptitudes and capacities of adolescents, e.g. humanities sciences, commerce, agriculture, engineering and technical, home science (for girls) and fine arts.

Every secondary school was expected to provide for as many of these streams as possible and at least for three of them. The vocational streams included in this pattern did not prepare the students for any vocation as such but merely formed an alternative channel of broad general education which would still enable them to enter the universities. Liberal central grants were made available for conversion of secondary schools to the multipurpose pattern. The progress made by 1965-66 is shown below.

| | *Multi-purpose* | *Total* |
|---|---|---|
| No. of High Schools | 508 | 20,766 |
| No. of Higher Secondary Schools | 1,878 | 6,711 |
| Enrolment in High Schools | 387,622 | 74,94,538 |
| Enrolment in Higher Secondary Schools | 1,204,400 | 38,23,526 |

These 'reforms' were extremely unfortunate. For one thing, they introduced specialisation at a very early stage; Students who had completed class VIII and were about 13-14 years' old were asked to choose their careers and had to be classified as belonging to pre-engineering and pre-medical sections. Dr. D. S. Kothari described this system to be as bad as that of child marriage. Secondly, the various streams provided in the scheme were taken up only by very few students and the wisdom of providing such costly courses for a few students in secondary schools of general education was seriously challenged. Even within a few years of the introduction of this scheme, therefore, the public opinion was ranged strongly against it. This is one of the ill- advised and costly changes that were tried out in the post-independence period and that bad ultimately to be given up. it is' 'reforms' of this type that have got a bad name for educational planning in the country.

## Obsession with Educational Pattern

Another and a more serious weakness of educational planning in the Post-independence period is what may be described as the obsession with the pattern of the school and college classes. It is difficult to explain or even to understand why a pattern of school and college classes which is the least important aspect of a national system of education should have been looked upon as its most important aspect and why it should have obsessed all concerned and dominated all educational planning in the post-independence period to such an extent that we are not still free from it. But there is no doubt that this obsession has done a great harm to education by diverting public attention and resources to wrong priorities.

In the pre-independence period, there was no such obsession with the pattern of school and college classes. The British administration allowed full freedom to the Provinces to organise their school education (i.e. education before the matriculation which was held by the universities as entrance for higher education) in any way they liked. But in so far as higher or post-matriculation education was concerned, an attempt was made to evolve a broadly uniform pattern of education, especially after the Indian Universities Act of 1904. But even this receded in the background between 1921 and 1947 when education was transferred to Indian and Provincial control. Inspite of this freedom and almost total absence of a desire to create a uniform pattern of school and college classes, a few common features did emerge though the inevitable process of co-ordination and mutual learning that is inescapable in a federal system. By 1944, the situation in the country was as follows:

— the duration of school education leading to the matriculation examination varied from province to province and could be from 10 to 12 years;

— the matriculation examination could be held by universities or by Secondary Education Boards;

— the intermediate course was of two years and the intermediate examination could also be held by universities or by special Boards;

— the undergraduate course was of two years and led to the first degree; but the duration of the courses for the first degree in professional fields like agriculture, engineering or medicine could be different and longer;

— the courses for the first degree were of two types-pass or honours-with the same duration. But there were exceptions as in Madras where the honours degree was taken after three years and where the second degree was awarded automatically after sometime or as in Allahabad where a honours degree was taken one year after the pass course and was followed by a one year course for the M.A. degree; and

— the duration of the courses for the second degree was also two years.

The Calcutta University Commission (1917-19) suggested the first major reform in this area, viz., the adoption of the pattern of 10+2+3 for the Calcutta University. This idea was also projected at the All-India level. The Calcutta University did not act upon it at all. But the Government of U.P. separated the intermediate classes from higher education proper and created a Board of High School and Intermediate Examination to look after all pre-university education. Some other Boards on the same pattern were also set up in North India. The three-year degree course did not materialise except in stray classes like the Madras Honours Course. There were also no sustained or 'intensive attempts on an All-India basis to adopt the pattern of 10+2+3, especially because the Government of India was almost divorced' from education from 1921 to 1947 as a result of the introduction of the system of dyarchy and transfer of education to Indian control under the Government of India Act, 1919.

The idea of another national pattern for the country as a whole was put forward by the Sargent Report or the Post-War Plan of Educational Development in India (1944) which differed from the Calcutta University Education Commission and recommended the pattern of 8+3+3,known commonly as the Higher Secondary pattern. As was pointed out earlier this Report was never accepted as a national policy. But somehow the idea of a national pattern of school and college classes was caught up and this pattern was actually introduced in Delhi Union Territory between 1945 and 1947. This raised controversies which were still alive when the University Education Commission (1948-49) was appointed. Naturally, the subject received considerable attention in its deliberations and as it agreed with the Calcutta University Commission, it recommended the pattern of 10+2+3. With these opposite recommendations, the controversy over the subject became sharper and the whole matter was referred to the Secondary Education Commission (1952). This Commission was broadly in favour of the Higher Secondary pattern but could not quite make up its mind whether the higher secondary course should be of eleven years as recommended by the Sargent Report or of twelve years as recommended by the Calcutta University Commission (1917-19) Basically, the controversy was between those areas where the duration of the total course leading to the first degree was fifteen years and those where it was fourteen years. Each of these areas thought that their system was better, was not prepared to change it, and was trying its best to make its own system the national pattern. It was this difficult situation that had to, be tackled between 1952 and 1954.

The solution that was ultimately devised was as follows:

— the highest emphasis was placed on the organisation of the three year degree course and this reform was mostly carried out between 1954 and 1965, with the help of liberal UGC grants, in all areas except U.P. and the City of Bombay;

— the higher secondary pattern of 8+3+3 was recommended with a transitional stage of 8+2+1+3 wherein the pre- university year could be in colleges.

This was a solution determined by considerations of finance and expediency and obviously, it was a definite concession to the view of the fourteen-year States. Naturally, they adopted the proposals with greater enthusiasm. But there were important exceptions also. As stated above, U.P. did not adopt the three-year course and refused to break up the 10+2 pattern. The Delhi Union territory and M.P. went the whole way and adopted the 8+3+3 pattern university. But the other States continued to have both the alternatives of 11 +3 or 10+1+3 as long-term measures. In the fifteen-year States, on the other hand, these reforms were given a cold shoulder. Kerala adopted the pattern of 10+2+3. None of these States reduced the duration to 14 years. They also did riot adopt the higher secondary pattern and when they. did, they usually adopted the pattern of 11+1+3. The net result therefore was more negative than positive. On the one hand, no national pattern of school and college classes ever emerged. On the other, the existing confusion of patterns became worse confounded; the controversy between 14 and 15 years States remained unresolved and the national obsession with the pattern as the single, most needed and radical reform of education was continued and strengthened further. Like the old man in the tale of Sindbad the Sailor, the pattern was riding the neck of educational reform in India almost continuously since 1944; it refused to alight and could not also be shaken off.

## Educational Opportunity

Equalisation of educational opportunity was one of the distinct objectives pursued during this period, although the results obtained were far from satisfactory because of inadequate resources and absence of a well-formulated policy and sustained implementation.

(1) From the quantitative point of view, a good deal of progress was made through the expansion of elementary, secondary and higher education, although the goal of universal elementary education was not reached. These issues have been discussed already.

(2) The education of girls received considerable attention and the progress made can be seen from the following data.

(3) The education of scheduled castes and scheduled tribes also received considerable attention.

It will be seen that the Scheduled Castes had a long way to go to reach equality with others which would be indicated by the proportion of their enrolment to total enrolment at each stage or in each sector being equal to their proportion in the total population. The scheduled tribes were, on the whole, even more backward. By and large, the wastage rates among the scheduled castes were higher than those for the total population, and those among the scheduled tribes, still higher. The overall performance of the Scheduled Caste and Tribe students was also less satisfactory.

(4) While the scheduled caste and scheduled tribe students received fairly liberal assistance at all stages, a notable scheme for their education was that of the post-matriculation scholarships. This began with a few hundred awards a little before independence. But by 1965-66, it had reached fairly large proportions. During this year, as many as 106, 250 students from the scheduled castes and 19,000 students from the scheduled tribe received post-matriculation scholarships. This financial support, coupled with

reservations in services, led to a considerable acceleration of their vertical mobility.

(5) There were great variations of educational development between the different States of India due to physical, historical, social, economic and cultural factors. States like Kerala, Tamil Nadu or Maharashtra were fairly advanced while those like M. P., Orissa and Rajasthan lagged behind. Even within the same State, some districts were fairly advanced while others were backward. Attempts to reduce these regional imbalances were made to some extent. But as the creation of new facilities was usually guided by market demands, the progress achieved, even by 1965-66, was not very satisfactory.

(6) Pre-primary education made some headway, mainly in urban areas where the rich and the well-to-do developed a demand for it and were prepared to pay for it as well. In the rural areas, some attempts were made by Government to establish pre-schools under the, social welfare programes. Even in 1965-66, the pre-schools known to the Education Department were only 3, 235 with an enrolment of 215, 005 pupils. In addition, there may have been about an equal number of pre-schools which were either unrecognised or provided by other agencies.

(7) The education of physically and mentally handicapped children received greater attention between 1947 and 1965. The Government of India developed a Central Institute for the training of the blind at Dehradun. In 1965-66, there were 12 schools for the mentally handicapped children with an enrolment of 771 and an expenditure of Rs. 424,635; and 179 institutions for the physically handicapped with an enrolment of 11,266 and an expenditure of Rs. 4, 856, 459. The field was largely in the hands of private enterprise which received State support.

The large expansion achieved during this period led to a considerable expansion of educational facilities in rural areas. Taking the system as a whole, 89 percent of the institutions and 71 percent of the enrolment were in rural areas in 1965-66. Naturally, the bulk of these was at the elementary stage. But 66 p.c. of the High Schools, 45 percent of the Intermediate colleges and 15 p.c. of the colleges of general education were also located in rural areas.

## Language Policy

In 1835, English was adopted as the language of the courts and of administration and it was made the medium of instruction in education. It also gradually became the language of the national trade commerce and industry. The main concepts of national education developed in the freedom struggle was that this domination of English would go and that English, along with other instructional. languages, would be nurtured mainly as a library language and as our window of the world, that Hindi would be the official language of the Union and the link language at the national level, and that regional languages should be adopted as media of instruction at all stages of education. Of all these ideas, only two were partly implemented by 1947; (1) the study of Hindi, on an optional basis, was greatly popularised in non-Hindi areas on grounds of patriotism; and (2) the regional languages were mostly adopted as media of instruction at the secondary stage under the long control of education by Indian Ministers between 1921 and 1947.

It was expected that the national leadership would complete the above revolution in language policy in a period of 15 years which, under the Constitution, was the time allowed to English to continue as the official language of the Union. But like the directive on universal elementary education, these policies also went away. The fascination for English, not only continued, but increased tremendously, especially as the ruling elite and super elite began to send their children to English-medium schools right from the pre-school stage. The hold of English over Central and State administration weakened, if at all, only to a marginal extent; and it continued its sway in courts, in public service examinations, and in national trade, industry and commerce. There were no planned attempt's made to introduce the regional languages as media of instruction at the university stage; and if some advance was made in this field, it was merely due to the pressures from below when students inadequately equipped with a working knowledge of English began to enter the universities in large numbers.

On the other hand, the efforts to boost up Hindi to the status of the official language of the Union or to make it a national link language did not succeed as anticipated. The official patronage extended to Hindi by the Government of India as well as by State Governments ill the Hindi region promoted the development of the language very greatly, although many were unhappy at the highly Sanskritised form it was assuming in contradiction to the spirit of Art. 351 of the Constitution which expected it to represent the composite culture of India. The three language formula was adopted for popularisation of Hindi in non-Hindi areas and given financial support for implementation. But it was not a great success in many areas and far less successful than Hindi films.

The hold of English over Central administration continued almost undiminished though Hindi was making some headway as an additional official language of the Union. It soon became obvious that Hindi will not become the official language of the union in 1965 and hence provision was made by law for the further, and almost indefinite continuance of English as an additional official language of the Union.

The Hindi lobby was very unhappy at these developments and extremely keen to put Hindi in the same privileged position as English as soon as possible. But its impatience and especially its Angreji Hatao compaigns did more harm than good and actually sparked off serious riots in Tamil Nadu in 1965. On the whole the cause of Hindi suffered both losses and gains during the period under review. While Hindi was actually spreading in non-Hindi areas slowly, imperceptibly and steadily, the public attitudes to the Hindi problem were hardening. For instance, the non- Hindi people claimed; (1) Hindi should hot be imposed on any State; (2) English and Hindi should continue as joint official languages of the Union for a long long period; (3) While Hindi may someday become the sole official language of the Union, English will still have its academic uses as India's window on the world and will always continue as an international link and as a supplementary national link as well; (4) If non-Hindi people are required to study Hindi, the Hindi people should study an Indian language (other than Sanskrit) preferably from the South; (5) There is no essential link between the study of Hindi and patriotism nor can the role of English in promoting the national struggle for freedom be ignored; (6) No special privileges should be available to those whose mother tongue is Hindi and those whose mother-tongues are other regional languages should not be made second class citizens; and (7) Hindi cannot be the medium of instruction in the universities, except in the Hindi zone.

The State Governments were, in their own way, making efforts to develop regional languages and adopting them for administrative purposes. These bad greater success especially as a new leadership from the people and rural areas which was inadequately equipped with English was emerging at the State level. But as stated earlier, the regional languages did not make much headway as media of instruction in the universities where academics infatuated with the use of English as a medium of instruction still held sway.

The Government of India appointed a Sanskrit Commission (1956-57) under the Chairmanship of Dr. Suniti Kumar Chatterjee; and in the light of its recommendations, tried to promote the study of sanskrit and especially the traditional methods of learning through various schemes like grant of scholarships and establishment of Sanskrit institutions or support to them, But the efforts did not succeed, mainly because of lack of job opportunities to the students so educated. There was also a consistent demand to include Sanskrit in the three-language formula but it could not be agreed to.

Urdu and Sindhi claimed for special assistance, and although something was done to help them, there was a general feeling that more could and should have been done. It will thus be seen that there was hardly any attempt to pursue a clear-cut language policy in a vigorous and sustained fashion. What operated in effect was a policy of drift and gradualism, due mainly to the inability to reconcile the basic commitments of the pre-independence period, with the realities of the post-independence situation.

## Role of Central Educational Bodies

The long divorce of the Government of India from education between 1921 and 1947 had reduced the significance of education At the national level. Between 1947 and 1965, education was regarded as a very important national concern, although a State subject, so that the role of the Ministry of Education become very significant. This development was also facilitated by the introduction of planning and by the fairly large financial resources that were made available to the Ministry for utilisation under the Central and Centrally sponsored sectors both of which expanded very greatly.

The Central Advisory Board of Education was also very active throughout the period under review and played a dynamic and important role in shaping educational policies. The expansion of the Central Sector and of central institutions dealing with education and culture at the national level was one of the major events of this period. Among these may be mentioned the University Grants Commission, some new Central Universities and institutions deemed to be universities or of national importance, the National Council of Educational Research and Training including Regional Colleges, of Education; the Academies, certain libraries and museums, and so on. While this activity was broadly welcomed, a frequent charge made was that the available resources were spread too thinly over a very wide area and that many of these Central institutions did not function satisfactorily.

In view of the increasing important role of the Centre in providing leadership, the problem of getting the services of competent educationists for the Ministry of Education assumed great significance. No attempt was however made to create an Indian Education Service. A kind of Central Educational Service was developed in the Ministry of Education. But the proposal was neither well planned nor well- implemented so that a basically good concept came into disrepute. At any rate, it became clear by 1965-66, that the Government of India had not adequately developed either the institutions or the personnel which would have enabled it to play its expected role of providing stimulating leadership.

## References

*India 2009: A Reference Annual (53rd edition)*, New Delhi: Additional Director General (ADG), Publications Division, Ministry of Information and Broadcasting, Government of India.

Setty, E.D. and Ross, E.L. (1987), "A Case Study in Applied Education in Rural India", *Community Development Journal*, 22 (2): 120–129, Oxford University Press.

Sripati, V. and Thiruvengadam, A.K. (2004), "India: Constitutional Amendment Making The Right to Education a Fundamental Right", *International Journal of Constitutional Law*, 2 (1): 148–158, Oxford University Press.

Vrat, Prem (2006), "Indian Institutes of Technology", *Encyclopedia of India (vol. 2)* edited by Stanley Wolpert, 229-231, Thomson Gale.

# 9

# History of Universities

A university is an institution of higher education and research, which grants academic degrees in a variety of subjects. A university provides both undergraduate education and postgraduate education. The word university is derived from the Latin universitas *magistrorum et scholarium*, roughly meaning "community of teachers and scholars".

## Early History of Universities

The original Latin word "universitas", first used in a time of renewed interest in Classical Greek and Roman tradition, tried to reflect this feature of the Academy of Plato. The original Latin word referred to places of learning in Europe, where the use of Latin was prevalent. The Latin term "academia" is sometimes extended to a number of educational institutions of non-Western antiquity, including China, India and Persia:

- Academies such as Taixue and Guozijian, succeeded by the medieval Academies of Classical Learning
- Taxila in Gandhara, Ancient India, now Pakistan and the Buddhist Nalanda University and Vikramasila University in Bihar, India.
- The Sassanid Academy of Gundishapur was founded in the 5th AD century in Persia/Iran.

The University of Constantinople, founded as an institution of higher learning in 425 and reorganised as a corporation of students in 849 by the regent Bardas of emperor Michael III, is considered by some to be the earliest institution of higher learning with some of the characteristics we associate today with a university. If a university is defined as "an institution of higher learning" then it is preceded by several others, including the Academy that it was founded to compete with and eventually replaced. If the original meaning of the word is considered "a corporation of students" then this could be the first example of such an institution.

If the definition of a university is assumed to mean an institution of higher education and research which issues academic degrees at all levels like in the modern sense of the word, then the medieval Madrasahs known as Jami'ah founded in the 9th century would be the first examples of such an institution. The University of Al Karaouine in Fez, Morocco is thus recognised by the Guinness Book of World Records as the oldest degree-granting university in the world with its founding in 859 by Fatima al-Fihri.

Also in the 9th century, Bimaristan medical schools were founded in the medieval Islamic world, where medical degrees and diplomas were issued to students of Islamic medicine who were qualified to be a practicing Doctor of Medicine. Al-Azhar University, founded in Cairo, Egypt in 975, was a Jami'ah university which offered a variety of postgraduate degrees (Ijazah), and had individual faculties for a theological seminary, Islamic law and jurisprudence, Arabic grammar, Islamic astronomy, early Islamic philosophy, and logic in Islamic philosophy.

## Ancient Indian Universities

Several sites on the Indian subcontinent were centres of learning in ancient times. Many were Buddhist monasteries.

— Nalanda, about 55 miles south-east of present-day Patna in Bihar

— Odantapuri, in Bihar (circa 550-1040 CE)

— Somapura, now in Bangladesh (from the Gupta period to the Muslim conquest)

— Jagaddala, in Bengal (from the Pala period to the Muslim conquest)

— Nagarjunakonda, in Andhra Pradesh

- Vikramasila, in Bihar (circa 800-1040 CE)
- Taxila (7th century BCE-460 CE) in Modern day Pakistan
- Sharada Peeth, in modern day Pakistan Administered Kashmir
- Valabhi, in Gujarat (from the Maitrak period to the Arab raids)
- Varanasi in Uttar Pradesh (8th century to modern times)
- Kanchipuram, in Tamil Nadu
- Manyakheta, in Karnataka
- Puspagiri, in Orissa
- Ratnagiri, in Orissa

## Nalanda

Nalanda is the name of an ancient university in Bihar, India. The site of Nalanda is located in the Indian state of Bihar, about 55 miles south-east of Patna, and was a Buddhist center of learning from 427 to 1197 CE. It has been called "one of the first great universities in recorded history." Some parts of Nalanda university were constructed by the great Mauryan Emperor Ashoka the Great e.g. the Sariputta Stupa. The Gupta dynasty also patronised some monasteries. According to historians, Nalanda flourished between 427 CE and 1197 CE, mainly on account of patronage of Buddhist Emperors like Harshavardhana and Pala kings of Pala dynasty. The ruins of Nalanda University occupy an area of 14 hectares. This university was completely built with Red Bricks. At its peak, Nalanda University attracted scholars and students from many parts of the globe e.g. China, Greece etc.

The name Nalanda is a Sanskrit word that means giver of knowledge. The Chinese pilgrim-monk Xuanzang gives several explanations of the name Nalanda. One is that it was named after the Naga who lived in a tank in the middle of the mango grove. Another—the one he accepted—is that Shakyamuni Buddha once had his capital here and gave "alms without intermission", hence the name.

### *Nalanda during the Period of Buddha (500 BCE)*

The Buddha is mentioned as having several times stayed at Nalanda. When he visited Nalanda he would usually reside in Pavarika's mango grove, and while there he had discussions with Upali-Gahapati and

Dighatapassi, with Kevatta, and also several conversations with Asibandhakaputta.

The Buddha visited Nalanda during his last tour through Magadha, and it was there that Sariputta uttered his "lion's roar," affirming his faith in the Buddha, shortly before his death. The road from Rajagaha to Nalanda passed through Ambalatthika, and from Nalanda it went on to Pataligama. Between Rajagaha and Nalanda was situated the Bahuputta cetiya. According to the Kevatta Sutta, in the Buddha's time Nalanda was already an influential and prosperous town, thickly populated, though it was not until later that it became the centre of learning for which it afterwards became famous. There is a record in the Samyutta Nikaya, of the town having been the victim of a severe famine during the Buddha's time. Sariputta, the right hand disciple of the Buddha, was born and died in Nalanda.

Nalanda was the residence of Sonnadinna. Mahavira is several times mentioned as staying at Nalanda, which was evidently a centre of activity of the Jains. Mahavira is believed to have attained Moksha at Pavapuri, which is located in Nalanda. King Asoka (250 BC) is said to have built a stupa in the memory of Sariputta. According to Tibetan sources, Nagarjuna taught there.

### *Education System*

Nalanda was one of the world's first residential universities, i.e., it had dormitories for students. It is also one of the most famous universities. In its heyday it accommodated over 10,000 students and 2,000 teachers. The university was considered an architectural masterpiece, and was marked by a lofty wall and one gate. Nalanda had eight separate compounds and ten temples, along with many other meditation halls and classrooms. On the grounds were lakes and parks. The library was located in a nine storied building where meticulous copies of texts were produced. The subjects taught at Nalanda University covered every field of learning, and it attracted pupils and scholars from Korea, Japan, China, Tibet, Indonesia, Persia and Turkey. The Tang Dynasty Chinese pilgrim Xuanzang left detailed accounts of the university in the 7th century.

### *Libraries*

The library of Nalanda, known as Dharma Gunj (Mountain of Truth) or

Dharmagañja (Treasury of Truth), was the most renowned repository of Buddhist knowledge in the world at that time. Its collection was said to comprise hundreds of thousands of volumes, so extensive that it burned for months when set aflame by Muslim invaders. The library had three main buildings as high as nine stories tall, *Ratnasagara* (Sea of Jewels), *Ratnodadhi* (Ocean of Jewels), and *Ratnarañjaka* (Delighter of Jewels).

### *Curriculum*

In an unattributed article of the Dharma Fellowship, the curriculum of Nalanda University at the time of Mañjusrimitra contained:

> ...virtually the entire range of world knowledge then available. Courses were drawn from every field of learning, Buddhist and Hindu, sacred and secular, foreign and native. Students studied science, astronomy, medicine, and logic as diligently as they applied themselves to metaphysics, philosophy, Samkhya, Yoga-shastra, the Veda, and the scriptures of Buddhism. They studied foreign philosophy likewise.

### *Influence on Buddhism*

A vast amount of what came to comprise Tibetan Buddhism, both its sutric Mahayana traditions and its (Vajrayana) traditions, stems from the late Nalanda teachers and traditions. The scholar Dharmakirti, one of the Buddhist founders of Indian philosophical logic, as well as and one of the primary theorists of Buddhist atomism, taught at Nalanda.

Other forms of Buddhism, like the Mahayana followed in Vietnam, China, Korea and Japan, found their genesis within the walls of the ancient university. Theravada Buddhism was also taught at Nalanda University, but its teachings were not developed further there, as Nalanda was not a strong centre of Theravada.

### *Decline and End*

In 1193, the Nalanda University was sacked by Bakhtiyar Khalji, a Turk; this event is seen by scholars as a late milestone in the decline of Buddhism in India. Khilji is said to have asked if there was a copy of the Koran at Nalanda before he sacked it. The Persian historian Minhaz, in his chronicle the Tabaquat-I-Nasiri, reported that thousands of monks were burned alive and thousands beheaded as Khilji tried his best to uproot Buddhism and plant Islam by the sword, and the burning of the library continued for several months and "smoke from the burning manuscripts hung for days like a dark pall over the low hills.".

The last throne-holder of Nalanda, Shakyashribhadra, fled to Tibet in 1204 CE at the invitation of the Tibetan translator Tropu Lotsawa. In Tibet he started an ordination lineage of the Mulasarvastivadin lineage to complement the two existing ones. When the Tibetan translator Chag Lotsawa visited the site in 1235, he found it damaged and looted, with a 90-year-old teacher, Rahula Shribhadra, instructing a class of about 70 students. Ahir considers the destruction of the temples, monasteries, centres of learning at Nalanda and northern India to be responsible for the demise of ancient Indian scientific thought in mathematics, astronomy, alchemy, and anatomy.

**Taxila**

Taxila is an important archaeological site in the Punjab province of Pakistan. It dates back to the Ancient Indian period and contains the ruins of the Gandharan city of Takshashila an important Vedic/Hindu and Buddhist centre of learning from the 6th century BCE to the 5th century CE. In 1980, Taxila was declared a UNESCO World Heritage Site with multiple locations. Taxila is situated about 32 km to the north-west of Islamabad Capital Territory-and Rawalpindi in Punjab-just off the Grand Trunk Road. Its elevation above the sea-level is 549 metres.

The ruins of Taxila consist of many different parts of the city buildings and buddhistic stupas which are located in a large area. The main ruins of taxila are divided into three major cities, each belonging to a distinct time period. The oldest of these is Bhir Mound which is as old as sixth century. The second city of Taxila is located at Sirkap and was built by Greco-Bactrian kings in the second century. The third and last city of Taxila is at Sirsukh and relates to the Kushan kings. In addition to the ruins of the city a number of buddhistic monastries and stupas also belong to the taxila area. Some of the important ruins of this category include the ruins of the stupa at Dharmarajika, the monastery at Jaulian, the monastery at Mohra Muradu in addition to a number of stupas.

The city of Taxila is mentioned by the Chinese monk Faxian (also called Fa-Hien), who visited ancient sites of buddhism in India. He came to Taxila in 405 CE. In his book "*A Record of Buddhistic Kingdoms*, Being an Account by the Chinese Monk Fa-Hien of his Travels in India and Ceylon in Search of the Buddhist Books of Discipline" he mentions the kingdom of Takshasila (or Chu-cha-shi-lo) meaning "the severed Head." He says that this name was derived from an event in the life of Buddha because this is the place "where he gave his head to a man".

Xuanzang (also called Hieun Tsang), another Chinese monk, visited Taxila in 630 CE. He mentions the city as Ta-Cha-Shi-Lo. The city appears to have already been ruins by his time.

Takshashila was an early center of learning dating back to at least the 5th century BCE. There is some disagreement about whether Takshashila can be considered a university. While some consider Taxila to be an early university or centre of higher education, others do not consider it a university in the modern sense, in contrast to the later Nalanda University. Takshashila is described in some detail in later Jataka tales, written in Sri Lanka around the 5th century CE.

Takshashila is considered a place of religious and historical sanctity by Hindus and Buddhists. The former do so not only because, in its time, Takshashila was the seat of Vedic learning, but also because the strategist, Chanakya, who later helped consolidate the empire of Emperor Chandragupta Maurya, was a senior teacher there. The institution is very significant in Buddhist tradition since it is believed that the Mahayana sect of Buddhism took shape there.

Some scholars date Takshashila's existence back to the 6th century BCE or 7th century BCE. It became a noted centre of learning at least several centuries before Christ, and continued to attract students from around the old world until the destruction of the city in the 5th century CE. Takshashila is perhaps best known because of its association with Chanakya. The famous treatise Arthashastra (Sanskrit for The knowledge of Economics) by Chanakya, is said to have been composed in Takshashila itself. Chanakya (or Kautilya), the Maurya Emperor Chandragupta and the Ayurvedic healer Charaka studied at Taxila. Generally, a student entered Takshashila at the age of sixteen. The Vedas and the Eighteen Arts, which included skills such as archery, hunting, and elephant lore, were taught, in addition to its law school, medical school, and school of military science.

**Vikramasila University**

Vikramasila University was one of the two most important centres of Buddhist learning in India, along with Nalanda University during the Pala dynasty. Vikramasila was established by King Dharmapala (783 to 820) in response to a supposed decline in the quality of scholarship at Nalanda. Atisha, the renowned pandita, is sometimes listed as a notable abbot.

Vikramasila (village Antichak, district Bhagalpur, Bihar) is located at about 50 km east of Bhagalpur and about 13 km north-east of Kahalgaon, a railway station on Bhagalpur-Sahebganj section of Eastern Railway. It is approachable through 11 km long motorable road diverting from N.H.80 at Anadipur about 2 km from Kahalgaon.

A fortified Vikramasila was destroyed by Muslim invaders fighting the Sena dynasty along with the other major centres of Buddhism in India around 1200. The remains of the ancient university have been partially excavated at village Antichak in the Bhagalpur district, Bihar state, India, and the process is still underway. Excavated remains represent the ruins of Vikramasila Mahavihara, the celebrated university founded by Pala king Dharmapala in late 8th or early 9th century A.D. It prospered for about four centuries before it collapsed in the beginning of 13th century A.D. It is known to us mainly through Tibetan sources, especially the writings of Taranath, the Tibetan monk historian of 16th-17th century A.D.

Vikramasila was one of the largest Buddhist universities having more than hundred teachers and about one thousand students. It produced eminent scholars who were often invited by foreign countries to spread Buddhist learning, culture and religion. The most distinguished and eminent among all was Atisa Dipankara, a founder of the Sarma traditions of Tibetan Buddhism. Subjects like theology, philosophy, grammar, metaphysics, logic etc. were taught here, but the most important branch of learning was tantrism.

Meticulous excavation at the site conducted initially by Patna University (1960-69) and subsequently by Archaeological Survey of India (1972-82) has revealed a huge square monastery with a cruciform stupa in its centre, a library building and cluster of votive stupas. To the north of monastery a number of scattered structures including a Tibetan and a Hindu temple have been found. The entire spread is over an area of more than one hundred acres.

The monastery, or residence for the Buddhist monks, is a huge square structure, each side measuring 330 metres having a series of 208 cells, 52 on each of the four sides opening into a common verandah. A few brick arched underground chambers beneath some of the cells have also been noticed which were probably meant for confined meditation by the monks.

The main stupa built for the purpose of worship is a brick structure laid in mud mortar which stands in the centre of the square monastery. This two terraced stupa is cruciform on plan and about 15 metres high from the ground level accessible through a flight of steps on the north side. On each of the four cardinal directions there is a protruding chamber with a pillared antechamber and a separate pillared mandapa in front. In the four chambers of the stupa were placed colossal stucco images of seated Buddha of which three were found in situ but the remaining one on north side was possibly replaced by a stone image after the clay image was somehow damaged.

The walls of both the terraces are decorated with mouldings and terracotta plaques which testify the high excellence of terracotta art flourishing in the region during Pala period (8th to 12th century A.D.). About 32 metres south of the monastery on its south west corner and attached with the main monastery through a narrow corridor is a rectangular structure identified as a library building. It was air-conditioned by cooled water of the adjoining reservoir through a range of vents in the back wall. The system was perhaps meant for preserving delicate manuscripts.

The architecture of the stupa and the themes of terracotta plaques of Vikramasila Mahavihara are comparable to the contemporary Somapura Mahavihara, Paharpur (Bangladesh). On plan both are very much alike except that Vikramasila monastery is larger and has fort like projections on its outer wall. A large number of antiquities of different materials, unearthed from this place in the course of excavation, are displayed in the site museum maintained by the Archaeological Survey of India.

## Medieval European Universities

Medieval universities are institutions of higher learning which was established during Gothic period and is a corporation. The first European medieval institutions generally considered to be universities were established in Italy, France, and England in the late 11th and the 12th centuries for the study of arts, law, medicine, and theology. These universities evolved from much older schools and monasteries, and it is difficult to define the date at which they became true universities, although the lists of studia generalia for higher education in Europe held by the Vatican are a useful guide.

Though some higher education institutions like the Nalanda University or University of Constantinople claim to be the oldest universities, the first universities in the modern sense (academic degree-granting higher education institutions) in western religious world were the University of Al-Karaouine (established in 859) and Al-Azhar University (established in 975). A different case is the University of Constantinople, which was founded in the 9th century as a secular institute of higher learning, to support the state administration. In China and the eastern world, there were many higher institutes of learning in the medieval era, the tradition of which traces back to ancient times, like the school Shang Hsiang.

The first degree-granting university in medieval Europe was the University of Bologna (established in 1088). The first universities in Europe were influenced in many ways by the Madrasahs in Islamic Spain and the Emirate of Sicily at the time, and in the Middle East during the Crusades. Medieval European universities were also influenced by a Gothic ethos: to build communities like communes (cities) themselves or guilds. With the increasing professionalisation of society during the 12th and 13th centuries, a similar demand grew for professional clergy.

Before the 12th century, the intellectual life of Europe had been relegated to monasteries, which were mostly concerned with the study of the liturgy and prayer; very few monasteries could boast true intellectuals. Following the Gregorian Reform's emphasis on canon law and the study of the sacraments, bishops formed cathedral schools to train the clergy in Canon law, but also in the more secular aspects of religious administration, including logic and disputation for use in preaching and theological discussion, and accounting to more effectively control finances. Learning became essential to advancing in the ecclesiastical hierarchy, and teachers also gained prestige. However, demand quickly outstripped the capacity of cathedral schools, each of which was essentially run by one teacher. In addition, tensions rose between the students of cathedral schools and burghers in smaller towns. As a result cathedral schools migrated to large cities, like Paris and Bologna.

The first universities in Europe (University of Bologna (1088), University of Paris (1160), University of Oxford (1167), University of Cambridge (1209), University of Palencia (1212), University of Salamanca (1218), University of Montpellier (1220), University of Padua (1222), University of Toulouse (1229) and University of Orleans (1235)) began as private enterprise of teachers and their pupils. Soon they realised they need protection against local city authorities. They petitioned secular power for privileges and this became a model. Emperor Frederick I in Authentica Habita (1158) gave the first privileges to students in Bologna. Another step was when Pope Alexander III in 1179 "forbidding masters of the church schools to take fees for granting the license to teach (licentia docendi), and obliging them to give license to properly qualified teachers".

## Characteristics

Initially medieval universities did not have a campus. Classes were taught wherever space was available, such as churches and homes. A university was not a physical space but a collection of individuals banded together as an universitas. Soon, however, some universities began to buy or rent rooms specifically for the purposes of teaching. Universities were generally structured along three types. The first type was in Bologna, where students hired and paid for the teachers. The second type was in Paris, where teachers were paid by the church. Third type Oxford and Cambridge were predominantly supported by the crown and the state, a fact which helped them survive the Dissolution of the Monasteries in 1538 and the subsequent removal of all the principal Catholic institutions in England. These structural differences created other characteristics. At the Bologna university the students ran everything — a fact that often put teachers under great pressure and disadvantage. In Paris, teachers ran the school; thus Paris became the premiere spot for teachers from all over Europe. Also, in Paris the main subject matter was theology, so control of the qualifications awarded was in the hands of an external authority—the Chancellor of the diocese. In Bologna, where students chose more secular studies, the main subject was law.

University studies took six years for a Bachelor's degree and up to twelve additional years for a master's degree and doctorate. The first six years were organised by the faculty of arts, where the seven liberal arts were taught: arithmetic, geometry, astronomy, music theory, grammar, logic, and rhetoric. The primary emphasis was on logic.

Once a Bachelor of Arts degree had been conferred, the student could leave the university or pursue further studies, in one of the three other faculties—law, medicine, or theology—in which to pursue the master's degree and doctorate degree. Theology was the most prestigious area of study, and the most difficult.

Courses were offered according to books, not by subject or theme. For example, a course might be on a book by Aristotle, or a book from the Bible. Courses were not elective: the course offerings were set, and everyone had to take the same courses. There were, however, occasional choices as to which teacher to use.

Students entered the University at fourteen to fifteen years of age. Classes usually started at 05:00 or 06:00. Students were afforded the legal protection of the clergy. In this way, no one was allowed to physically harm them; they could only be tried for crimes in a church court, and were thus immune from any corporal punishment. This gave students free rein in urban environments to break secular laws with impunity, a fact which produced many abuses: theft, rape and murder were not uncommon among students who did not face serious consequences. This led to uneasy tensions with secular authorities. Students would sometimes "strike" by leaving a city and not returning for years. This happened at the University of Paris strike of 1229 after a riot (started by the students) left a number of students dead; the University went on strike and they did not return for two years. As the students had the legal status of clerics which, according to the Canon Law, could not be held by women, women were not admitted into universities.

A popular textbook for university study was called the Sentences (*Quattuor libri sententiarum*) of Peter Lombard; theology students and masters were required to write extensive commentaries on this text as part of their curriculum. Much of medieval thought in philosophy and theology can be found in scholastic textual commentary because scholasticism was such a popular method of teaching. Most universities of international excellence in Europe were registered by the Holy Roman Empire as a Stadium Generale. Members of these institutions were encouraged to disseminate their knowledge across Europe, often giving lecture courses at a different Studium Generale.

**Research Universities**

European research universities have a long history that arguably dates back to the founding of the University of Bologna in 1088, although the University of Paris and the University of Magnaura are other contenders for this position. In the 19th and 20th centuries, European universities focused on science and research, and their structures and philosophies have shaped the university as we now know it. The original medieval universities are thought to have arisen from schools in churches before developing into what can now be definitively considered the "university." Aims of early universities included training professionals, investigating science, improving society, and teaching students to research and think for themselves. Many external influences, such as eras of humanism, Enlightenment, Reformation, and revolution, shaped research universities during their development, and the discovery of the New World in 1492 added human rights and international law to the university curriculum.

By the 18th century, universities published their own research journals, and by the 19th century, the German and the French university models had arisen. The German, or Humboldtian model, was conceived by Wilhelm von Humboldt and based on Friedrich Schleiermacher's liberal ideas pertaining to the importance of freedom, seminars, and laboratories in universities. The French university model involved strict discipline and control over every aspect of the university.

Universities concentrated on science in the 19th and 20th centuries, and they started to become accessible to the masses after

1914. Until the 19th century, religion played a significant role in university curricula; however, the role of religion in research universities decreased in the 19th century, and by the end of the 19th century, the German university model had spread around the world. The British also established universities worldwide, and higher education became available to the masses not only in Europe. In a general sense, the basic structure and aims of universities have remained constant over the years.

The first European university is often considered to be the University of Bologna, founded in 1088, although some were differ on this statement based on the intangibility of the definition of "university." In addition, the concept of the University of Bologna as the "mother of European Universities" was created as a symbol for Italy's national unity, which detracts from the legitimacy of its being considered the first. If the term "university" requires that a single corporate body be made up of students and professors of different disciplines, rather than that a corporate body simply exists, the University of Paris, founded in 1208, can be considered the first university; however, the University at Magnaura Palace was founded much earlier, in the 9th century. The University of Magnaura can be defined as a university because it brought prominent scholars together to create a "focal point of medieval Greek science and culture". The first universities in Europe were influenced in many ways by the Madrasah institutions in Islamic Spain, the Emirate of Sicily, and the Crusader states.

Traditional medieval universities are thought to have arisen from schools in churches, which began to require more structure as a result of their increasing popularity. This need, along with the advancing complexity of society, which required specialised training for administrators, lawyers, doctors, notaries, and ecclesiastics, and the rediscovery of ancient knowledge, such as new translations of Aristotle and Roman law, led to the development of student guilds, or universitates, and eventually the definitive university. Early universities, according to Professor of sociology and general editor of *A History of the University in Europe* Walter Rüegg, were meant to allow people to develop "knowledge for the sake of knowledge;" however, around the 16th century, knowledge was seen to be valuable as a part of the civil community. Universities at this time aimed to train clergymen, lawyers, government officials, and doctors. At the same time, according to Rüegg, people studied in order to further scientific investigation and attend to the demands of society. Science during the 16th century was an essential part of university curriculum, incorporating "openness to novelty" and the search for the means to control nature into the course of study.

The European University proliferated in part because groups decided to secede from the original universities to promote their own ideals; the University of Paris fostered many universities in Northern Europe, while the University of Bologna fostered many in the South. Some leaders also created universities in order to use them to increase their political power and popularity. For example, Frederick II, Holy Roman Emperor founded the University of Naples in 1224 to train lawyers and administrators who could rival the University of Bologna's influence, which served the hostile Lombard League.

The structure of these early classes involved a master reading from texts and commenting on the readings, as well as students learning by teaching other students. Masters also offered disputed questions to their classes for discussion. Moving into the 18th century, professors became less focused on simply training university teachers and more focused on "forming the minds of the elite" of a larger society.

While humanistic ideas of the 14th-16th century Renaissance were slow to catch on, they eventually spread from France, to Germany, to England during the 16th century Reformation. Under the influence of the increasingly popular humanist mode of thought, university education began to include the preparation of students for lives of civility, civilisation, and culture, along with a response to social concerns. Important to the medieval university curriculum were the trivium and quadrivium, two classifications of the liberal arts intended to prepare students for further learning, usually in the areas of theology, law, or medicine. Trivium included the three verbal disciplines: grammar, rhetoric, and logic, while Quadrivium included the four mathematical disciplines: arithmetic, geometry, astronomy, and music. The discovery of the New World in 1492 prompted additions to the European University curriculum, as subjects such as human rights and international law became relevant to current times.

Newly conquered Spanish territories raised questions about aboriginals' rights, and discussion stemmed from the Bible, medieval natural law theories, and humanistic ideas of toleration. Rüegg links the idea of the 'New' World to the idea of 'new' knowledge as opposed to the old works of the ancients. In the mid-16th century, scholarly and scientific journals became a popular way to "spread innovations among the learned," and by the 18th century, universities were publishing their own research journals. Enlightenment in the 18th century also encouraged the transition from the "preservation and transmission of accepted knowledge" to the "discovery and advancement of new knowledge," although newer universities more quickly adapted ideas of Enlightenment and Absolutism than older ones.

## MODERN UNIVERSITIES

The end of the medieval period marked the beginning of the transformation of universities that would eventually result in the modern research university. Many external influences, such as eras of humanism, Enlightenment, Reformation, and revolution, shaped research universities during their development. BME is considered the oldest university of technology in the world. The legal predecessor of the university was founded in Hungary in 1782 by Emperor Joseph II, named Institutum Geometrico-Hydrotechnicum. This University represented a new type of universities.

Moving into the 19th century, the objective of universities evolved from teaching the "regurgitation of knowledge" to "encourag[ing] productive thinking." Two main university models, the German and the French, arose and gave rise to other models such as the British and Russian. The German model, conceived by Wilhelm von Humboldt, was also known as the Humboldtian model. In 1810, Humboldt convinced the King of Prussia to build a university in Berlin based on Friedrich Schleiermacher's liberal ideas; the goal was to demonstrate the process of the discovery of knowledge and to teach students to "take account of fundamental laws of science in all their thinking, " thus, seminars and laboratories started to evolve. Humboldt envisioned the university education as a student-centred activity of research:

> Just as primary instruction makes the teacher possible, so he renders himself dispensable through schooling at the secondary level. The university teacher is thus no longer a teacher and the student is no longer a pupil. Instead the student conducts research on his own behalf and the professor supervises his research and supports him in it.

Freedom was an important concept in the German university model, and the system of professors was based on competition and freedom: although professors served as state functionaries, they had the freedom to choose between several states, and their identity and prestige arose from the specialisation of scientific disciplines.

The French University model lacked the freedom of the German model, consisting of severe discipline and control over the curriculum, awarding of degrees, conformity of views, and personal habits. French university professors trained at the École Normale Supérieure, and much of their prestige depended on their schools' reputations. By 1866, though, the German model had begun to influence the strict French model.

The German university model was also used in Russian universities, which hired lecturers trained in Germany and which dedicated themselves to science. At the same time, Russian universities were meant to train the bureaucracy in the same way as the French grandes écoles. Throughout the 19th and 20th centuries, Russian universities underwent much variation in their degrees of strictness and control.

British universities also modelled themselves after the German university. They enjoyed a great deal of freedom because the state granted them an autonomy that allowed them initiative and flexibility. The Universities of Oxford and Cambridge emphasised the importance of research, arguably more authentically implementing Humboldt's idea of a university than even German universities, which were subject to state authority.

Overall, science became the focus of universities in the 19th and 20th centuries. Students could conduct research in seminars or laboratories and began to produce doctoral theses with more scientific content. According to Humboldt, the mission of the University of Berlin was to pursue scientific knowledge. The German university system fostered professional, bureaucratically regulated scientific research performed in well-equipped laboratories, instead of the kind of research done by private and individual scholars in Great Britain and France. In fact, Rüegg asserts that the German system is responsible for the development of the modern research university because it focused on the idea of "freedom of scientific research, teaching and study."

European research universities ultimately developed lasting traditions of university education that spread around the world. By the end of the 19th century, the German university model had spread throughout Europe, to the United States, and to Japan. In America, the Spanish, and then the English and French, founded universities in lands that they conquered in the early 16th century. These universities aimed to fulfil the needs of colonists, spread religion, provide professional training to colonists, and help overseas rulers with effective administration. By the 19th century, the British had established institutes of higher learning in Canada, Australia, and the Cape Colony, all of which were modelled after European universities. Japan, the Near East, and Africa all had universities based on European models in the 19th century. These universities disseminated Western European science and technology and trained natives to develop resources. Entering into the 20th century, higher education became available to the masses of the world as a result of urbanisation and industrialisation. Some of these universities promoted the aims of rulers, while others had a revolutionary impact on the power structure of the countries in which they were located. Generally speaking, the most basic structure and aims of research universities have remained constant over the years; according to author Clark Kerr, universities "are among the least changed of institutions."

The funding and organisation of universities varies widely between different countries around the world. In some countries universities are predominantly funded by the state, while in others funding may come from donors or from fees which students attending the university must pay. In some countries the vast majority of students attend university in their local town, while in other countries universities attract students from all over the world, and may provide university accommodation for their students.

Across the world there are differing standards for the legal definition of the term "university" and formal accreditation of institutions. There is no nationally standardised definition of the term in the United States, although the term is primarily used to designate research institutions and is often reserved for doctorate-granting institutions, but some US states, such as Massachusetts, will only grant a school "university status" if it grants at least two doctoral degrees.

In many regions of the world, a university is any institution of higher education and research which grants autonomously a range of academic degrees in several fields, from bachelor's degrees to doctorate degrees, including masters' degrees, as well as honoris causa degrees and agrégation/habilitation diplomas in the places where these are used. Independently performed research conducted by universities includes both fundamental research and applied research.

## References

Stanley Aronowitz, (2000) *The Knowledge Factory*. Boston: Beacon.

Clyde W. Barrow, (1990) *Universities and the Capitalist State: Corporate Liberalism and the Reconstruction of American Higher Education, 1894–1928*, University of Wisconsin Press.

Sigmund Diamond, (1992) *Compromised Campus: The Collaboration of Universities with the Intelligence Community, 1945–1955*, Oxford University Press.

Olaf Pedersen, (1998) *The First Universities : Studium Generale and the Origins of University Education in Europe*, Cambridge University Press.

Walter Rüegg, general editor, *A History of the University in Europe*. Cambridge: Cambridge University Press.

# 10

# Role of Government in Education

Education is today largely paid for and almost entirely administered by governmental bodies or non-profit institutions. This situation has developed gradually and is now taken so much for granted that little explicit attention is any longer directed to the reasons for the special treatment of education even in countries that are predominantly free enterprise in organisation and philosophy. The result has been an indiscriminate extension of governmental responsibility. The nature and content of the National Educational Policy as well as the manner and success of its implementation obviously depends on the role of the Government of India in education. In this chapter we shall briefly discuss the role of the Government of India in education as it has evolved over the years, its present status and future prospects.

## Indian Government and Education

### 1833-1870

The East India Company was made to accept responsibility for the education of the Indian people in 1813. But the Government of India did not then exist; the authority of the Governors of the three Presidencies of Bengal, Bombay and Madras was supreme and subject only to the control of the Court of Directors of the Company in England. Between 1813 and 1833, therefore, education was an exclusive responsibility of the Provincial Governments. This situation however changed completely in 1833 when the Charter Act of that year created the office of the Governor-General of India and vested in him the sole authority to govern all the Company's possessions in India.

This was basically a political decision taken with the object of creating a powerful and supreme agency within the country itself to strengthen the administration of the existing territories as well as to facilitate the conquest of new ones. But it made education, like every other subject, an exclusive responsibility, of the Government of India in which all revenues were vested and which alone could authorise appropriations therefrom. At one stroke, the Provincial Governments thus lost all their authority over education and became merely the agents of the Government of India to administer it on its behalf. They could not create a single post, however low, nor sanction a rupee of expenditure, nor make any change in policies, however small, without the approval of the Government of India. This system of a total centralisation of authority continued till 1870. It would have been almost unworkable but for the fact that, In actual practice, the Government of India allowed a good deal of freedom to the Provincial Governments to adjust educational policies to their local needs and respected their proposals and advice.

During this period, there were two main occasions when the Government of India issued orders which, in substance, were tantamount to the enunciation of a National Policy on Education although this expression was not then used. The first refers to the orders issued by Lord William Bentinck, on the basis of a Minute recorded by Macau- lay, that the objective of modern education in India ought to be the promotion of European literature and science among the people of India and that English should be the medium of education.' The second was the Educational Despatch dated 19th July 1854 issued by the Court of Directors. It is a long document of 100 paragraphs which laid down the broad principles and programes for educational development in India. It confirmed the orders issued earlier by Lord Bentinck and, among other things, authorised:

(1) the establishments of universities at Bombay, Calcutta and Madras,

(2) the creation of Education Departments in the Provinces,

(3) the establishment of a graded network of schools and colleges in all parts of the country,

(4) the provision of grants-in-aid to private schools, (both missionary and Indian),

(5) training of teachers,
(6) encouragement to the education of women, and
(7) employment of educated Indians in government services.

This policy statement continued to govern all educational developments in India till 1882.

**1870-1921**

In 1870, Lord Mayo initiated a system of decentralisation and delegation of authority. The centralised administration introduced in 1833 had served its purpose. The whole of India had been conquered, the so-called Sepoy Mutiny quelled, and the British rule fully consolidated in all parts of the country. On the other hand, the weaknesses of the system which led to delays and wastefulness in expenditure and created an irresponsible attitude in the Provincial Governments came to the surface and began to gall. A move for decentralisation was, therefore, inevitable, and it came none too soon.

Under the orders issued by Lord Mayo, the Provincial Governments were made responsible for all expenditure on certain services and were given, for that purpose, a fixed grant-in-aid and certain sources of revenue. This system continued to be in force up to 1876-77 when a system of 'shared revenues' was introduced. Under this system, certain revenues were designated as exclusively 'Central', certain others were designated as exclusively 'Provincial' and the remaining were designated as 'Divided' and their receipts were shared between the Central and Provincial Governments according to an agreed contract which remained in force for a period of five years at a time.

Thus the quinquennial contracts were revised in 1882-83, 1886-87, 1891-92 and 1896-97. In 1904, they were declared to be quasi-permanent i.e., not to be changed except in a grave emergency, they were declared to be permanent. It will thus be seen that, under these financial arrangements, the entire expenditure on education was to be borne by the Provincial Governments within the resources allocated to them. A delegation of administrative powers naturally followed this transfer of financial responsibility., It may be said, therefore, that between 1870 and 1921, most of the administrative and financial authority over education was gradually transferred to the Provincial

Governments; and the Government of India merely retained a theoretical right of the control and general supervision as a sequel to its ultimate responsibility to the British Parliament.

It must be made clear however that, when necessary, the Government of India did not hesitate to intervene, to review educational progress, and to issue such directives to Provincial Governments as it felt to be necessary. The first such occasion to intervene arose when there was an insistent demand that the progress of education in India since the Educational Despatch of 1854 should be reviewed. The Government of India, therefore, appointed the first Commission on Education in India, viz. the Indian Education Commission (1882) and on the submission of its report, issued orders laying down a new National Policy on Education. Its main fêatures were:

(1) emphasis on the spread of primary education and education among girls, scheduled castes and scheduled tribes;

(2) full encouragement to Indian private enterprise in secondary and higher education; and

(3) creation of local bodies at the District and Tehsil levels (with considerable participation of the Indian people) and their association with the administration of primary education.

These policies continued to be in force till the end of the nineteenth century.

The second occasion for a strong and sustained intervention arose when Lord Curzon became the Governor-General of India. He was of the view that Indian education had grown too fast at the secondary and university stages, that its administration had become flabby because of undue freedom given to Indian private enterprise, that standards had deteriorated and that the uncontrolled expansion of secondary and higher education was leading to indiscipline and disaffection against Government. He was, therefore, of the view that the Government of India should no longer be a 'king log' and that a policy of intensive central interest in education must be enunciated and sustained. He created the office of the Director-General of Public Instruction in India under the Central Government (1897). He also convened a Conference of the Directors of Public Instruction in the Provinces at Simla (1900), appointed the Indian Universities

Commission (1902), passed the Indian Universities Act (1904) in the Central Legislature, and issued the Government Resolution on Educational Policy in 1904. He also initiated a system of large Central grants to the Provinces for educational development and these continued to be in vogue for several years afterwards. An Indian Education Service (IES) was also created in 1897 and its officers held all key posts in the Education Departments. A Second Government of India Resolution on Educational Policy was also passed in 1913. The two Resolutions of 1904 and 1913 may also be described as National Policies on Education and form a continuing sequence with the orders of Lord Bentinck, the Educational Despatch of 1854, and the Resolution of the Government [of India] on the Recommendations of the Indian Education Commission (1884).

It may be incidentally mentioned that the Government of India started a practice of compiling and publishing quinquennial reviews to the progress of education in India from 1882. Such reviews were published for 1886 87, 1891-92, 1996-97, 1901-02, 1902-07, 1907-12, 1912-17, and 1921-22.

**1921-1947**

This period of active Central control and financial support of education came to an end in 1921 when, under the Government of India Act, 1919, education in the Provinces was transferred to the control of Indian Ministers responsible to legislatures with an elected majority. As a corollary to this basic decision, the role of the Government of India (which continued to be responsible to the British Parliament) in education had to be limited to the minimum. Under the Government of India Act, 1919, therefore, the responsibilities of Government were divided into Central and Provincial lists in the first instance and then the latter were divided into reserved and transferred. Because of various conflicting proposals made on the subject, education was treated as partly all-India, partly reserved, partly transferred with limitations and partly transferred without limitations. The following powers were reserved to the Government of India.

1. The Banares Hindu University and such other new universities as may be declared to be all-India by the Governor-General-in Council

2. College for Indian chiefs and educational institutions maintained by the Governor-General-in-Council for the benefit of members of His Majesty's Forces or other public servants, or their children.
3. The authority to legislate on the following subjects was reserved for the central legislature, mainly with a view to enabling the Government of India to take suitable action on the report of the Calcutta University Commission.
   (a) Questions regarding the establishment, constitution and functions of new universities;
   (b) Questions affecting the jurisdiction of any university outside its province; and
   (c) Questions regarding the Calcutta University and the reorganisation of secondary education in Bengal.

Except for the above matters reserved for the Government of India the whole of the education wag transferred to the control of Indian Ministers with one exception, viz. education of Anglo-Indians find Europeans was reserved. There were also some restrictions on the control which the Ministers could exercise in certain matters (e.g. the IES).

It was also decided to stop all further recruitment to the IES so that the 'service would fade out within a few years. Needless to say the system of Central grants which had made such a useful contribution to educational development also disappeared.

The Hartog Committee (1928) examined this situation with concern and said: "we are of the opinion that the divorce of the Government of India from education has been unfortunate: and holding as we do, that education is essentially a national service, we are of opinion that steps should be taken to consider a new relation of the Central Government with this subject. We have suggested that the Government of India should serve as a Centre of educational information for the whole of India and as a means of coordinating the educational experience of the different provinces. But, we regard the duties of the Central Government as going beyond that.

We cannot accept the view that it should be entirely relieved of all responsibility for the attainment of universal primary education. It may be that some of the provinces, inspite of all efforts, will be unable to provide the funds necessary for that purpose, and the Government of India should, therefore, be constitutionally enabled to make good such financial deficiencies in the interests of India as a whole".

This view was carefully examined when the Government of India Act, 1935, was passed. But as the basic condition, viz., the transfer of education to popular control in the Provinces side by side with the Government of India continuing to be responsible to Parliament remained unchanged, the policy underlying the Act of 1919, was continued with some modifications which reduced the authority of the Government of India over education and correspondingly increased that of Indian Ministers over it at the provincial level. The actual provisions made in the Government of India Act, 1935, abolished the old distinction between reserved and transferred subjects and the limitations placed on the powers of the education ministers. The whole of education thus became a transferred subject, except the following matters which were reserved for the Government of India:

*(i)* The Imperial Library, Calcutta: the Indian Museum, Calcutta the Imperial War Museum: the Victoria Memorial, Calcutta and any similar institution controlled or financed by the Central Government;

*(ii)* Education of the Defence Forces;

*(iii)* The Banaras Hindu University and the Aligarh Muslim University;

*(iv)* Preservation of ancient and historical monuments.

With these radical changes in the constitutional position, the question of the Government of India issuing any Resolutions on the National Policy on Education did not even arise; and in fact, no Government of India Resolution on National Educational Policy was issued for 55 years between 1913 and 1968. However, attempts were made to strengthen the advisory and coordinating role of the Government of India.

The quinquennial reviews of education in India continued to be published and were actually brought out in 196-27, 1931-32, 1936-37, and 1946-47. A Central Advisory Board of Education consisting of all Education Ministers in the Provinces was first constituted for this purpose in 1921. It was, however, abolished in 1924 as a measure of economy. It was revived again in 1935; and its one great achievement was to prepare the Post-War Plan of Educational Development (1944). It proposed to create, in a period of 40 years, an educational system in India which would be like that in England in 1939. The plan however was never accepted by Indian public opinion.

## 1947-2009

The subject came again for discussion in 1950 when the Constitution was being adopted on the basis of a Federal Government at the Centre. It could have been possible at this time to define a more effective Central role in education. But the general public opinion was strongly in favour of vesting almost all authority over education in the Slates; and the mere fact that the Congress was in power at the Centre and in all the States made it almost seem unnecessary to vest any constitutional authority over education in the Centre. Once again, therefore, the basic policy of the Government of India Act, 1919, was continued with one change, viz. certain additional powers were now vested in the Centre. In fact, the Constitution makes Education basically a State subject (Entry 11 of the State List), subject to certain powers reserved in the Central (Entries 63-66) and Concurrent Lists (Entry 25). These are quoted below for ready reference:

## List I: List of Union Functions

The Institution known at the commencement of the Constitution as the Banaras Hindu University, the Aligarh Muslim University and the Delhi University and any other institution declared by Parliament by law to be an institution of national importance;

Institutions for scientific or technical education financed by the Government of India wholly or in part and declared by Parliament by law to be institutions of national importance;

Union agencies and institutions for:

*(a)* professional, vocational or technical training, including the training of police officers; or

*(b)* the promotion of special studies or research; or

*(c)* scientific or technical assistance in the investigation or detection of crime.

Co-ordination and determination of standards in institutions for higher education or research and scientific and technical institutions.

**List II: List of State Functions**

Education including universities, subject to provision of entries 63, 64, 65 and 66 of List I and entry 25 of List III.

**List III: List of Concurrent Functions**

Vocational and technical training of labour. The academic opinion in India has never been fully reconciled to this constitutional decision which makes education an almost total responsibility or the States and the Subject therefore has continued to be debated over the last 30 years. On the whole, three definite categories of views have emerged:

(1) The first view, held by a minority, and mostly among State level politicians is that the authority over education should be transferred to the State Governments to a still greater extent that the Ministry of Education should be abolished, and that almost all the funds meant for the development of education should be provided in the State sector, thus abolishing the Centrally sponsored sector and reducing the Central Sector to the minimum;

(2) The second view which prevailed throughout the period between 1947 and 1976, was that there need be no' change in the! constitutional role of the Government of India in education. But education should be regarded as a national concern, and steps should be taken to see that the advisory and coordinating roles of the Government of India are considerably strengthened. This has been the most dominating view in the post-independence period.

(3) The third view, also held by a minority was that education should be brought into the concurrent list. This was supported by the Committee of Members of Parliament under the Chairmanship of Shri Sapru (1963) which recommended that higher education should be brought on the concurrent list. The proposal however did not get support among the State Governments and had to be dropped.

The problem was discussed by the Education Commission (1964- 66) Unfortunately, the members of the Commission could not reach a concensus on the subject. The majority of members were for the status quo and for the continuance of education in the State list. They recommended that "there is plenty of scope, within the present Constitutional arrangement, to evolve a workable Centre-State partnership in education and that this has not been exploited to the full. The case for amending the Constitution can only be,, made after this scope is fully utilised and found to be inadequate.

All things considered we recommend that an intensive effort be made to exploit fully the existing provisions of the Constitution for the development of education and evolution of a national educational policy. The problem may then be reviewed again say, "after ten years." The debate on the subject would have gone on indefinitely had not the emergency intervened. Smt. Indira Gandhi, who was then in need of some respectable ideas for inclusion in her omnibus proposals for amendment to the Constitution, suddenly picked upon the subject and brought education on the concurrent list. The Janata Government which came to power with a pledge to undo all the Constitutional amendments made in the emergency declared its intension to put education back in the State List. It did not succeed, mainly because or the opposition from the Congress. But Dr. P.C. Chunder has declared in Parliament that the policy of his government is to act as if education is in the State list.

If history is to be written in modern parlance, it is interesting to note that education has been in the exclusively Central list between 1833 and 1870, in the Concurrent list between 1870 and 1921, in the exclusive State list between 1921 and 1947, mostly in the State list with some special powers to the Centre between 1947 and 1976, and in the Concurrent list from 1976 onwards.

The Central government of India formulated the National Policy in Education (NPE) in 1986 and also re-enforced the Programe of Action (POA) in 1986. The government initiated several measures including the setting up of Navodaya Vidyalaya selective schools in every district, advances in female education, inter-disciplinary research and establishment of open universities. India's NPE also contains the National System of Education, which ensures some uniformity while taking into account regional education needs. The NPE also stresses on higher spending on education, envisaging a budget of more than 6% of the overall national budget. While the need for wider reform in the primary and secondary sectors is recognised as an issue, the emphasis is also on the development of science and technology education infrastructure.

The government objective for the Sarva Shiksha Abhiyan (SSA), started in 2001, is to provide education to children between 6–14 years by 2010. The programe focuses specially on girls and children with challenged social or financial backgrounds. The SSA also aims to provide practical infrastructure and relevant source material in form of free textbooks to children in remote areas. The SSA also aims at widening computer education in rural areas.

Women from remote, underdeveloped areas or from weaker social groups in Andra Pradesh, Assam, Bihar, Jharkhand, Karnataka, Kerala, Gujarat, Uttar Pradesh, and Uttarakhand, fall under the Mahila Samakhya Scheme, initiated in 1989. Apart from provisions for education this programe also aims to raise awareness by holding meetings and seminars at rural levels. The government allowed 340 million rupees during 2007–08 to carry out this scheme over 83 districts including more than 21,000 villages.

Currently there are 68 Bal Bhavans and 10 Bal Kendra affiliated to the National Bal Bhavan. The scheme involves educational and social activities and recognising children with a marked talent for a particular educational stream. A number of programes and activities are held under this scheme, which also involves cultural exchanges and participation in several international forums.As a part of the tenth Five Year Plan (2002–2007), the central government of India outlined an expenditure of 65.6% of its total education budget of Rs. 438250 million, or (Rs. 287500 million) on elementary education; 9.9% (Rs. 43250 million) on secondary education; 2.9% (Rs. 12500 million) on adult education; 9.5% (Rs. 41765 million) on higher education; 10.7% (Rs. 47000 million) on technical education; and the remaining 1.4% (Rs. 6235 million) on miscellaneous education schemes. According to the United Nations Educational, Scientific and Cultural Organisation (UNESCO), India has the lowest public expenditure on higher education per student in the world.

## ROLE OF GOVERNMENT: COMPREHENSIVE ANALYSIS

So far, we have discussed the Constitutional Role of the Government of India in education. It must be pointed out however that the constitutional role of the Government of India in education is only one aspect of its actual role which must be examined in its totality. The other aspects of this role which modify the constitutional position very substantially are:

(1) public opinion,

(2) financial relations,

(3) political situation, and

(4) administrative arrangements.

It is only an integrated view of all these aspects that can give real insights into the nature of the problem and enable us to devise practicable reforms.

**Public Opinion**

In a truly democratic set-up, the administration of education which concerns every individual intimately must be highly decentralised. The general practice in this regard is that school education or at least elementary education which has to be provided for every child, should be controlled by the local community. This, for instance, is the tradition in U.S.A., where the people are extremely alert on educational issues and where the principle of local control of school education is strongly rooted in the historical traditions of the country. In a situation of this type, the State itself has a minor role in school education and the Federal Government, even less. The position regarding secondary and higher education, however is rather different. Secondary education is usually under local control if it is provided on a universal basis. Otherwise, it is generally provided by a larger community or the State; and higher education, except in a few big cities, is generally managed by the State or by the State and the Federal Government in some kind of partnership. On the basis of this broad general practice, it should ordinarily be expected that in India elementary education should be administered at the local community level, secondary education at the district or State level, and higher education at the State level or at the State and national levels.

Unfortunately, the historical traditions in our country have been different so that local control of education at the community or district level has failed to develop adequately. It is true that we did have a tradition of some local control of education because, in the pre-British days, schools were established and controlled by the local communities rather than by the Princes who, at best, extended their patronage to a few learned scholars or schools of higher learning. But these schools, more often than not, were enterprises of individuals or of small interested groups within the community rather than of the community as a whole. Even this limited tradition also died out when Government accepted responsibility for providing education.

In the old British Indian Provinces, an attempt was made to associate local bodies at the community and district level with the provision of elementary education. This tradition has survived but has neither become vital or dynamic. In the Princely States, on the other hand, no such effort was ever made. In the post-independence period also the local control of education was not encouraged except for the Panchayati Raj experiment which has been tried earnestly only in a few areas. Consequently, the present position is that the vast masses of the people who are mostly illiterate have no interest in education as now imparted in the formal system and the tradition of local control in education is also mostly non-existent.

Public interest in education in India is mainly confined to the educated and elite groups who are the principal beneficiaries of the formal educational system and who mostly belong to the top 30 percent of the income groups. Their main interest is in secondary and higher education where, apart from other things, their own private enterprise provides the bulk of the educational institutions. Moreover, it is the children of this elite which form about 70 percent of the enrolment in secondary education and about 80 percent of the enrolment in higher education. The basic issues that interest this elite are, therefore, the location and opening of new secondary schools, colleges and universities, their curricula and grants, in-aid and the expansion of elementary education.

As these, issues are mostly decided at the State level, the concept of education as essentially a State responsibility gets the strongest-public support. The view, gets further strengthened from the fact that, the State is probably the most convenient level from which a basic social service like education can be administered. The sap e view also finds still further support in the State levy leadership whose image and power-base largely depends upon the control of educational institutions, teachers and students. It is these supports which made education a Stale subject under the Constitution and which also continue to legitimise the position. In fact, one may even assert that education as a State responsibility is at present so well entrenched in the public mind that it is extremely difficult, if not actually impassible, to alter this situation.

One need not necessarily quarrel with this view and may agree that education may basically remain a State responsibility. But one cannot also accept a State absolutism in education and an over-concentration of authority at the State level. The power of the state, in education has therefore, to be limited to a considerable extent in the larger interests of education itself. This is generally attempted in three ways.

(a) The first is administrative decentralisation where authority over education, and especially over school education, is transferred to the local community at the municipal, village, Tehsil or District levels. As pointed out earlier, this trend is weak in the country, partly because the earlier tradition of local control or popular involvement in education has almost died out, partly because such decentralisation can be most effective in elementary and adult education which continue to be our neglected sectors, and partly because the local leadership at the village, Tehsil or District level is still weak in comparison with that at the Stale level and cannot assert itself. Consequently, the unfortunate public view that the State and Central levels are the only two that really matter in education, gains undue currency and strength. This trend also finds support in the general attitudes of linguistic and other minorities and weaker sections like Scheduled Castes and Tribes who find that the local levels are generally oppressive and that their oppresiveness increases as one goes down to lower levels so that their hopes of justice and fair treatment lie mainly at the State and national levels.

(b) The second is academic decentralisation, i.e., to free the educational process from bureaucratic control by respecting university autonomy which the universities should, in their turn, share with their departments and affiliated colleges, by enabling the schools to prepare their own curricula and to hold their own examinations, and in short by so delegating authority to educational institutions and their teachers that the teaching-learning process becomes free, joyful and independent of State control. Unfortunately these concepts have not gained strength either within the teaching profession or among the general public. On the other hand, the contrary trends have gained an upper hand and the academic control of the State over education, schools and teachers has increased, rather than decreased, since 1947.

*(c)* While we have thus been unable to check State absolutism in education either through decentralisation to local bodies or through academic decentralisation, we have had a somewhat better success to control State authority in education through centralisation, i.e., by giving a larger voice to the Central Government in educational matters. One powerful group that supports this demand is that of the national bureaucracy which can be transferred to any part of the country and the large trade and industrial interests that have also acquired a national character. These groups are generally in favour of a national system of education with common curricula and text books in all parts of the country—a situation which can be created only if the Central Government can have an over-riding voice in education. The university and research, system which can be best planned on a national basis also supports the same trend. Further support comes from another important group, viz., teachers, who would like to fight for uniform scales of pay and emoluments in all parts of the country and who realise that they can become a tremendous force if organised on a national basis. They are, therefore, in favour of an increasing role in education for the Centre and against any devolution of authority to the local bodies. A large section of the, intellectual elite also recognises the need for a national policy in education from the point of view of national integration and takes the stand that while the "diversity" implied in the State control of education is both necessary and desirable, it is equally important to provide the 'unity' in this diversity through a national educational policy. It, must also be pointed out that the national leadership that grew in the freedom struggle initiated a large and intensive debate on education at the national level and that this tradition still continues unabated. Consequently,

education has become, throughout the last hundred years or so, a great national concern although it remains State subject in administration. The public support for the role of the Government of India in education arises essentially from these social and political groups and from these national concerns which cannot be ignored, although not all of them are healthy and desirable, To the extent they succeed, there will be a curb on the State authority in education and a legitimate basis for the formulation and implementation of a national policy on education.

**Financial Relations**

The Centre-State relations in financial support of education are obviously very important. Where the centre can give large grant-in-aid for educational development, it always gets considerable control over it and is in a strong position to implement national policies on education, irrespective of any constitutional provisions on the subject. Prior to 1870, the Government of India did exercise almost complete control over education because it sanctioned all the funds needed for it. This authority decreased in actual practice between 1870 and 1902 when, under the system of financial devolution initiated in that year, the entire responsibility for financing education was gradually transferred to the Provincial Governments. Lord Curzon initiated a system of specific-purpose Central grants for educational development which continued even after he left. They therefore enabled the Central Government to play a major role in expanding and improving education between 1902 and 1921.

After the attainment of independence, the desire of the Government of India to expand and improve education led to the formulation of national decisions on several important issues and to the revival of Central grants to help their speedy implementation. For instance, the creation of the University Grants Commission in 1956 was partly meant to provide additional and specific-purpose grants to State Governments for the development of higher education. Similar grants were provided for engineering education under the advice of the All India Council of Technical Education. The Indian Council of Agricultural Research has provided special grants for the development of agricultural universities and agricultural education, research and training; and the Central Ministry of Health and the Indian Council of

Medical Research have provided similar assistance respectively for medical education and research.

In addition to these, efforts were made to give specific-purpose grants for educational development through successive five-year plans. The education chapter of each Five Year Plan is essentially a statement of a national policy on education and of the programes intended to implement it. A system, therefore, arose under which all schemes included in the Plans were divided into three categories:

(1) Central i.e., those which were to be implemented by the Central Government and funds for which were also provided in the Central Sector;

(2) Centrally-Sponsored i.e. those which were to be implemented by the State Governments, but funds for which were provided at the Centre and were later made available to the State Governments for specific approved schemes; and

(3) State i. e. those which were to be implemented by the State Governments and funds for which were also provided in the State plans. In the first and the second plans, the number of Central and Centrally-sponsored schemes was large and there were special Central grants even for State schemes.

From the third plan onwards, these policies have greatly changed, mainly because of the pressure from the States, in two directions:

(1) The number of centrally-sponsored schemes is being continually reduced, and

(2) Central plan assistance is given, not for individual State schemes of educational development and not even for all education taken together, but for the State plan as a whole, subject to only one condition, viz., the allocation for elementary education is earmarked.

It is not however easy in practice to enforce this earmarking rigidly; and the net effect of all these changes is that the capacity of the Government of India to enforce its 'advice' on the State Governments through the indirect method of centrally-sponsored schemes or specific purpose grants has been greatly reduced.

The Education Commission (1964-66) recommended the enlargement of the Central sector in education and the revival of the

Centrally-sponsored grants on a large scale to implement national policies in education. But this recommendation has not yet been accepted by the Government of India.

On the other hand, the recommendations of the Seventh Finance Commission have adopted a hew approach altogether. The policy adopted by the first six Commissions was to transfer only such resources to the States as would enable them to cover the deficit in their budgets at the end of the plan period so that the State Governments bad to depend very largely. on the Centre for financing their developmental plans.

The Seventh Finance Commission has changed this policy and transferred substantial resources to the States so that they have larger autonomy to finance their development plans. This has changed the situation substantially. In the first place, the Centre now has more limited resources to expand the Central Sector. The proposal of the Commission to expand the Centrally sponsored sector has also run into hot weather.

The State Governments have been pleading, since 1966, to abolish all the Centrally sponsored schemes. They are succeeding continuously and now the Centrally-sponsored schemes, especially in education, have been reduced to the minimum and they appear to be on their way out. One is not sure therefore what financial levers, if any the Centre may continue to have to influence State educational policies. if these levers disappear, it will not make much difference whether education remains in the concurrent list or is retransferred to the State list.

**Political Aspects**

The political aspects of the problem also need some attention. it is obvious that the chances of enunciating and implementing a strong national policy are greater when the same political party is in power at the Centre and in the States. This, for instance is the situation in the USSR where, inspite of a very large constitutional delegation of authority over education to the States, a uniform national system of education has been created and maintained by the Communist Party. In India also, national policies in education have depended for their success, not so much on Constitutional provisions as on the strength of the Congress party and the capacity of the national leadership to assert itself. Between 1921 and 1947, the Congress continually reiterated the view that India should have a national system of education which, necessarily implied the enunciation and implementation of a national policy on education. The idea also worked politically to some extent so long as the Congress remained in power at the Centre and in all States, say, between 1947 and 1967. The State Governments were then generally of the view, that a national policy in education was desirable and were more amenable to advice from the Centre, But differences began to surface when non-Congress governments were formed in some States such as Kerala or Tamil Nadu, The language problem in particular proved to be extremely difficult.

**Administrative Aspects**

Administrative arrangements play an important role in posting a national policy on education. If there is a basic decision to have a national policy on education, steps, are usually taken to create an effective administrative machinery to implement it. On the other band, if there is an effective administrative machinery, it does help, in its turn, to enunciate and implement a national policy on education.

Over the last 120 years or so, however, policy and administration have not always moved in unison.

(a) In 1855, steps were taken to create Education Departments in the Provinces which had no legal authority over education while, in the Government of India which had all the authority over education, there was no adequate machinery to look after this subject which was consequently dealt with partly in the Home Department and partly in the Political Department. Between 1833 and 1870, therefore, the authority over education was largely exercised by the Provincial Government inspite of the fact that all authority was centralised and vested in the Government of India.

(b) On the other hand, there was a deliberate policy, between 1870 and 1921, to delegate increasing authority over education to Provincial Governments. But there was a good deal of administrative centralisation simultaneously. For instance, the Indian Education Service (IES) was created in 1897; and as stated already, Lord Curzon created the office of the Director General of

Public Instruction at the Centre. A separate Department of Education was created in 1910 and the Bureau of Education was established in 1915. These measures, combined with the introduction of Central grants for education gave a considerable lever to the Government of India to enunciate and implement a national policy on Education.

*(c)* Between 1921 and 1947, however, there was a constitutional divorce between the Government of India and education; and, at the same time, the IES was abolished, the educational services were fully provincialised, and even a separate Department of Education and the Bureau of Education were abolished as a measure of economy in 1923. Consequently, the Central machinery to enunciate and implement a national educational policy became the weakest in modern history.

*(d)* Between 1947 and 1978, the constitutional authority of the Centre in education has been increased; and side by side, a separate Ministry of Education has been created at the Centre, strengthened from time to time and, more often than not, placed under a Minister of the. Cabinet rank. This has strengthened the administrative basis for a national policy on education. But the demand to create an Indian Education Service has not yet been conceded, inspite of the recommendation of the Education Commission (1964-66).

Administrative measures can also buttress the 'advisory' role of the Centre. For instance, the Central Advisory Board of Education was created in 1921 from this point of view, but it was abolished in 1923 as a measure of economy. It was, however, revived in 1935 and has continued to function ever since. Sporadic attempts continue to be made to strengthen its role; and their success has varied from time to time, depending mainly on the personality of the Union Education Minister and the willingness of the Government of India to back tip the 'advice' of the Board with financial support. It has, in practice, made a fairly significant contribution to the evolution of national policies on Education. While its comparative weakness as an institutional mechanism for the formulation and implementation of national policies in education is recognised, it has not yet been possible to find a better alternative solution to the problem.

Yet another administrative step taken is to create and strengthen national institutions which could educate public opinion, give guidance to State level personnel and provide advanced level training facilities. It is from this point of view that Central institutions like the National Council of Educational Research and Training (NCERT), the National Staff College of Educational Planners and Administrators, the Central Institute of English and Foreign Languages, the Central Institute of Hindi, Central Hindi Directorate, the Central Institute of Indian Languages, and the Central Sanskrit Organisation were created. This programe has yielded some good results but we are far from realising, the full potential of this strategy.

## References

Jayant Pandurang Nayaka, Syed Nurullah (1974), *A students' history of education in India (1800-1973)*, Macmillan.

Manoranjan Mohanty (2004), *Class, caste and gender: Volume 5 of Readings in Indian government and politics*, SAGE.

Jean Drèze, Amartya Sen (2002), *India: development and participation*, Oxford University Press,

UNESCO Education Sector, (2004) *The Plurality of Literacy and its implications for Policies and Programs: Position Paper*. Paris: United National Educational, Scientific and Cultural Organisation.

# 11

# Evolution of Modern Education System

India made its tryst with destiny on 15th August 1947. Independence meant the important task of rebuilding the nation and in this, education had an important place. It convened two conferences in January 1948, within a few months from attaining Independence viz. The Conference of the Central Advisory Board of Education (CABE) and an All India Conference of Provincial Ministers of Education. At these Conferences, consideration was given to urgent educational problems confronting independent India and some important and far- reaching decisions were made including the one of attainment of compulsory basic education.

Following independence in 1947, Maulana Azad, India's first education minister envisaged strong central government control over education throughout the country, with a uniform educational system. However, given the cultural and linguistic diversity of India, it was only the higher education dealing with science and technology that came under the jurisdiction of the central government. The government also held powers to make national policies for educational development and could regulate selected aspects of education throughout India.

At the time of Independence, there were 1,40,794 Primary schools (1,26,982 for boys and 13,812 for girls), each school serving an area of approximately 5 miles; there were 12,899 middle/secondary schools (11,081 for boys and 1,818 for girls), there were 20 Universities and 591 colleges (459 Arts and Science colleges and 132 professional). The enrolment in primary schools stood at 115.38 latch

(84.28 lakh boys and 31.10 lakh girls) representing 36.3% of the school-going population at the primary school stage (6 to 11 years). The literacy percentage in accordance with the census data of 1951 was 16.67% only (24.95% for male and 7.93% for female). Thus, the education system was beset with a number of problems e.g. fewer educational institutions, regional imbalance, gender disparities, absence of vocational and technical education, lack of uniform curricula and an emphasis on English education in the main.

The need for a literate population and universal education were given due recognition during the freedom struggle. Mahatma Gandhi while leading the freedom struggle against colonial rule advocated basic education and proposed an alternative village and community based system of education.

The adoption of the 1968 Policy, which was based on the recommendations of the Education Commission (1964-66), marked a significant step in the history of education in post-Independence India. Since then, there has been a considerable expansion in the educational facilities all over the country at all levels. While several prominent educational institutions were established in different parts of the country, particular attention was paid to the creation of basic educational facilities in the rural areas. Efforts were also initiated to adopt a common structure of education throughout the country and to lay down a common scheme of studies for boys and girls.

While these achievements were impressive by themselves. the general formulations incorporated in the 1968 Policy neither, got translated into a detailed strategy of implementation nor, were accompanied by the assignment of specific responsibilities and financial and organisational support. Problems of access, quantity, quality, relevance and financial outlay, as a result, accumulated over the years.

It was in response to this that the new National Policy on Education (NPE) was adopted in May, 1986 after a comprehensive appraisal of the existing educational scenario. The Policy laid great emphasis on developing a national system of education, the elimination of disparities in the educational system and provision of more facilities through qualitative interventions. It proposed to decentralise educational administration with a view to make it more responsive to the needs of the people.

One of the significant aspects of the NPE, 1986 is the greater concern for the empowerment of women, and access to education to disadvantaged sections of the society, educationally backward minorities and the disabled. The Policy gave added impetus to the launching of a large-scale programe of non-formal education, boldly acknowledging that the school system cannot reach all children. In order to nurture rural talent, the establishment of Navodaya Vidyalayas (model schools) with residential facilities, was also part of the NPE, 1986. It also called for greater rigour and discipline in academic pursuits, autonomy and accountability, experimentation and innovation, nurture of excellence and modernisation of processes at different levels of education.

The NPE, 1986 in consonance with the earlier Policy, also proposed that the implementation of its various parameters be reviewed every five years. It also called for appraisals at short intervals to "ascertain the progress of implementation and the trends emerging from time to time." Accordingly, a review of the 1986 Policy was conducted during 1990-92. The review broadly endorsed the National Policy on Education (1986). Based on an in-depth review of the whole gamut of educational situation and formulated on the basis of national consensus, the NPE enunciated a comprehensive framework to guide the development of education in its entreaty. While that framework continues to be of relevance, the development during the last few years and the experience gained in the implementation of the Policy had necessitated certain modifications. These modifications were introduced in May, 1992.

Universalisation of elementary education, equalisation of educational opportunities, women's education and development, vocationalisation of secondary education, consolidation of higher education, modernisation of technical education, improvement of quality, content and process of education at all levels continue to be the themes of national endeavour in the field of education. One of the significant changes is that the focus in elementary education has now shifted from enrolment, per se, to retention and achievement.

The revised Policy resolves to ensure "that free and compulsory education of satisfactory quality is provided to all children upto 14 years of age before we enter the twenty-first century." In order to achieve this a national mission is proposed to be launched for the achievement of this goal. In fact, the experience of the National Literacy Mission has proved that the mission mode is the most effective strategy for achieving total literacy. The total literacy campaigns will be the means for achieving total adult literacy. The revised policy formulations have also extended the scope of vocational education by including generic vocational courses.

Consequent on revision of the Policy, the Government also prepared a revised Programe of Action (POA) in August, 1992. The POA, 1992 emphasises that the first and the foremost task is to reform the management of education and calls for developing an ethos of cost effectiveness and accountability at all levels of educational planning and administration. It advocates that efficiency should be rated not by the ability to consume budget and demand more but by performance and delivery. The POA envisages preparation of action plans at the state and district levels in tune with the situational imperative.

The POA calls for launching a national mission to ensure the achievement of universalisation of elementary education by the year 2000 as set out in the modified Policy. It has also proposed alternative channels of schooling like voluntary schools and non-formal education centres for those who cannot attend conventional full-time schools. It has suggested improvement of facilities in schools through revamped Operation Blackboard to be extended to upper primary stage. The POA notes that the total literacy campaign has emerged as a viable model. It has transformed the perception of universal adult literacy from one of the hopeless dreams to an achievable prospect.

The POA perceives the problem of universalisation of elementary education as, in essence, the problem of the girl child and stresses the need to increase participation of girls at all stages of education, particularly in streams like science, vocational, technical and commerce education where girls are grossly under-rated. The POA stresses the need for re-orienting the education system to promote women's equality and education. It advocates need for institutional mechanism to ensure that gender sensitivity is reflected in the implementation of all national programes. It also calls for curbing the unplanned proliferation of sub-standard institutions.

## EDUCATIONAL PLANNING

The Constitution of India places Education in the concurrent list. The NPE 1986 explains the concept of concurrency as a meaningful partnership involving "a new sharing of responsibility between the Union Government and the States in respect of this vital area of national life. This concept enables the Centre and the States to make concerted efforts for the development of education maintaining a broad uniformity in standards and structures.

Educational planning in the country is essentially the joint endeavour of the Central and the State Governments. The Planning Commission at the Centre and the State Planning Departments decide the policy and approach to be adopted. At the Central level a planning and monitoring division in the Department of Education (DOE) works in close liaison with the education division of the Planning Commission.

Actions related to education at the national level including planning and policy-making are guided and coordinated by the Central Advisory Board of Education (CABE), the members of which include Ministers of Education of all States and Union Territories and leading educationists of the country. A few national level institutions specialising in particular aspects of education, assist and advise the Central and State Governments in the formulation and implementation of policies and programes in their respective areas. Special mention may be made in this regard, of organisations such as the National Institute of Educational Planning and Administration, the National Council of Educational Research and Training and the University Grants Commission.

### Organisation and Structure of the Education System

Decisions regarding the organisation and structure of education are largely the concern of the States. Within the overall policy framework, each State independently determines the educational structure to be adopted, particularly at the school stage.

Some variations can be found in the educational structure within the school stage. The primary and upper primary or middle stages together constitute the elementary stage. It has been envisaged that there should be a common structure for the elementary stage consisting of 5 years of primary schooling followed by 3 years of upper primary/ middle school education. It is visualised that the States where the first ten years are divided into four years of primary, three years of upper primary and three years of secondary schooling, will attempt to switch over to 5+3+2 pattern by 1995. At present, corresponding to the number of years spent at the elementary stage, the secondary stage consists of 2 to 3 years of schooling which marks the completion of the ten years of general education programe.

After the age of 14 years, a child can either join the secondary school providing general education programes or alternatively a vocational school or an Industrial Training Institute which equips her/ him with specialised vocational skills. A person who completes 10 years of general education has similar choice either to take up academic courses at the higher secondary level preparing to join collegiate education or opt for vocational streams within the higher secondary programe or through specialised institutions such as Polytechnics and Industrial Training Institutes. Completion of higher secondary education qualifies the individual for entering first degree programes. Admission to professional courses such as engineering and medicine, at this stage, is highly competitive. Even demand for admission to different programes in arts, science and commerce fields vary considerably.

## Institutions and Coverage

During the period between 1950-51 and 1990-91, the number of primary and upper primary level institutions grew from 223 thousand to about 705 thousand, registering more than a three-fold increase. In terms of the overall growth rate, the increase was to the tune of percent for primary level and percent for upper primary level institutions.

## Enrolment and Retention

In terms of growth of enrolment, the period since 1947 could be divided into two phases. The first phase corresponds to the period beginning with the fifties and ending with the seventies. It was characterised by the gradual slowing down of growth rates. The second phase corresponds to the eighties, characterised by an upswing in enrolment coverage.

For primary education, the annual growth rate for the fifties was percent which declined to percent in the sixties and percent in the seventies. During the eighties, however, the enrolment growth rates increased to percent. Beginning with 1980-81 and up to 1990-91 the data indicate a siginficant increase in enrollments at all levels. This is more pronounced at the secondary level, followed by upper primary and primary levels respectively, indicative of the intensity of the thrust, resulting from the expanding base of the educational hierarchy.

The proportion of children moving up from the primary to upper primary level has been increasing. This inter-stage transition was 1 percent in 1950-51; 1 percent in 1960-61; 2 percent in 1970-71; 2 percent in 1980-81 and in 1990-91 it reached 3 percent. However, in spite of the increase in inter-stage transition ratio, the absolute number of dropouts, or those not continuing in the system, is much larger.

Another important facet of expenditure on education which the POA, 1992 has highlighted is the increased strees on cost-effectiveness. It is increasingly being realised that "Progress should cease to be driven by budgets and instead should stress process and outcomes; efficiency should be rated not by the ability to consume budget and demand more but by the performance and delivery." There is an emerging consensus that the failure to achieve Universalisation of Elementary Education is more due to systemic deficiencies than due to resources per se. The systemic deficiencies are being remedied to ensure better cost effectiveness.

## Trends and Perspectives

The Government of India, in August this year brought out a detailed plan of action entitled 'Programe of Action, 1992' (POA) translating the National Policy on Education, 1986 as modified in 1992, into concrete action points. While delineating We future course of action, POA recapitulates aria analyses the past experience and presents the current situation.

### Early Childhood Care and Education

The National Policy on Education (NPE) has given a great deal of importance to Early Childhood Care mid Education (ECCE). It views

ECCE as a crucial input in the strategy of human resource development (HRD), as a feeder and support programe for primary education and as a support service for working women of the disadvantaged sections of the society. It has also taken into account the holistic nature of ECCE and has pointed out the need for organising programes for the all-round development of the child. It specifically focuses on the need for early care and stimulation of children belonging to the vulnerable sections of the society. Since the age span covered by ECCE is from conception to 6 years, emphasis has been given to a child centred approach, play way and activity based learning in place of formal methods of teaching and early introduction of the three R's. The importance of community involvement has also been highlighted. Emphasis has been given to establishing linkages between Integrated Child Development Service (ICDS) and other ECCE programes. The Revised Policy Formulations reiterate the postulates of NPE, 1986 on ECCE. The existing ECCE programes include:

*(i)* ICDS.

*(ii)* Scheme of assistance to voluntary organisations for conducting Early Childhood Education (ECE) centres.

*(iii)* Balwadis and day-care centres run by voluntary agencies with Government's assistance.

*(iv)* Pre-primary schools run by the State Governments, Municipal Corporations and other governmental and non-governmental agencies.

*(v)* Material and child health services through primary health centres, subcentres and other agencies.

ICDS is currently the biggest programe of early childhood development, with 290 thousand Anganwadis serving nearly 14 million children and about million mothers; 9 percent ICDS projects are located in rural and tribal areas and percent in urban slums. Besides the ICDS, by the end of 1991-92, there were 12,470 creches with a coverage of about 300 thousand children below 5 years, 4395 ECE centres in 9 Educationally Backward (EB) States and the Balwadi Nutrition Programe serving nearly 230 thousand children in the age-group of 3-5 years. The aim of ECCE is dig every child should be assured access to the fulfilment of all basic needs. As such efforts will be made towards universalisation of ICDS by A.D. 2000. Over the recent years, a number of initiatives have been taken to make the programes more specific. These *inter alia*, include training for the personnel, revision of the content of the programes, provision of adequate instructional and play materials and enlisting community and parental participation wherever possible in resource mobilisation, planning and implementation.

**Elementary Education**

Provision of free and compulsory education to all children until they complete the age of 14 years is a Directive Principle of the Constitution of India. Since 1950 determined efforts have been made towards the achievement of this goal. Over the years there has been an impressive increase in the number and spread of institutions as well as enrolment rates. Universal provision of institutions has been substantially achieved at the primary stage. According to the Fifth AR India Educational Survey (1986), 9 percent of the rural population had primary schools/sections within a walking distance of 1 km. and 8 percent of the rural population was served with middle schools/ sections within a walking distance of 3 km.

Universalisation of Elementary Education (UEE) in its totality is still an elusive goal and much ground is yet to be covered. Dropout rates continue to be significant. retention of children in schools is low and wastage considerable. In 1987-88, drop-out rates were 4 percent in classes IN and 6 percent in classes I-VIII. Despite increased participation of girls, disparity still exists. Though the participation of girls in primary education (classes IN) increased from 2 percent in 1950-51 to 4 percent in 1990-91, it was still below the normative percentage of about 50 percent. The participation of girls in upper primary classes (classes VI-VIII) was lower, it increased from 1 percent in 1950-51 to 3 percent in 1990-91. The participation of SCs and STs is now more or less in proportion to their share in population at the primary level, but the sex disparity persists among SCs and STs. In classes IN, SC girls account for 3 percent of SC students and in classes VI-VIII 3 percent (1990-91). The corresponding percentages of ST girls are 3 percent and 3 percent respectively.

The NPE, 1986, and its POA gave unqualified priority to UEE and introduced many innovations. First, the emphasis was shifted from enrolment *per se* to enrolment as well as retention. As the POA, 1986 put it crisply "enrolment by itself is of little importance if children do not continue beyond one year, many of them not seeing the school for more than a few days." Secondly, the NPE, 1986 sought to adopt an array of meticulously formulated strategies based on micro-planning, and applied at the grass root level all over the country, to ensure children's retention at school. POA, 1986 sought to replace enrolment drives by participative planning in which the teachers and the villagers would formulate family-wise and child-wise design of action to ensure that every child regularly attended school or non-formal education centre and completed at least five years of schooling or its nonformal equivalent. Thirdly, the NPE, 1986 recognised that unattractive school environment, unsatisfactory condition of buildings and insufficiency of instructional material function as demotivating factors for children and their parents. The Policy, therefore, called for a drive for a substantial improvement of primary schools and provision of support services.

The scheme of Operation Blackboard was conceived to meet this challenge. The launching of this scheme has greater significance in that it was a manifestation of the Union's intent to shoulder its sham of responsibilities in this vital area of national life, a responsibility arising from Education being in the Concurrent List. Fourthly, the NPE, 1986 commended the adoption at the primary stage of a child-centred and activity-based process of learning. Fifthly, the NPE, 1986 and its POA postulated a large programe of restructuring of teacher education, preservice as well as in-service.

Last but the most important, the NPE, 1986 sought to address the most difficult aspect of access, viz., access to education for millions of girls and working children who, because of socioeconomic compulsions, cannot participate in school system. As rightly pointed out by the NPERC, it was for the first time, in 1986, that an educational policy had admitted that the school would not reach all children and that a large and systematic programe of Non-Formal Education (NFE) has to be an integral component of the strategy to achieve UEE. NFE, as envisaged by the NPE, 1986 and its POA, would have enough flexibility to enable the learners to learn at their own pace and at the same time would have quality comparable with formal education.

Most of the directives of NPE and POA, 1986 have been operationalised by the Union and States/UTs. The number of primary schools has increased from 529 thousand in 1985-86 to 558 thousand in 1990-91; and the number of upper primary schools has increased from 135 thousand to 146 thousand during the same period. By March, 1992, Operation Blackboard covered 414 thousand (77%) schools in 5385 (84%) Community Development Blocks and 1142 (29%) Municipal areas. Owing to resource constraint all the primary schools of the country could not be covered as envisaged. About 70,000 (46%) teachers have been appointed as against 152 thousand single teacher schools identified for coverage. Over 100 thousand (43%) class rooms have been constructed as against the target of 239 thousand. Following the guidelines in the National Curricular Framework, the National Council of Educational Research and Training (NCERT) revised the entire school syllabi and brought out revised textbooks for classes I to XII. Based on the National Curricular Framework and the NCERT syllabi/textbooks, the States have also undertaken measures of curriculum renewal and development of new textbooks for different stages of school education for their introduction into the school system in a phased manner.

Guidelines for operationalising microplanning have been prepared and distributed to the State Governments. The concept of microplanning and local level capacity building have been given currency and efforts launched to decentralise educational planning and management vide new schemes or experimental projects. The resulting impact of these measures is expected to be felt during the coming years.

A positive externality, rather unanticipated, of the Total Literacy Campaigns, has been that in many districts covered by the campaign an upsurge in the demand for primary education is noticeable. In quite a few districts "out of school" children in the age group 914 were covered by the campaigns. Further, in these districts the awareness generated among parents is leading to better participation of children in primary schools. This pleasant experience has reconfirmed the need to pay more attention to the "demand side" in strategies for achieving UEE and highlighted the need for a disaggregated approach to the problem of UEE whereby districts, not States, and specific disadvantaged groups the girls of SCs and STs should become the basis for future planning.

Significant developments have taken place in the area of learner achievement. The NPE, 1986 spells out the Minimum Levels of Learning (MLL) and states that "to promote equality it will be necessary to provide equal opportunity to all not only in access but also in the condition for success. Besides, awareness of the inherent equality of all will be created through the core curriculum. Minimum Levels of Learning will be laid down for each stage of education." In pursuance of this policy and based on the report of a Committee appointed by the Ministry of HRD in 1990 and the recommendations of the Central Advisory Board of Education (CABE), MLL had been laid down for the primary stage with the intention of reducing the curriculum load and making it more relevant and functional for those children who have no support for learning at home or outside the school, who are not likely to avail of the opportunity of education beyond this stage and who must learn here what is required to sustain them throughout their lives and enable them to function in their world as socially useful and contributing individuals. It is now acknowledged that UEE cannot be accepted as having been achieved unless children passing out of school acquire MLL. Achievement has come to be assigned equal importance alongwith access and retention.

Another important development was the World Conference on Education for All (EFA) held in March 1990, in Jomtien, Thailand. The Conference was organised by UNESCO, UNICEF, UNDP and the World Bank and attended by 155 member states of United Nations and several donor agencies. The Conference adopted a declaration calling upon all member states and international agencies to take effective steps for achieving EFA by the year A.D. 2000. The Conference advocated a holistic concept of basic education in lieu of a pectoral approach segregating sections like Primary Schooling, Non-formal Education, Adult and Continuing Education in separate compartments. In order to homes increased donor interest in the basic education, as a result of the Conference, it was decided to formulate comprehensive basic education projects in educationally backward States.

The failure to universalise elementary education and literacy is not only a question of lack of resources but also of systemic deficiencies. The additional resources that may be available under external assistance should, therefore, be used for educational reconstruction which should go beyond the conventional measures such as opening new schools, construction of school buildings and appointing teachers. It is necessary to adopt a holistic approach, and to address:

*(i)* the educational needs of the working children, girls and disadvantaged groups, and

*(ii)* issues of content, process and quality.

Projects should also be used to develop sustainable and replicable models in different programes related to basic education. Therefore, these projects should be developed and implemented in the true spirit of meaningful participation between the Centre and States as envisaged in NPE. It would also be necessary to implement these projects in a mission mode with effective and participative management structures and with involvement of local community, teachers and NGOs.

Two such externally assisted projects, viz., the Bihar Education Project with UNESCO assistance and the Lok Jumbish Project in Rajasthan with the assistance of Swedish International Development Agency have been launched. The CABE further decided that project formulation should be a process of capacity building.

While reiterating the priority for UEE as well as the policy frame outlined by NPE, 1986, the Revised Policy Formulations (RPF) brought about following modifications:

*(i)* Achieving essential levels of learning has been specifically incorporated as one of the thrust areas in para 5.5; this is a logical consequence of the increasing importance that came to be attached to MLL alongwith access and retention.

*(ii)* Scope of Operation Blackboard (OB) has been enlarged to provide three reasonably large rooms and three teachers in every primary school; it has also been decided to extend OB to the upper primary stage.

*(iii)* It has been specifically laid down that at least 50 percent of the teachers recruited in future should be women.

*(iv)* Taking a realistic view of the enormous task of achieving UEE in its entirety (access, retention as well as achievement), the RPF envisage that free and compulsory education of satisfactory

quality should be provided to all children upto 14 years of age before the commencement of the twenty-first century.

*(v)* Taking note of the effectiveness of the Mission mode in social sectors, particularly literacy, the RPF envisage launching of a national mission to ensure the achievement of UEE by the year 2000.

In the Eighth Plan the strategy for UEE envisages adoption of disaggregated target setting and decentralised planning. An analysis of the educational indicators reveals that within each State, even in the educationally backward ones, there are areas and districts which are almost within reach of universalisation, while even in the educationally advanced States there are districts which are still quite backward. The attempt, therefore would be to prepare district specific and population-specific plans for UEE within the broad strategy frame of Microplanning through people's participation and introduction of Minimum Levels of Learning (MLL) in schools to improve learner achievement. Microplanning will provide the framework for universal access and universal participation while MLL would be the strategy frame for universal achievement.

In order to reduce disparities a disaggregated approach will be adopted through district planning by classifying districts into four categories:

*(i)* High literacy districts in which access and enrolment are almost universal and community awareness for education is already high;

*(ii)* Total literacy campaign districts in which community mobilisation for educational needs has been successfully generated by the National Literacy Mission;

*(iii)* Low literacy districts in which the provision of education facilities is unsatisfactory and the delivery system functions without any community involvement; and

*(iv)* Externally assisted project districts with a different management structure and sufficient financial support.

The strategies with regard to access, participation, achievement, environment building, community participation, etc. will be different for these four categories of districts. Under this broad strategy of district planning and based on the experience gained in implementation of NPE, and the RPF, the following strategies are proposed:

*(i)* Adoption of alternative channels of schooling like voluntary schools and NFE centres for those who cannot avail of conventional full-time schooling.

*(ii)* Microplanning through involvement of teachers and the community in order to design and implement a familywise, child-wise plan of action for universal access/enrolment and participation.

*(iii)* Making parents aware about their responsibility for ensuring the completion of elementary education by their children and for providing at home the facilities and encouragement needed for this purpose.

*(iv)* Establishment of linkages between programes of pre-school and primary education, and between programes of literacy and UEE, in total literacy campaign districts.

*(v)* Improvement of school facilities through revamped Operation Blackboard and connecting it to MLL strategy. It will also be extended to upper primary stage.

*(vi)* Decentralisation of educational management for making the schools function so as to ensure universal enrolment, retention and achievement.

*(vii)* Introduction of MLLs at primary and upper primary stages including coverage of the non-formal education channel..

*(viii)* Revision of process and content of elementary education to make teaching-learning child centred, activity based and joyful.

*(ix)* Introduction of continuous and comprehensive evaluation with focus on remedial measures.

*(x)* Modification of teacher training programes in view of changed strategies and programes.

*(xi)* Improvement of the monitoring system for UEE.

*(xii)* Launching a National Mission to achieve the goals envisaged in the revised Policy.

Further efforts would be made to develop district specific projects, with specific activities, clearly defined responsibilities, definite time-schedule and specific targets. Each district project will be prepared within the major strategy framework and will be tailored to the specific needs and possibilities in the district. Apart from effective UEE, the goals of each project will include the reduction of existing disparities in educational access, the provision of alternative systems of comparable standards to the disadvantaged groups, a substantial improvcment in the quality of schooling facilities, obtaining a genuine community involvement in the running of schools, and building up local level capacity to ensure effective decentralisation of educational planning. That is to say, the overall goal of the project would be reconstruction of primary education as a whole in selected districts instead of a piecemeal implementation of schemes. An integrated approach is more likely to achieve synergies among different programe components.

**Non-formal Education**

The role of non-formal part-time education in providing education to working children, and children in habitations without schools has been recognised since the Education Commission of 1964-66. During 1979-80, the scheme of Non-Formal Education (NFE) was introduced as an alternative strategy to impart education to children, who for various reasons cannot attend formal schools. The NPE envisaged a large and systematic programe of NFE to achieve UEE. The scheme was revised in its content and emphasis in 1987-88. Although its focus is on the ten educationally backward States, namely, Andhra Pradesh, Arunachal Pradesh, Assam, Bihar, Jammu & Kashmir, Madhya Pradesh, Orissa, Rajasthan, Uttar Pradesh and West Bengal, it has been extended to cover urban slums, hilly, tribal and desert areas and areas with concentration of working children in the other States as well. Financial responsibility is borne by the Central and State Governments in the ratio of 50:50 for general (co-educational) and 90:10 for girls NFE centres. Assistance to the extent of 100 percent is provided to voluntary agencies for running NFE centres and for experimental and innovative projects.

The (revised) NFE scheme has been visualised as child-centred, environmentoriented, flexible system to meet the educational needs of the comparatively deprived geographical areas and socio-economic sections of the society. Other features of the scheme are its organisational flexibility, relevance of curriculum, diversity in learning activities to relate them to the learner's needs and decentralised management. The programe is being implemented on a project basis, generally co-terminus with the community development Block comprising about 100 NFE Centres.

In order to strengthen the NFE Scheme the following strategies are being adopted:

*(i)* Provision of NFE centres will be based on the Microplanning exercise carried out for UEE. NFE centres will invariably cater to the needs of children, especially girls, who are not able to or who cannot attend the formal school.

*(ii)* The community will be involved in ate setting-up, and supervision of all NFE centres.

*(iii)* The NFE instructors will be identified with the help of the community. Special efforts will be made to appoint women instructors wherever possible.

*(iv)* Training of NFE personnel, especially instructors, will be given top priority. Adequate training and re-orientation will, be provided.

*(v)* Training responsibility will be shared by the project, District level institutions like DIETs, DRUs, State level institutions like SCERT, and National institutes like NCERT and NIEPA.

*(vi).* Project administration will be strengthened for effective decentralisation of management. Necessary administrative and management inputs will be provided at the State and District levels.

*(vii)* Arrangements will be made for testing of children in the NFE stream with reference to an equivalent Stage in the formal system and specific instructions issued to facilitate lateral entry into the formal system for students of the NFE stream.

*(viii)* Efforts will be made Lo link non-formal courses with the Open Schools.

*(ix)* The NFE programe will be linked with the scheme of public libraries, Jana Shiksha Nilayams, etc.

*(x)* In total literacy campaign districts follow-up programes will be taken up for children in the agegroup 9-14 to go beyond NLM literacy norms. This will form apart of the post-literacy and continuing education programe of the district.

*(xi)* Vocational and technical courses of wide variety will be provided for children and youth who pass out of the Non-Formal stream. Shramik Vidyapeeth and Vountary agencies will be involved in this process.

*(xii)* Voluntary agencies will be encouraged to undertake projects of NFE, especially in areas where the formal school system is not able to meet the demands of UEE.

**Adult Literacy**

The National Literacy Mission (NLM) which was launched on 5th May, 1988, with the objective of imparting functional literacy to 80 million adult illiterates in the age-group 15-35 by 1995 has entered its fifth year of operationalisation. The Mission has confirmed in more than one sense that eradication of illiteracy is not a utopian idea but something which is possible, feasible and achievable. The first positive indication came from the provisional figures of the 1991 census released by the Registrar General and the Census Commissioner of India. The literacy rate for the population aged 7 and above in the country increased from 4 percent in 1981 to 5 percent in 1991, registering an increase of percent. Whereas the male literacy in creased from 5 percent to 6 percent, the female literacy increased from 2 percent to 3 percent. For the first time, the country achieved the distinction of having larger number of literate persons (35 million) than the illiterate ones (32 million).

Several exciting and interesting developments have taken place in the area of literacy and adult education since the launching of National Literacy Mission in 1988 in general and the call for "Education for All" in the Jomtien World Conference held in March, 1990 in particular.

The mass campaign for eradication of illiteracy launched in Eranakulam district of Kerala in 1989, with the active involvement of persons of all walks of life, achieved significant success and the district achieved the distinction of becoming the first fully literate district in the country on 4th February, 1990. Encouraged by this success, Total Literacy Campaigns were launched to cover the entire States of Kerala and Goa and the Union Territory of Pondicherry. At present, 156 districts in the country are covered by the Total Literacy Campaigns either fully or partially. The entire State of Kerala, the Union Territory of Pondicherry, Burdwan and Midnapur districts in West Bengal, Bijapur and South Kannad district in Karnataka, Sindhudurg and Wardha districts in Maharashtra, Puddukottai and P.T.T. Sivaganga districts in Tamil Nadu have already concluded the Total Literacy Campaigns and have achieved success ranging between 65 to 75 percent. Other campaigns are in different stages of implementation.

The number of students participating in the National Literacy Mission crossed one million by 1991-92. All the other existing programes were also reviewed and revised to conform to the principle of area approach for total literacy. The thrust areas under the National Literacy Mission include continuous environment building conducive to literacy, use of IPCL (Increased Pace and Content of Learning) materials in all literacy programes and organisation of mass campaigns for total literacy in a definite timeframe as dominant strategy for eradication of illiteracy in all programes of adult education.

After experimenting with successive and alternative models of adult literacy, NLM has now settled down to a model which has given lot of hope and faith that illiteracy can be overcome in a time-bound manner with planned and co-ordinated efforts and with mobilisation of all sections of the society. In addition to 156 districts already covered by the Total Literacy Campaigns, 200 additional districts would be covered by such campaigns by the close of 1997-98.

The mass campaign approach is now accepted as a possible achievable and feasible approach. There is now an active and competitive participation of State Governments to take up the TLCs. The District Collectors who were primarily pre-occupied with problems of maintenance of law and order, peace and tranquility and implementation of government funded development programes and had hardly any acquaintance with the adult education programes, are now in the vanguard of TLCs and are providing the leadership, motivation, direction and organisational support for these campaigns.

The emphasis in adult literacy programe has completely shifted from mere enrolment of learners in the adult education centres in the traditional centre based approach, to attainment of certain predetermined levels of literacy and numeracy in a given area with a definite time frame. The basic features of this dominant strategy for eradication of illiteracy i.e. they being areaspecific, time-bound volunteer-based and result-oriented have been introduced in all other programes being undertaken for combating illiteracy in the country. Media is being involved in literacy promotion as a tool of dissemination of information, as a tool of mobilisation, motivation and sensitisation, as a tool of learning/sharing information, ideas and experiences, and as a tool of social action for change. Both print and non-print media including the traditional folk art forms are being harnessed in promoting literacy.

## Secondary Education

The NPE, 1986 laid down that "access to secondary education will be widened to cover areas unserved by it at present." There has been a significant increase in the number of secondary and higher secondary schools and in enrolment during the period from 1987-88 to 1990-91. During this period enrolment at secondary stage increased by 1percent and at the higher secondary stage by 1 percent. The number of secondary schools increased from 54,845 in 1987-88 to 59,468 in 1990-91; corresponding figures for higher secondary schools are 16,460 and 19,151 respectively. The ratio of secondary and higher secondary schools to upper primary schools had declined from 1:in 1987-88 to 1: in 1990-91.

Gender disparities in enrolments are significant. In 1990-91 girls accounted for 33 percent of the enrolment at the secondary stage and 32 percent at the higher secondary stage. The SCs and STs also lag behind in regard to enrolment. Thus, SCs account for 1percent at the secondary stage and percent at the higher secondary stage; corresponding figures for STs being percent and 3 percent respectively.

Though a considerable degree of uniformity has been achieved in regard to common education structure of 10+2+3, there is considerable diversity regarding the location of the +2 stage. In quite a few States it is not part of the school system.

The secondary stage is divided into two very distinct sub-stages secondary (upto class X) which is the stage of general education and higher secondary (classes XI and XII) which is marked by differentiation and diversification. The national system of education, as stated in the NPE, 1986 envisages a National Curricular Framework. Such a framework has already been prepared for the secondary education though its implementation has been uneven. The work of curriculum revision for the secondary stage was undertaken in almost all the States and the Union Territories (UTs). The NCERT also prepared the guidelines, syllabi and textbooks for all stages of school education. For the higher secondary stage, however, the Curricular Framework has not yet been authorised. The NCERT had developed a draft document in 1988 but that document requires to be reviewed keeping in view the emerging concerns. However, several States used the draft National Curricular Framework for the higher secondary stage prepared by the NCERT.

The Revised Policy Formulations take note of the increased demand for secondary education and go beyond NPE, 1986 by calling for a planned expansion of secondary education facilities all over the country. Secondly, they call for higher participation of girls, SCs and STs, particularly in science, vocational and commerce streams. Thirdly, they call for reorganisation of Boards of Secondary Education and vesting them with autonomy "so that their ability to improve the quality of secondary education is enhanced." Fourthly, they envisage that effort will be made to provide computer literacy in as many secondary level institutions as possible so that the children are equipped with necessary computer skills to be effective in the emerging technological world.

**Vocational Education**

The NPE, 1986 advocated a systematic, well-planned programe of vocational education which would be a distinct stream intended to prepare students for identified occupations. It envisaged that vocational courses would ordinarily be provided at the higher secondary (+2) stage but flexibility was provided to start vocational education after class VIII. The NPE, 1986 set a target to cover 10 percent of higher secondary students under vocational courses by 1990 and 25 percent by 1995. A substantially funded centrally sponsored scheme for vocationalisation of secondary education was started with effect from February 1988. The scheme was taken for implementation in all States and Union Territories excepting Tripura, Daman and Diu, Dadra & Nagar Haveli and Lakshadweep. At the end of 1991-92, 12,543 vocational sections were approved in 4400 schools, thereby creating facilities for diversion of about lakh students at the +2 stage. This accounts for percent of students enrolled at the +2 stage. Although quantitatively the implementation of the vocational education scheme at the +2 stage has been fairly substantial, in qualitative terms, there remains much to be done. Vocationalisation of education is identified as a priority area in the Eighth Five Year Plan.

The NPE, 1986 had also mentioned the need for non-formal and need-based vocational programes mainly, though not exclusively, for disadvantaged groups. The NPE, 1986 also envisaged vocational courses at the tertiary level for facilitating vertical mobility. While some beginning has been made in these areas, they will receive impetus during the Eighth Plan. The Revised Policy Formulations retain the policy framework laid by the NPE, 1986 but for two modifications. First, the target for coverage under vocational courses has been revised ten percent of the higher secondary students by 1995 and 25 percent by 2000. Secondly, they envisage children at the higher secondary level being imparted generic vocational courses which cut across several occupational fields and which are not occupation specific.

**Higher Education**

India today has one of the largest systems of higher education comprising over 190 Universities and 7,000 colleges having an enrolment of over million students with a 263 thousand strong faculty. Several important schemes have been introduced in the last few years to restore the integrity, discipline and credibility of the system and to elevate the standards of higher education in the country. The all-India screening test for recruitment of teachers introduced in December, 1989 continues.

A code of ethics and procedure for assessment and evaluation of teachers has been evolved. The system of Academic Staff Colleges for reorientation and refresher courses for teachers has been introduced. A beginning has been made for granting autonomy to selected colleges and university departments. Academic calendar has been prepared and would be continuously monitored. Andhra Pradesh has set tip a State Council of Higher Education and other States are considering setting up State Councils to coordinate development and growth of higher education in the States. Common research facilities of international standards in the fields of Nuclear Science, Astronomy, Astrophysics and Atomic Energy have been set up to provide research facilities and services. Model curricula for all disciplines have been prepared by expert committees and circulated to universities for adoption. Special assistance is being given for starting courses in emerging areas like Biotechnology, Aunospheric Science, Oceanography, Electronics and Computer Science. Finally alternate models of university management are also being considered.

The Indira Gandhi National Open University (IGNOU) which was established by an Act of Parliament in September, 1985 for the introduction and promotion of the Open University and distance education systems in the educational pattern of the country and for the coordination and determination of standards in such systems, has emerged as a strong alternative at the level of higher education. The IGNOU has adopted an integrated multimedia instructional approach consisting of printed material, audio and video cassettes and counselling sessions organised during the weekend.

In pursuance of its role as national apex body for promotion, coordination and determination of standards in distance education, IGNOU has set up a Distance Education Council (DEC) as a statutory authority of the University. The DEC is initiating steps for the establishment of a network of open universities and other distance education institutions in the country.

## Technical and Management Education

Technical education, which in our context also includes management education, is one of the most crucial components of human resource development with great potential for adding value to products and services and for improving the quality of life of the people. As a result of the efforts made during the successive Five Year Plans in the past on the development of technical education, the expansion of technical education in the country has been phenomenal during the past four decades.

There are, at present, over 200 recognised technical education institutions at the first degree level and more than 500 at the diploma level with the annual admission capacities of 40,000 and 80,000 students respectively. Facilities for Masters and Doctoral programes in engineering and technology have also been created in 140 institutions with an intake of about 10,000 students per year. Five Indian Institutes of Technology (IITs) established at Mumbai, Delhi, Kanpur, Kharagpur and Chennai have emerged as premier centres of technical education in India. The sixth IIT is in the process of being established at Guwahati in Assam. Specialised institutions like National Institute for Training in Industrial Engineering, National Institute of Foundry and Forge Technology, School of Planning and Architecture, Indian School of Mines, Technical Teachers' Training Institutes and premier technical universities like University of Roorkee, Anna University, Birla Institute of Technology (Pilani), Indian Institute of Science, Bangalore and Banaras Hindu University (Institute of Technology) are important centres of technical education.

In the area of management education, Indian Institutes of Management have been setup at Ahmedabad, Kalkata, Bangalore and Lucknow. Besides, there are more than 350 degree institutions and 800 diploma institutions at the State level. The National Technical Manpower Information System has been set up by the Government of India to monitor the supply and utilisation of engineering and technical manpower in the country so as to ensure a well planned development of technical education.

Some professional bodies in the fields of engineering, technology and management conduct formal and non-formal education/training programes for fresh students as well as the working professionals and also contribute to professional development in their respective areas of activities.

The NPE, 1986 underlined the need for reorganising the technical and management education system to effectively deal with the changes in the economy, social environment, production and management processes and rapid expansion of knowledge and advances in science & technology. The NPE, 1986 laid specific guidelines for the qualitative and quantitative development of the technical and management education sectors; establishment of linkages amongst the concerned agencies; manpower assessment and technical education forecasting; increasing effectiveness of technical education management system; proper delivery systems; measures to achieve greater cost effectiveness and generation of resources through suitable means.

The various initiatives taken after the NPE include:

*(i)* *AICTE*: As one of the most significant achievements in the sector of technical education, the All India Council of Technical Education (AICTE) was conferred statutory status under the AICTE Act in 1987. The Council has started functioning with an independent secretariat through the various Boards of Studies and the Regional Committees. There is, however, an urgent need to strengthen the AICTE in terms of its professional and administrative functions through a process of decentralisation.

*(ii)* *Scheme of Continuing Education:* The scheme was started through the Indian Society for Technical Education for upgrading the skills of working professionals under which more than 200 course modules were produced which provided training to about 10,000 working professionals.

*(iii)* *Industry Institute Interaction and Entrepreneurship and Management Development Programes:* A scheme of industry-institute interaction for forging effective and closer interaction between technical institutions and the industry was launched. This also included establishment of an industrial foundation at IIT, Delhi and technological transfer and innovation. A scheme of entrepreneurship development for catering to the developmental needs of the non-corporate and unorganised sectors was also launched through the technical institutions.

*(iv)* *Curriculum Development:* A scheme for restructuring the curriculum development centres was launched for effecting curriculum development on the basis of realistic needs of the industry and the users.

*(v)* *Strengthening the scheme of Modernisation and Removal of Obsolescence and Thrust Areas of Technical Education:* Greater emphasis was given for covering more institutions by modernising their laboratories, workshops and teaching processes and by adopting new emerging areas of engineering and technology. This, however, needs massive financial inputs

and a strong monitoring and evaluation system as compared to the one that exists.

(vi) *World Bank Assisted Projects for Development of Technician Education*: A massive project with the assistance of World Bank was launched to enable the State Governments to upgrade their polytechnics in capacity, quality and efficiency with the total cost of Rs. 1650 crore to be implemented in two phases (1992-98) with a target of covering 500 approved polytechnics in 16 States and one Union Territory.

(vii) *Review of IIMs and TTTIs:* The IIMs and the TTTIs were reviewed by two separate National Review Committees in order to assess the present status and impact so as to give them a new thrust and direction.

(viii) *Review of Community Polytechnics:* The Scheme of Community Polytechnics was reviewed by a National Expert Committee in terms of its impact, coverage and effectiveness on the socioeconomic upliftment and poverty alleviation. The number of Community Polytechnics was also substantially increased.

(ix) *Apprenticeship Training*: In order to provide training for the 10+2 vocational students under the amended Apprentices Act, additional vocational subjects were included under the purview of the Act.

**Open Education**

The open learning system augments opportunities for education, ensures access, is cost-effective and promotes a relevant, flexible and innovative system of education. The initial experience of the Indira Gandhi National Open University (IGNOU) and the State Open Universities, as well as the National Open School underlines the tremendous potential of the open learning system.

The IGNO which launched its academic programes in 1987 has made significant progress. The University presently offers Bachelor's degree programes in thirteen disciplines, a Master's degree in Business Administration, and several diploma and certificate programes. The annual enrolment has increased from about 4,400 in 1987 to over 62,000 in 1992. The three State Open Universities, namely, Dr. B.R. Ambedkar Open University in Andhra Pradesh

(BRAOU), the Kota Open University (KOU) and the Yashwantrao Chavan Maharashtra Open University in Maharashtra (YCMOU) together admitted about 65,000 students in 1992. The distance education institutions (open universities and institutes of correspondence education of conventional universities) accounted for about 1 percent of the enrolment in higher education in 1990-91.

Several new programes in employment-related areas are being developed by the IGNOU. Advanced Diploma programes in Construction Management, Advanced Diploma in Irrigation and Water Resources, Postgraduate Diploma in Journalism and Mass Communication, Bachelor's Degree in Nursing and Master's Degree in Distance Education and Library and Information Science are some of the new programes under development by the IGNOU. The State Open Universities have also launched a number of relevant programes in Electronics, Horticulture, Education and Communication besides the diploma and degree programes in Humanities, Commerce and Social Sciences. The Directorates of Correspondence Education of the conventional universities have also been diversifying their programes. These institutions are presently offering a large number of diploma and certificate programes in technical/professional areas.

The IGNOU has setup a Distance Education Council as a statutory body for the promotion, coordination and determination of standards of the open university/distance education system.

— The Distance Education Council will take steps for networking the State Open Universities and other distance education institutions, for sharing courses and programes, and developing a pattern and structure for the open university programes that would facilitate student mobility among programes as well as institutions.

— The open university/distance education programmes would be structured on a modular pattern with provision for transfer of credits. Students will have the facility of registering for courses of their choice which, in appropriate combinations, will enable them to obtain certificates, diplomas or degrees.

— The Distance Education Council will encourage joint development of programes and courses by IGNOU, State Open Universities and the Directorates of Correspondence Education of conventional universities.

— It will also recommend financial assistance from IGNOU to state open universities for their development and for undertaking specific projects.

The Distance Education Council will ultimately assume the responsibility for developing the existing correspondence education programes on a selective basis and converting them into distance education programes of an acceptable quality. However, for the time being, the responsibility for the development of distance education programes in the conventional universities will remain with the UGC. There would be close consultation between the UGC and the IGNOU in the development of such programes.

Electronic media will be progressively involved in the expansion of open learning. Doordarshan (Television) is already telecasting programes of the IGNOU three days a week for 30 minutes. The All India Radio (AIR) stations of Hyderabad and Bombay are broadcasting selected IGNOU programes. The Hyderabad station of All India Radio has setup a transmission network in Andhra Pradesh for broadcasting the programes offered by the BRAOU. A few of the institutes of correspondence education have made arrangements with the All India Radio for broadcasting their lessons. Distance education requires as a matter of prerequisite multimedia instruction and its success will substantially depend on the availability of facilities for broadcasting and telecasting. Efforts will be made during the Eighth Plan period to augment and network these facilities so that these programes can reach a larger number of students.

Measures will be taken to promote the mobility of students among open universities and among the traditional universities and open universities. A significant development in this regard is the signing of the Memorandum of Understanding between the University of Pondicherry and the IGNOU which provides for recognition of each other's degrees and diplomas as well as transfer of credits for courses successfully completed by students between the two universities. Efforts will be made to promote similar arrangements with other universities.

The National Open School (NOS) already established, will be strengthened and developed to widen access to education at the secondary and higher secondary levels. Efforts will be made to establish open schools in different States so that secondary education is significantly expanded through different regional languages.

The possibility of launching vocational education programes through the open learning system will be explored. For this purpose, meaningful linkages will be established with workstations, industries and other organisations. Such bilateral initiatives will help administer the theoretical and practical components of the vocational education packages.

The possibility of setting up a national consortium on open schooling will be explored in order to initiate coordinated steps in such areas as policy issues, priorities, long-term national and state needs, establishment of resource centres for development of materials, development of human resources for the open learning system, monitoring and evaluation of its performance, etc.

The open learning system at the secondary and tertiary levels will focus attention on education and training in areas related to employment and self-employment. It will seek the involvement of the existing institutions and organisations in commerce, industry, the service sectors as well as rural development organisations, including the mobilisation of the material and human resources in such organisations in the development of appropriate programes and their delivery. Efforts will be made to develop close co-operation and collaboration between open education institutions and the agencies which use trained manpower both in the public and the private sectors as well as the professional organisations in various fields.

The open learning system will take steps to meet the continuing education needs of the manpower already employed in different sectors. It will help develop programes in close cooperation with the concerned employing organisations; for training and retraining of manpower, for the upgradation of skills for application of new technologies and also in providing opportunities to serving personnel to improve their qualifications for their professional advancement.

## TEACHER EDUCATION

A Centrally sponsored scheme of Restructuring and Reorganisation of Teacher Education is being implemented since 1987-88. It aims at strengthening the teacher education system in the country so as to provide effective training and academic support to schools and adult and non-formal education systems. The centrally sponsored scheme of teacher education has the following main components.

Mass Orientation of about five lakh School Teachers (MOST) annually till 1989-90 to familiarise them with the major thrusts envisaged in the NPE and LO improve their professional competence.

Setting-up of about 400 District Institutes of Education and Training (DIETs) either by upgrading suitable existing Elementary Teacher Education Institutions or, where necessary, by establishing new ones so as to provide total academic and training support to the elementary and adult education systems at the district level:

— Strengthening of about 250 Secondary Teacher Education Institutions (STEIs), development of about 50 of them as Institutions of Advanced Study in Education (IASEs) and the rest as Colleges; of Teacher Education (CTEs);
— Strengthening of SCERTs; and
— Establishment and strengthening of Departments of Education in Universities by the UGC.

Setting up DIETs, CTEs and IASEs is a long-gestation activity. Yet, about 150 DIETs have become operational and have started conducting training programes. Appraisal of few such institutions sanctioned during 1987-88 is being undertaken through external agencies.

A National Council of Teacher Education was setup in 1973 to maintain standards of teacher education. The Council is being conferred statutory powers to enable it to discharge its responsibilities more effectively, including through accreditation of teacher training institutions.

## EDUCATION AND WOMEN'S EMPOWERMENT

Education for Women's Equality is a vital component of the overall strategy of securing equity and social justice in education. The National Policy on Education, 1986 makes a strong and forthright statement on the intervening and empowering role of education. It emphasises the provision of special support services and removal of factors which result in discrimination against women at all levels of education.

The Policy and Programe of Action brings out clearly the need and will to devise institutional mechanism in order to ensure that gender sensitivity is reflected in the implementation of educational programes across the board. Education for Women's Equality is too important to be left to the individual commitments or proclivities of persons in charge of implementing programes. Therefore all agencies and institutions in the field of education are to be made sensitive and responsive to the gender dimension of educational inequities.

Some of the special efforts made to promote education of girls are indicated below:

— Under the Scheme of Operation Blackboard, Government of India has provided assistance for creation of 93,303 posts of primary school teachers mainly to be filled by women. According to the latest reports, 69,926 posts of teachers have been filled up of which 4 percent are women teachers.

— Ninety percent assistance was given for NFE Centres meant for girls. The cumulative number of NFE Centres for girls is 81,282.

— The Mahila Samakhya (Education for Women's Equality) Project is under implementation in the States of Gujarat, Karnataka and Uttar Pradesh with the main objective of motivating women to participate in education and providing non-formal, adult and vocational education.

By conscious action, admission of girls to the extent of 28 percent in Navodaya Vidyalayas has been ensured.

At the level of higher education, both general and technical, there has been a phenomenal expansion of educational opportunities for women. The response of women to avail these growing opportunities has been overwhelming as reflected by the trend in women's enrolment in all faculties and at all levels of education. Women's education at the university and college levels has been diversified and re-oriented in tune with the changing requirements of society, industry and trade. More and more women have been competing for admission to specialist and professional courses year after year.

Women's enrolment in higher education institutions has grown from a mere million in 1950-51 to 1 million in 1990-91, recording an increase of more than 36 times over the 40 year period. The number of women enrolled, per 100 men enrolled, during this period has gone up more than 3 times from 14 in 1950-51 to 48 in 1990-91. The enrolment of women as percentage of total enrolment has increased progressively from 2 percent in 1981-82 to 2 percent in 1985-86 and to 3 percent in 1990-91. The number of colleges meant exclusively for women has also gone up from 644 in 1981-82 to 874 in 1990-91 recording an increase of over 35 percent during the decade.

The University Grants Commission is assisting universities in promoting Women's studies to undertake research projects, development of curricula, training and extension as a motivator for various adult education programes and as a critical instrument for social and academic development. The Commission has a Standing Committee on Women's Studies which reviews, advises and monitors the implementation of the Scheme.

## References

Geeta Gandhi Kingdon (March 2007), *The progress of school education in India*, Global Poverty Research Group, Economic and Social Research Council.

Jean Drèze, Amartya Sen (2002), *India: development and participation*, Oxford University Press.

Mahendra K. Premi, *India's Literacy Panorama, Seminar on the Progress of Literacy in India: What the 2001 Census Reveals*, Education for All in India.

Vanlalchhawna (2006), *Higher education in North-East India: unit cost analysis*, Mittal Publications.

# 12

# Educational Development: Theoretical Issues

The task before independent India was to remove the infirmities of the inherited structure of the educational system and transform it into a social force geared to the socioeconomic transformation of the Indian polity from colonial underdevelopment to self-reliant development. Within such a conceptual frame, education was conceived as being intertwined with the developmental process as one of its important components. It took quite some time to clearly outline the following multifaceted tasks:

— first, to quantitatively expand the inherited miniscule in such a manner that quality and quantity move together in symbiosis,

— second, to strengthen the linkage between education and the labour market and bridge the gap between work and knowledge,

— third, to evolve a desirable transition matrix within the educational sector– to universalise primary education, to vocationalise secondary education, to relate specialism to self-reliant development and to import substitution in the world of the intellect,

— fourth, to reduce regional disparities in the spread of education so as to make its benefits available to all regions of the country,

— fifth, to widen the socioeconomic base of the educational system through programes of protective discrimination as well as of proper incentives so as to reduce, and ultimately eliminate, the differentials between the scheduled and the non-scheduled, the

rural and the urban as well as the male and female population,
sixth, to transform the essentially teacher and teaching-oriented education into an essentially learning and learner-oriented education and to emphasise the creativity of the learner rather than the assimilation of "received" truth, and

— seventh, to develop education meaningfully in such a manner that it contributes to national integration, humanism and love for nature.

Let us critically assess the advances made in the achievement of the above objectives and the inadequacies of the national responses to the above tasks.

Since the advent of independence, this old but rejuvenated country embarked on its tryst with destiny and is currently engaged in modernising itself and building perhaps the largest and the most complex educational system in the world. Every sixth student in the world enrolled at the primary level, every seventh at the secondary level and every eighth at the tertiary level is an Indian. The number of students enrolled at the primary level is more than double the population of Spain and approximates three times the population of Canada. The number of students enrolled at the secondary level is roughly twice the population of Australia. The number of students enrolled at the higher level approximates the population of New Zealand. This number is 3.5 times the number of teachers in the USSR, six times that in the USA and nine times that in France. There are over 500,000 primary schools in India-more than 15 times that in the United Kingdom. The number of colleges in India is equal to the number of schools in Malaysia and approximates the population of Nauru. The large system is highly complex and is composed of institutions ranging from single teacher schools to universities with about three million students on their rolls, from schools moving with nomadic groups on camel backs to centres of scientific education and research which throw satellites into space.

The most critical weakness of the contemporary situation lies in the anaemic and dysfunctional linkage between education and the world of work and the consequent lack of correspondence between the output of the educational system and the inputs of the labour market. The Kothari Commission had particularly drawn attention to the importance of work experience, the transition from "the world of school to the world of work" and the development of requisite manpower for the country with practical training in industry as an integral part of education.

The introduction of 'SUPW' (Socially Useful Productive Work) as a third dimension and as a qualitatively new approach to education was expected, in the words of the Patil Committee, "to occupy the central place in the school curriculum". In spite of the great hopes that were linked with this innovation, those who are aware of the ground realities are highly critical of its net outcome. It has been observed that quite often the SUPW has been reduced to a ritual and is, not rarely, handled by a group of teachers who impart only some of their own prejudices against work to the students. Some critics have, perhaps uncharitably, stated that the acronym 'SUPW' in practice stands for "Some Useful Periods Wasted". The vocationalisation of secondary education has met with no greater success. It has been said that there has been vocalisation about vocationalisation in the country, rather than vocationalisation itself. The most painful aspect of the situation is that, though the Union Government has been the initiator and the principal advocate of vocationalisation, it has hardly found a significant place in either the Kendriya Vidalayas or the schools under the Central Board of Secondary Education. Till a few year back, only 1.2 percent of the students at the higher secondary stage were found to have offered vocational courses.

In spite of the progress made in the quantitative expansion of education and the narrowing of the gaps between different social groups, inequities within the educational system of the country continue to be quite sharp. While the literacy rate for non-scheduled urban population in Ernakulam district of Kerala is 83.30 percent, it is heartening to note that Ernakulam has not the unique honour of having achieved 100% literacy the same for the Scheduled Tribe women in rural areas of Jhabua district of Madhya Pradesh is only 0.96 percent. Inequities get compounded in the case of the Scheduled Caste women in the rural areas of the backward regions. The end product of layer upon layer of inequities is a malignancy which is rendering Indian education into an anaemic and diseased orgainsm.

The relative deprivation of women in the field of education is particularly significant because it underlines all other attributes of deprivation. The Scheduled Castes are deprived no doubt; but scheduled caste women are more deprived than their man folk, the rural population is deprived no doubt but the rural women are more deprived than their menfolk. A movement for women's education in the Indian social context is, therefore, very much more than a movement for women's education. It strikes at the very roots of the parasitic system of social inequities intertwining with the Indian polity, continuously sucking out blood and rendering it anaemic and weak. Women's education is an instrument for the liberation not only of women but of the Indian society as a whole.

The national component in the Indian educational system has been considerably eroded under parochial pressures. The fragmented system has become a serious constraint on the inter-regional mobility of manpower. The 10+2+3 system wits introduced on the basis of a national consensus. It is, therefore, unfortunate that it has taken more than a decade to implement it in all the states. The introduction of the core national curriculum in the school system is still a dream.

Regionalism, communalism and casteism still get reflected in the school textbooks both explicitly and implicitly. This is particularly true in the history and geography curriculum. "Hindu" period or the "Muslim" period of history still continue to haunt the history classrooms. Chauvanist and parochial statements and attitudes sow prejudices in the minds of the young, which later on germinate and produce strains and stresses in the polity. Geography textbooks are replete with environmental determinist explanations. National resources are presented as regional and an approach is inculcated among the young to view resource development not within the frame of a territorial division of labour in the national economy but as resource utilisation within a number of separate closed systems.

The vast system of education continues to be essentially teaching and teacher oriented. The learning process has yet not come to acquire the central focus of the pedagogic exercise. The creativity of the young, which is the basic instrument of history, has yet not been given the attention that it deserves. The end-of-term external examination continues to be the most dominant element on the academic scene, disrupting the learning process and rendering a large portion of pedagogy as essentially dysfunctional. "Covering the syllabus", dictating notes or writing "made-easy" books, is becoming a substitute for the Socratic tradition. Searching for hints, mugging up answers to "expected" questions, using unfair means in the examination are becoming a substitute for learning. The "abolition" of the examination system at many stages in the school has thrown the baby with the bath water. At the university level, all attempts to introduce examination reforms have unfortunately met with a dismal failure. The external and essentially dysfunctional examination continues to be the be-all and end-all of most of our educational endeavours.

## Issues of Unity in Diversity

The social ethos of India reflects a high degree of unity in diversity. The factors that have led to the emergence of this unique feature of the Indian polity are not far to seek. We shall examine the spatial aspects of the ethos, by identifying, on the one hand, the factors leading to regional differentiation and diversities, and, on the other, the factors which operate as bonds of unity. Let us examine the factors that operationalise differentiation in the Indian space.

First, the large geographical spread of the sub-continent provides fertile ground for the germination and flowering of regional diversities in the social mileu. India is the seventh largest country in the world, approximating in size with the continent of Europe minus the USSR. It would have been surprising indeed, if the degree of regional differentiation in a country of such dimension had been less marked than it is.

Second, differentiation in the natural landscapes has contributed to the emergence of different forms and patterns of man-nature interactions in the different regions of India. Ranging from the senile topography of the Deccan to the youthful contours of the Himalayas, from the highly differentiated system of the highest peaks of the world to the unvarying monotony of the extensive plains, from the intricate maze of channels in the Bengal delta to the almost complete absence of surface flow in the Thar, from the wettest parts of the world to some of the driest, from the dense growth of tropical forests in the north-east to the vast extensive tracts where not a blade of grass grows – the extent of diversity in the natural environment of India is of an astoundingly high order.

The Indian people have, for millenia, interacted and come to terms with these different environments and, as a consequence, their responses to their specific landscapes have acquired distinctly regional forms. The food they eat, the clothes they wear, the houses they live in, the economic activities they carry out, the dialects they speak, the ballads they sing, the festivals they organise, the myths and legends that embody their emotional responses—all of these acquire a regional stamp.

Third, the differing sources of the waves of immigration to the sub-continent from the surrounding territories in a process spread over millennia, the different routes of the dispersal of these into this vast land and the consequent concentration of diverse ethnic elements in different regions have created a social mosaic with distinct concentrations their ethnic distinctiveness merging into each other in the vast intervening tracts. Three important regional concentrations may be distinguished:

*(i)* the south, with its long coastline permitting maritime links with the peoples across the sea;

*(ii)* the north-west, with convenient openings for the peoples of the vast expanses of Central and West Asia across the Himalayan wall at Khyber and Bolan; and

*(iii)* the north-east, the passes of which permitted the immigration of the Mongoloid peoples into the valleys and the Himalayan territories which show an interlacing of northern and southern elements in differing magnitudes enmeshed with each other within this mountain domain.

Fourth, the formation of regional identities of the agricultural communities in different regions at different points of time within a range of about 3,000 years has contributed to the strengthening of the regional forms in the social sphere. This process of region formation has been further sharpened by the continuity of the historical tradition of an essentially agricultural society.

In the light of the above, the unique feature of the social situation in India is not the extent of its plurality but the fact that social diversity has been based on and sustained by an underlying unity which has grown with time. The factors that have led to strengthening of this underlying unity of the social ethos in India may now be examined.

First, in spite of the differences in the natural environment of the various regions, the monsoonal rhythm of the seasons provides a strong element of uniformity. The alternating of the dry and the wet seasons and the concentration of the life-giving rains into a few months of the year are, by and large, all India phenomena, even though the magnitude of the dryness of the dry season and the wetness of the wet season varies greatly from one part of the country to the other. The music and fragrance produced by rain drops falling on the parched thirsty earth generate intense emotional responses in the Indian people almost everywhere from the and Thar to the humid north-east. The Kajari of Bhojpur and the Malhar of Braj have their counterparts in almost all parts of India. The rain-fed subsistence agriculture – and the village community based on it – is, in more senses than one, a gift of the monsoon. The all-pervasiveness of the monsoon – in spite of the many regional variations -has provided the natural base for a certain degree of uniformity in man-nature interactions throughout the length and breadth of the country. The unity of India is strongly rooted in this commonness.

Second, the horizontal spread of cultural and socioeconomic attributes from different parts of the country to each other and the constant and ever-growing give and take through inter-regional contacts and exchanges, have generated a process of cultural synthesisation which has put its stamp on regional categories and has created strong bonds of integration. The foremost of all these integrative forces in the basal matrix of Indian culture was provided by the spatial spread of Vedic and Puranic traditions during the ancient period itself from the Indo-Gangetic Plains south, north and eastwards, bringing the whole of the sub-continent-from Kashmir to Kanyakumari and from the desert wastes of Sindh to the lush valleys of Kamrup – under its influence. The unifying role of this horizontal spread became strong and meaningful to the extent it had the capacity to assimilate within itself elements of regional traditions, getting itself enriched in this process. This give and take operated at two levels. First, Brahmanical learning through the medium of Sanskrit provided strong bonds of cultural unity among the religious and the intellectual elite in the country as a whole. A similar role was played by Persian and English in the later periods of history. Secondly, and perhaps, in a more important sense, it was the cultural synthesis achieved through the preachings of Bhakti and Sufi saints in rural India which has left an indelible imprint on the cultural ethos of India. Though Kabir and Nanak, Tukaram and Chisti, Ramanuj and Reshi spoke in different dialects, their message was essentially the same-the unity of mankind and the brotherhood of man. Perhaps nowhere else in the world does one find such apparently diverse traditions as those associated with Hinduism and Islam getting intertwined so intricately into a composite matrix as reflected in the Kabirbani, the Taj Mahal, the Rag Darbari or the Kangra miniatures. The integration of India is strongly rooted in this composite matrix.

Third, the development of inter-regional economic linkages and the emergence of a national home market during the past two hundred years or so, though constrained by the negative influences of Imperialist exploitation, have played an important role in unifying the country. The British, by striking at the roots of the self-sufficiency of the village community, brought the bulk of rural India into a largely unified all-India market. The establishment of a network of railways and other means of communication greatly facilitated this process. The requirements of the economy also generated inter- district and inter-state migration on a considerable scale, breaking the age-old isolation of regional groups from each other. Of special significance in this connection was the rural-urban migration stream which brought together into urban agglomerations people who spoke different dialects or professed different faiths but were citizens of a new India. The attempts made since 1947 to correct the distortions introduced by the British in the regional structure of the country and the accelerated rate of socioeconomic development have furthered the consolidation of the national home market, and have thus strengthened the foundations of Indian nationhood.

## Regional Disparities

While diversities are essentially a positive element and provide colour as well as vitality to the country, disparities are essentially a negative element and lead to economic debility as well as social tensions. The starting-point of an analysis of regional disparities in India cannot but be the recognition that though many crucially important modifications of the positive kind have been introduced within it since its tryst with destiny, the regional structure of underdevelopment established by the imperialist power still persists in terms of some of its characteristics.

The spatial structure of the colonial India acquired its basic contours during the second phase of the colonial rule—that of British industrial capital (1813-1914) particularly with the development of the railway network—and got further crystallised during the third phase that of British finance capital (1914-47). The spatial dimension of the colonial pattern of accumulation essentially consisted in impounding even the very limited growth impulses within the socio-economic enclaves. The national market, which was the off- spring of the forced intrusion of the metropolitan capital accumulation process, was not the symbiotic result of interlacing local, sub-regional and regional markets from the base upwards.

The system of exchange between the metropolitan bridges from the various arms of which the enclaves hung down created vortexes of exchanges in the dependent economy, interconnected by a tenuous currency and transport network. Through these vortexes, the surplus was siphoned off mainly to the metropolitan economy, a part getting impounded in the system of satellite enclaves.

The port-oriented centrifugal transport network led to the partial fragmentation of the home market and weakened the centripetal forces in the economy. The hinterlands of the three ports of Bombay, Calcutta and Madras were more strongly linked with London through the network orientation and freight policies than with each other. Considerable degree of external integration coexisted with internal fragmentation.

The emergence of the dysfunctional pockets of underdevelopment around the ports distorted the industrial map of colonial India, leaving the resource-rich regions by and large, industrially backward. In 1948, the presidency states around the three ports accounted for 76.7 percent of the total industrial workers, 77.0 percent of the total value of the net industrial production, 82.9 percent of the value of engineering and electrical goods and 87.2 percent of the value of chemical goods in the country. The corresponding percentage figures for the minerally rich states of Bihar, Orissa and Madhya Pradesh were 9.61, 9.54 and 5.10, respectively. The same distorted picture is reflected in the fact that the three portbased states accounted, in 1946-47, for 74.28 percent of rupee and 67.26 percent of sterling capital in registered industries.

With the shift in the nature of State power after Independence, the country faced the challenge of moving away from underdevelopment to development, of removing the constraints on vertical shifts within the workforce and of the organising the space economy as would be commensurate with the requirements of a developing society. The economic history of contemporary India is the history of both successes and failures in meeting this challenge.

The basic policies of the new State were directed towards modifying the pre-existing structure of colonial underdevelopment with a view to adapting it to the requirements of a higher rate of domestic capital accumulation. The limitations of the strategy, termed as the second way of development by Dobb and Takahashi, were, therefore, further compounded in the newly independent countries like India due to the legacy of the colonial model in space economy. Under such circumstances, regional disparities were bound to get accentuated further, not withstanding the emergencey of certain new centres in less developed areas in response to directed public investment. The experience, for instance, of the Durgapur-Chittaranjan, the Ranchi or Bhilai complex, shows that even large-scale public investment had only a marginal impact on the regional economy as a whole and the tendency of growth impulses getting impounded within a few agglomerations continued.

Public investment in agriculture also went along the same lines. The very idea of the high-yielding variety package programe implicit in the "green revolution strategy"-by definition-sharply accentuated regional disparities, because of the concentration of inputs heavily subsidised by the State in restricted pockets, Between the early sixties and middle seventies, 20 percent of the net sown area of the country had come under the impact of the green revolution by eating up about half of the technological inputs used in the country. Once again, the results expected of this concentrated application of public investment in selected pockets did not fructify because the assumption of propagation-through percolation and diffusion-of growth impulses from the centre to the periphery, characteristic of Anglo-Saxon regional development theory, proved to be considerably feeble in the

Indian context. For similar reasons, the strategy of developing the backward areas, initiated and sponsored by the Planning Commission also failed to produce the desired results.

As we note the enclave agglomeration is no longer a mere outpost of the metropolitan economy. It is, however, still a major trade outlet that becomes the centre of conglomerate big business, metropolitan collaboration capital, and major state institutions. Its basic functional character, however, remains unchanged; it continues to be the focal point of the suction mechanism for commodity, income, capital and labour force flows. The specific features of its pattern and attributes of spurious urbanisation remain basically intact.

Apart from the old "satellite centres" of tertiary activity and mining and plantation areas, a new set of satellite centres of public investment now subserve the main agglomerations. These public sector townships are different from the old satellite centres in that they are usually location sites of heavy industry and are not merely centres of tertiary activity. However, in course of time, they may develop into subsidiary agglomerations with increasing share of tertiary sector. The growth impulses of public investment in these new centres continue to be impounded and fail to affect the neighbourhood substantially. One moves from the most advanced centre of ferrous metallurgy to Jhum cultivation covering five thousand years in 50 kilometres.

Because of the massive public investment in agriculture, focused on the water supply variables, a sharp gradation of the hinterland of primary produce has taken shape. Areas of sub-marginal subsistence are mostly concentrated in the dry lands, followed by the areas of uncertain water supply. However, thanks to the accentuation of vertical inequality in the HYV areas, pockets of sub-marginal subsistence persist therein as well. The circumstances of sub-marginal subsistence continue to be reproduced, as before, in pockets of squalor all along the urban spectrum. In some cases, these pockets may be eliminated from the heartland of urban areas and pushed to their peripheries, because of sky-rocketing costs of urban land in response to massive public investments.

## Integration and Differentiation

It follows from the above discussion of the main features of diversities and disparities in India that the two are products of different socio-ecological processes, play contrasting roles in development and call for different operational strategies and policy approaches. Diversities have evolved over millennia and constitute the basic material of which the Indian nation is made. Unity and diversity of India are not opposites which can grow at each other's cost. They are symbiotically linked and support and sustain each other. Any attempt to overemphasise either of these would disturb the delicate balance.

Diversities are not irritants to be gradually eliminated from the polity. Unity is not a yoke to be thrown away in the interest of the liberation of subjugated "nations","nationalities" or "homelands". Those who view India as a monolith and those who view it as a mechanical mixture of diverse elements put together by the British—both are in error and do not understand the characteristic feature of the Indian polity, that has made India what it is. They may appear to be contradictory on the surface but they both strike at the unity and integration of India. India is a unity in diversity; and we can ignore it only at great peril. to ourselves.

The challenge posed by the accentuation of regional disparities is, however, highly disquieting and should be met by a forward-looking policy of balanced regional development. The operationalisation of the territorial division of labour along with and as a complement to the sectoral division would lead to regional specialisation in productive endeavours through the unfolding of resource-based production cycles and the maturation of economic regions. This would simultaneously and definitionally lead to the consolidation of the home market and the strengthening of interregional dependencies in the country. Differentiation and integration would thus proceed together within the developmental process, supporting and strengthening each other.

The demand for more power to the states or to the Centre loses much of its significance in this context. If development proceeds on the basis of a territorial division of labour and the maturation of economic regions, the states and the Union would both become strong – the former through specialisation/differentiation and the latter through interdependency/ integration. On the other hand, if the development impulses are feeble and the process of region formation is anaemic, the states and the Centre would both be weak and infirm.

In the context of development, power is exercised for the optimisation of growth with equity and not on grounds of the division of spoils among wielders of power. It is significant that while in one case of Pakistan, the demand for more power to the provinces is rooted not in the Punjab, the developed province, but in the relatively less developed provinces like Baluchistan and NWFP; in the case of India, it is mainly concentrated in the relatively more developed states like the Punjab, Tamil Nadu and West Bengal and not in the less developed states like Uttar Pradesh, Bihar or Madhya Pradesh. Even in a relatively less developed state like Jammu and Kashmir, there is a popular movement for the status of a Centrally administered territory in the most backward part of the state, i.e. in Ladakh. The political economy behind the demand for more powers to the states/provinces cannot obviously be the same in Pakistan and India.

The flowering of cultural diversities within the framework of an Indian ambience is a positive feature reflecting its unity in diversity. Endeavours to "Indianise" Indians in the name of unity are as deplorable as efforts to carve out "homelands" or erode the Union. Regional disparities may, however, be considered to be the consequence of persisting attributes of underdevelopment and its minimisation constitutes one of the key tasks of socioeconomic transformation. It may, therefore, be asserted with some confidence that national policies should be directed towards the flowering of diversities and liquidation of disparities within the national framework of integrated differentiation accompanying the development process.

Viewed in this context, the centralisation-decentralisation contradiction is a false contradiction. This is particularly true in the sphere of resource development. Let us take the example of water management. As long as kutcha wells are being used, management can be highly dispersed or "decentralised" -the household being the unit of decisionmaking. But the system of Ganga-Kavery connecting canals can be managed only by a strong Union Government. If the waters of the northwestern rivers, which are mostly the snow melt of the Himalayas, were to be considered the property of the Punjab, or the oil drilled at Bombay High that of Maharashtra, regional as well as national development would be in serious jeopardy.

Decentralisation is not a mantra, and centralisation is not a dirty word. Both are the two sides of the same coin of development. There is some avoidable confusion in this regard due to the fact that the term "decentralisation" is defined negatively-as being away from the Centre, and not positively in terms of people's participation in the making of decisions that affect their lives, and enjoying the powers to implement them. If it is so defined, one arrives at the model comprising systems of interdependencies nesting into larger systems as their subsystems, of fields within fields.

The gravitational field of the moon is contained within the field of the earth, which, in its turn, is contained within the field of the sun. There are not mutually exclusive and equivalent areas of influence but a multi-level and hierarchical system comprising subsystems. The relative influence wielded by each in a given situation depends on the specificity of the specific conjunction. The sun is far more "powerful" than the moon, but the latter exerts greater influence than the former on the tidal phenomenon over the globe.

In the context of the approach, as outlined above, it would be erroneous to reduce the complexities of the process of integrated differentiation in a developing society to the question of state-centre relations. Such a reduction would have some justification – at least on juridical grounds—if India had been a federation. It is not; India is a Union, not a federation of states. This distinction is of the essence. Sovereignty lies with the people of India, who have given themselves a Constitution. The powers of the states or the zilla parishads or the village panchayats are all derived from the sovereignty of "we the people of India". In the case of a federation, sovereignty lies with the people of the federating units and the powers of the Centre are derived from the multiple sovereignties.

The present debate on the relative powers of the Centre and the state is, therefore, being carried on within a dysfunctional frame of reference. The complexities of the problems of integrated differentiation can be properly appreciated within the framework of a multi-level system of autonomies and accountabilities–from the individual, the household, the village/town/city/ metropole, the block, the district, the substate, the state, the zone to the nation, and, in fact, to the globe and the ecosystem. Each has a field nesting into the higher order field from the micro, through the meso, to the macro. Each has its autonomy and is accountable in terms of its autonomy; for only robots are not accountable and only slaves have no autonomy. It is thus that the unfolding of the process of integrated differentiation may be facilitated; unity getting strengthened in symbiosis with diversity, specialisation developing in conjunction with interdependency; and autonomy flourishing in tandem with accountability.

## Impacts of Colonial Education

Having provided the backdrop of the regional dimension of socioeconomic processes as they evolved over time on the Indian soil since the advent of colonialism, it would be desirable to focus attention on some of the internal forces of self-articulation within the educational sphere itself:

The most potent of the contradictory pulls regulating the trend of educational development are those exerted by tradition and modernity. The contradiction is resolved by the modernisation of tradition itself through a simultaneous process of rejection of the moribund, the dead and the obsolete in tradition and of the assimilation of its live, vital and relevant elements into the modem. This is how astrology transformed itself into astronomy by, for example, rejecting the geocentricity of the solar system but assimilating some of its mathematical formulations. The modem does not generate in a vacuum; it grows in the womb of tradition. It does not replace it; it transforms it. The modem is modernised tradition, a new wave in the ocean of time. If the modem rejects the whole of tradition, it ceases to be, modem. It becomes rootless and anaemic, a spurious product-glossy but emphemeral-destined for the dustbin of history. If tradition does not eschew the obsolete by modernising itself, it ceases to be tradition. It becomes sterile, a stagnant pool of decay and degeneration.

The rejuvenating process of the modernisation of tradition proceeded, albeit at a slow pace and having many ups and downs, within all the major civilisations of the earth till the Industrial Revolution and the emergence of industrial and financial capital on the scene. This was a turning-point in history. While the Greco-Roman tradition, which had survived the suffocating atmosphere of the Inquisition, modernised itself and flourished in the metropolitan countries of Western Europe on the basis of the flowering of rationalism and humanism, the traditions of the colonial empires faced crises of an unprecedented magnitude.

The overseas territories within temperate latitudes provided lebensraum for European immigrants, who with rifles in their hands, liquidated whole peoples and, out of sheer benevolence, permitted civilisations to breath their last peacefully in the soil killing the ambience of encapsulated reservations. This brutal genocide was called colonisation and a new genre of literature, paintings and films arose to glorify the civilising mission of the wild West. Imported modernity flourished in the graveyard of native traditions both in America and Australia.

The situation was different in the tropics. They provided an arena not for colonisation but for colonialism. Traditions in these lands which were deeply rooted in the native soil and were, as in the case of India, the quintessence of millennia of social experience froze-so to say—into immobility, and became sterile, atrophied and fossilised. The obsolete, backward-looking and decaying elements of tradition were not allowed to the a natural death, fertilising the soil for the sprouting of newer shoots.

The colonial powers preserved the festering sores of casteism and communalism, parochialism and obscurantism so as to pollute the atmosphere of national resurgence and to induce ideological debility in the system. Over this osing substratum of decaying tradition was superimposed a thin veneer of rootless modernity imported from across the seas. These structural inadequacies were expressing themselves most sharply in the sensitive sphere of educational underdevelopment. While the pathshalas, gurukuls and madrasas continued to teach the outdated doctrine of geocentricity as late as in the first half of the twentieth century, Macaulay's educational system could produce only graduated flunkeys. While tradition was dying, modernity was powerless to be born. Modern renaissance in India, as in most colonial countries, was, therefore, neither really modem nor substantively a renaissance. It is, no doubt, true that the anti-imperialist struggle for national independence inspired the search for alternative models of education; but, perhaps, with the possible exception of the intellectual contributions of Rabindranath Tagore and Jawaharlal Nehru, the tradition-modemity gap could not be satisfactorily bridged.

Since the distortions introduced into the educational system by the colonial power had far-reaching consequences, as they had in the case of economic processes, and as some of these still persist, poisoning the atmosphere of our academic endeavours, it may be worth while to identify some of the main characteristics of the educational system inherited by independent India.

First, the system was quantitatively a miniscule with only a marginal section of the teeming millions inhabiting the vast subcontinent within its orbit of influence. The literacy rate in a country where the concepts of zero and the decimal system were evolved, was abominably low. In 1951, after about two centuries of the 'civilising' role of the British, literacy rate was 16.67 percent and the enrolment per lakh of population for elementary schools was 4,500 and for secondary schools 418. The level of enrolment in higher education approximated to the corresponding figures in the present day Swaziland and Somalia and was less than those in Lesotho and Zambia.

Second, education in colonial India responded to the needs of alien administration rather than to those of socioeconomic development. With the share of the secondary sector in the work force and agricultural productivity per hectare as well as per worker declining as a result of the operation of the colonial mechanism, education was not required to become an input into productivity and provide the scientific– technological base as well as trained manpower for economic development. It was instead expected to produce graduated cogs and wheels for the administrative machinery. The distance between education and work which had grown over millennia was bridged in the countries of the West under the impact of the Industrial Revolution. Such a revolution was not allowed to take place in the countries of the third world and as a consequence the linkages between work and education which were traditional

Third, the multi-level educational system was highly pyramidal with very acute angles at the base. The transition rates from the primary to the middle, from the middle to the secondary, from the secondary to the higher secondary, from the higher secondary to the lower tertiary and from the lower tertiary to the higher tertiary were exceptionally low. The tertiary stage showed an even more alarming picture. Postgraduate and research work, which provides the basic inputs for self-reliance, constituted a disproportionately small share in the total enrolment in higher education-11.5 percent for the former and 0.8 percent for the latter.

Most of higher education was concentrated at the undergraduate level. What made the situation even more dysfunctional was the fact that the undergraduate base was structurally delinked from the rest of higher education by the emergence on the academic scene of that rare species found only in the academically semiarid lands of the colonies designated as the affiliated "Degree Colleges". It is not difficult to imagine the soulless ambience of institutions where the faculty was required only to "cover the syllabus" prescribed by external agencies and prepare students for an end-of-term essay type examination conducted by external agencies.

Fourth, education in colonial India—particularly at higher levels—was concentrated in and around port cities. This enclavisation of education was an important element of the spatial system of underdevelopment wherein newly established ports of Calcutta, Bombay and Madras acted as apex points for the colonial suction mechanism and part of the surpluses generated in the subjugated economy were impounded in their conurbations. These port towns became the headquarters of "presidency" universities.

Fifth, the socio-economic base of education in colonial India was extremely narrow. Its gates were closed to the vast majority of the toiling people. Such segments of population wherein economic and social deprivations were combined with each other as in the case of Scheduled Castes and Tribes, found it almost impossible to enter the sacred precincts of educational institutions. The rural areas, inhabited by the vast majority of the Indian people, were almost completely devoid of educational facilities. The level of female education was particularly low. It was on their frail shoulders that the whole system of inequities rested. For example, literacy rate for predominantly tribal district of Koroput in 1931 was only 1.73 percent as against the national average of 9.50 percent for the general population. The corresponding figure for females was only 0.72 percent.

Sixth, education in colonial India was essentially teaching, and not "learning", oriented. The teacher-student relationship was based on the assumption that knowledge is essentially "received" and an uncritical acceptance of the gospel truth was therefore the most efficient method of learning. The products of such a system of education could be evaluated with the help of an examination which put the marks of differing "qualities" on the commodities being produced in the teaching shops for the employment market, primarily in the so-called service sector. The ability to uncritically accept the "received" truth could be best judged by a uniform external end-of-term and comprehensive essay-type examination.

Seventh, the educational system of colonial India was intended to weaken the forces of national integration, which were growing on the basis of the strengthening of the national home market, on the one hand, and under the impact of the national movement, on the other. The virus of communalism, casteism and regionalism was injected into the polity through the instrumentality of the curriculum. Hindus and Muslims, for example, were taught in the school that there was nothing common between the two. Not only was their religion different but they were taught to believe that different periods of history were associated with each, that they wore different kinds of dresses and spoke different languages.

## References

Government of India (1992), *Programe of Action on the National Education Policy*, Ministry of Human Resource Development, New Delhi.

*India 2009: A Reference Annual (53rd edition)*, New Delhi: Additional Director General (ADG), Publications Division, Ministry of Information and Broadcasting, Government of India.

Vaidyanathan, A., and P. R. Gopinathan Nair, eds. *Elementary Education in Rural India: A Grassroots View*. Thousand Oaks, Calif.: Sage, 2001.

Salmi, J. (1992), "Perspectives on the Financing of Higher Education", *Higher Education Policy*, Vol.5, No. 2, pp.13-19

Rani, Geetha, P. (2003), "Financing Education in India in the Economic Reform Period: Focus on Intra-sectoral Allocation of Resources to Education", in *Globalisation and Challenges of Education*, (ed), NIEPA.

# Bibliography


Baber, Zaheer (1996), *The Science of Empire: Scientific Knowledge, Civilization, and Colonial Rule in India*, State University of New York Press.

Bandyopadhyay, Sekhar (2004), *From Plassey to Partition: A History of Modern India*, New Delhi and London: Orient Longmans. Pp. xx, 548.

Bhattacharya, Sabyasachi, ed. *The Contested Terrain: Perspectives on Education in India.* New Delhi: Orient Longmans, 1998.

Blackwell, Fritz (2004), *India: A Global Studies Handbook*, United States of America: ABC-CLIO, Inc.

Bose, Sugata; Jalal, Ayesha (2003), *Modern South Asia: History, Culture, Political Economy*, London and New York: Routledge, 2nd edition. Pp. xiii, 304.

Clyde W. Barrow, (1990). *Universities and the Capitalist State: Corporate Liberalism and the Reconstruction of American Higher Education, 1894–1928*, University of Wisconsin Press..

Compayre, Gabriel; Payne, W. H. *History of Pedagogy* (1899), translated by W. H. Payne, 2003, Kessinger Publishing.

Cordasco, Francesco. (1976). *A Brief History of Education: A Handbook of Information on Greek, Roman, Medieval, Renaissance, and Modern Educational Practice*, Rowman & Little field.

Coulson, Joseph. (1999). "Market Education: The Unknown History". Transaction Publishers.

Elder, Joseph W. (2006), "Caste System", *Encyclopedia of India (vol. 1)* edited by Stanley Wolpert, 223-229, Thomson Gale.

Ganeri, Anita. (1999). *Looking Back: India Under the Mughal Empire 1526-1858*. Austin, Texas: Raintree Steck-Vaughn.

Geeta Gandhi Kingdon. (2007), *The progress of school education in India*, Global Poverty Research Group, Economic and Social Research Council.

Ghosh, Suresh Chandra. (2001). *The History of Education in Ancient India*, c. 3000 B.C. to A.D. 1192. New Delhi: Munshiram Manoharlal.

Government of India. (1992), *Programe of Action on the National Education Policy*, Ministry of Human Resource Development, New Delhi.

Hailman, W. N. (1874). *Twelve lectures on the history of pedagogy, delivered before the Cincinnati teachers' association.* Wilson, Hinkle & Co.

Hartmut Scharfe (2002). *Education in Ancient India.* Brill Academic Publishers.

Hasan, Mushirul, ed. (1998). *Knowledge, Power and Politics: Educational Institutions in India.* New Delhi: Lotus.

*India 2009: A Reference Annual (53rd edition)*, New Delhi: Additional Director General (ADG), Publications Division, Ministry of Information and Broadcasting, Government of India.

Jayant Pandurang Nayaka, Syed Nurullah (1974), *A students' history of education in India (1800-1973)*, Macmillan.

Jean Drèze, Amartya Sen (2002). *India: development and participation*, Oxford University Press,

John F Richards, (1996). *The Mughal Empire*, Vol I.5, *New Cambridge History of India*, Cambridge University Press.

Judd, Dennis (2004), *The Lion and the Tiger: The Rise and Fall of the British Raj, 1600-1947*, Oxford and New York: Oxford University Press.

Kulke, Hermann; Rothermund, Dietmar (2004), *A History of India*, 4th edition. Routledge.

Kumar, Nita. (1999). *Lessons from Schools: The History of Education in Banaras.* New Delhi and Thousand Oaks, Calif.: Sage.

Mahendra K. Premi, *India's Literacy Panorama, Seminar on the Progress of Literacy in India: What the 2001 Census Reveals*, Education for All in India.

Manoranjan Mohanty (2004), *Class, caste and gender: Volume 5 of Readings in Indian government and politics*, SAGE.

Markovits, Claude (ed) (2005), *A History of Modern India 1480-1950 (Anthem South Asian Studies)*, Anthem Press.

Metcalf, Barbara; Metcalf, Thomas R. (2006), *A Concise History of Modern India (Cambridge Concise Histories)*, Cambridge and New York: Cambridge University Press.

Michael Chiappetta, (1953) "Historiography and Roman Education," *History of Education Journal* 4, no. 4: 149-156.

Mookerji, Radha Kumud. (1990) *Ancient Indian Education: Brahmanical and Buddhist.*

*ndia 2009: A Reference Annual (53rd edition)*, New Delhi: Additional Director General (ADG), Publications Division, Ministry of Information and Broadcasting, Government of India.

Olaf Pedersen, (1998). *The First Universities : Studium Generale and the Origins of University Education in Europe*, Cambridge University Press.

Peers, Douglas M. (2006), *India under Colonial Rule 1700-1885*, Harlow and London: Pearson Longmans.

Prabhu, Joseph (2006), "Educational Institutions and Philosophies, Traditional and Modern", *Encyclopedia of India (vol. 2)* edited by Stanley Wolpert, 23–28, Thomson Gale.

Raman, S.A. (2006). "Women's Education", *Encyclopedia of India (vol. 4)*, edited by Stanley Wolpert, 235-239, Thomson Gale.

Rani, Geetha, P. (2003), "Financing Education in India in the Economic Reform Period: Focus on Intra-sectoral Allocation of Resources to Education", in *Globalisation and Challenges of Education*, (ed), NIEPA.

Robb, Peter (2004), *A History of India (Palgrave Essential Histories)*, Houndmills, Hampshire: Palgrave Macmillan.

Salmi, J. (1992). "Perspectives on the Financing of Higher Education", *Higher Education Policy*, Vol.5, No. 2, pp.13-19

Sarkar, Sumit (1983). *Modern India: 1885-1947*, Delhi: Macmillan India Ltd. Pp. xiv, 486.

Savage-Smith, Emilie (1985). *Islamicate Celestial Globes: Their history, Construction, and Use*, Smithsonian Institution Press, Washington, D.C.

Setty, E.D. and Ross, E.L. (1987). "A Case Study in Applied Education in Rural India", *Community Development Journal*, 22 (2): 120–129, Oxford University Press.

Sigmund Diamond, (1992)*Compromised Campus: The Collaboration of Universities with the Intelligence Community, 1945–1955*, Oxford University Press.

Spear, Percival (1990), *A History of India, Volume 2*, New Delhi and London: Penguin Books.

Sripati, V. and Thiruvengadam, A.K. (2004), "India: Constitutional Amendment Making The Right to Education a Fundamental Right", *International Journal of Constitutional Law*, 2 (1): 148–158, Oxford University Press.

Stanley Aronowitz, (2000). *The Knowledge Factory*. Boston: Beacon.

Stein, Burton (2001), *A History of India*, New Delhi and Oxford: Oxford University Press.

UNESCO Education Sector, (2004). *The Plurality of Literacy and its implications for Policies and Programs*: Position Paper. Paris: United National Educational, Scientific and Cultural Organisation.

Vaidyanathan, A., and P. R. Gopinathan Nair, eds. (2001). *Elementary Education in Rural India: A Grassroots View*. Thousand Oaks, Calif.: Sage.

Vanlalchhawna (2006), *Higher education in North-East India: unit cost analysis*, Mittal Publications.

Vrat, Prem (2006), "Indian Institutes of Technology", *Encyclopedia of India (vol. 2)* edited by Stanley Wolpert, 229-231, Thomson Gale.

Walter Rüegg, general editor, *A History of the University in Europe*. Cambridge: Cambridge University Press.

Wolpert, Stanley (2003), *A New History of India*, Oxford and New York: Oxford University Press.

Yun Lee Too, (2001). *Education in Greek and Roman antiquity*. Boston: Brill.

# Index